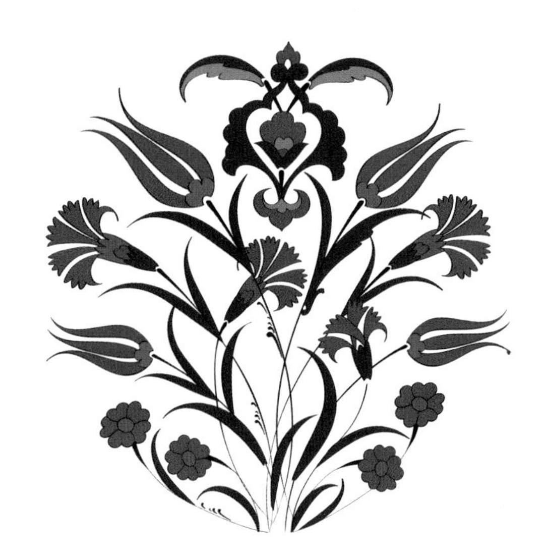

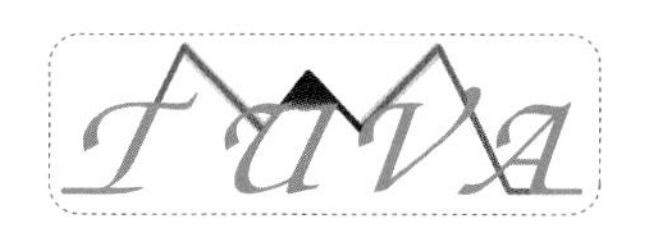

Maria Diaz

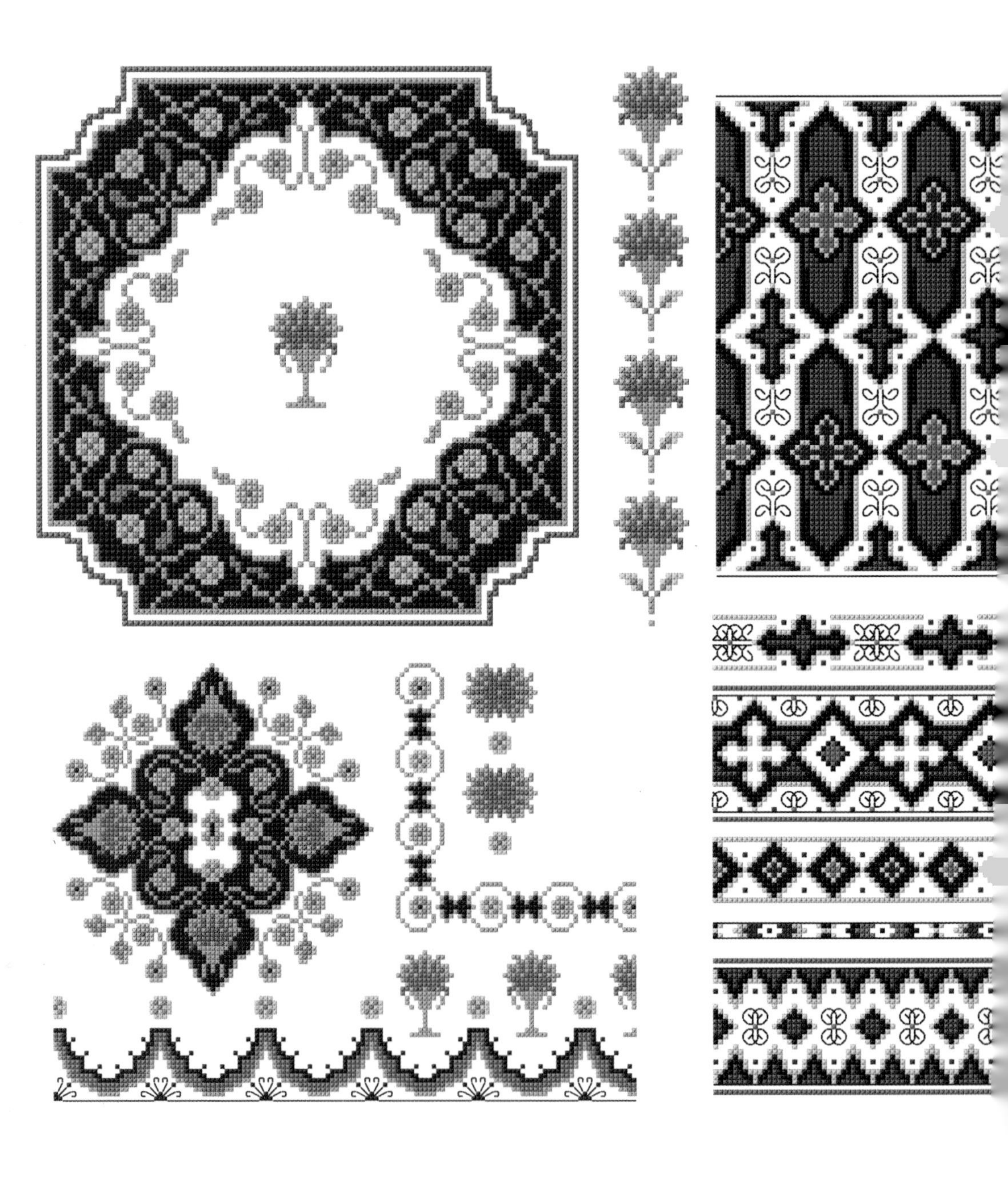

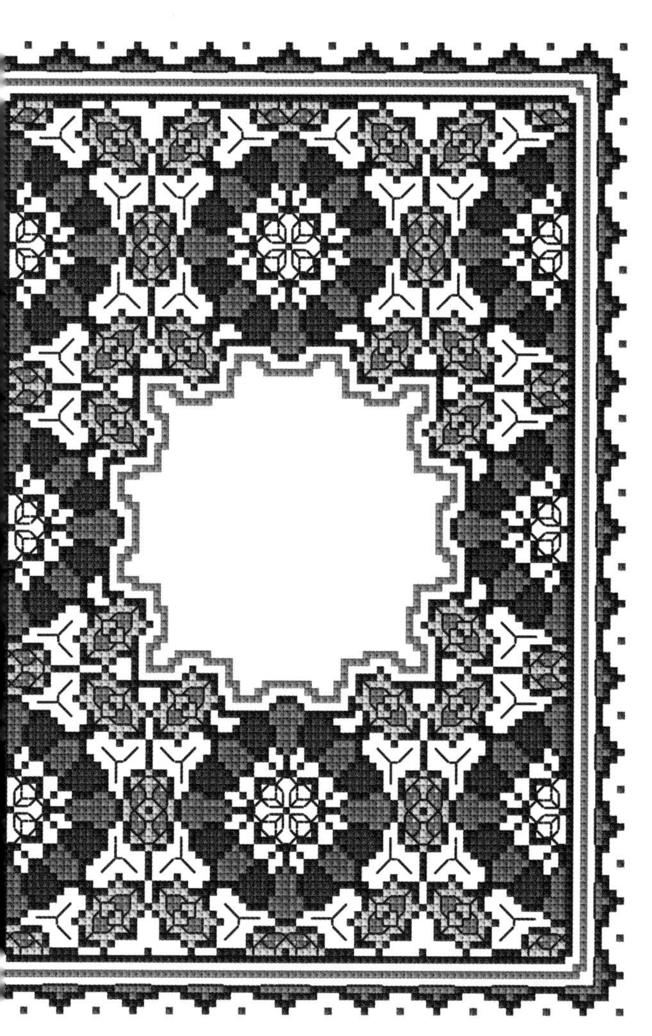
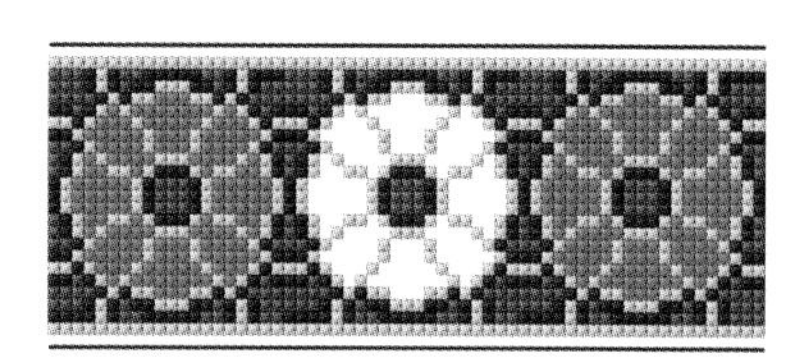
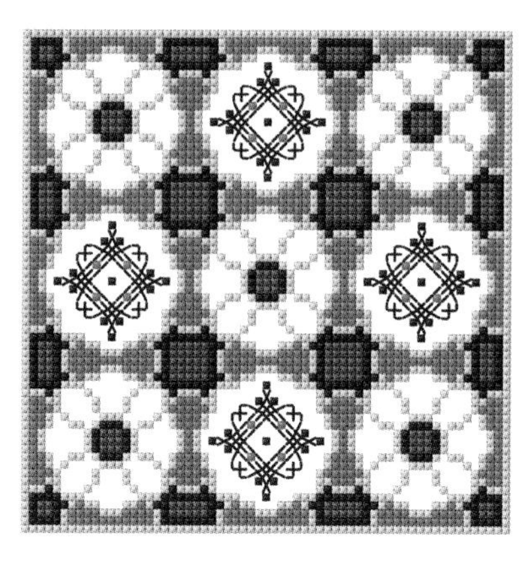

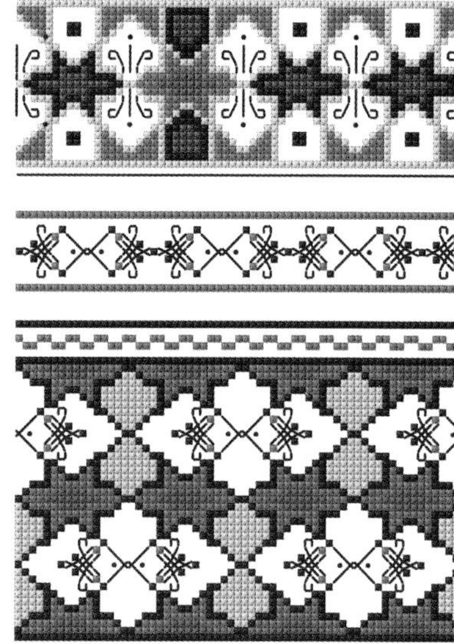

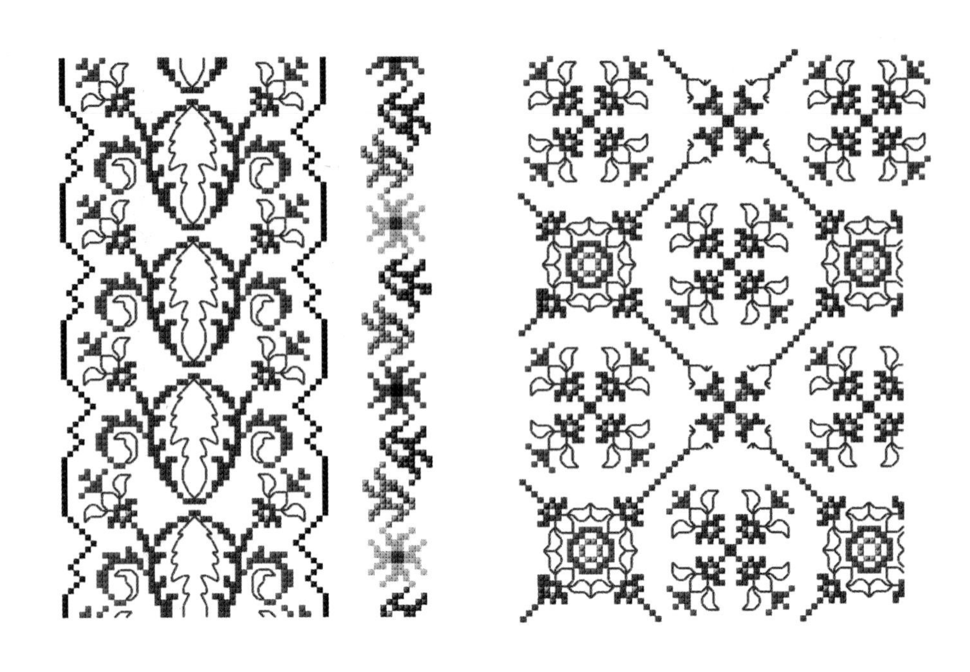

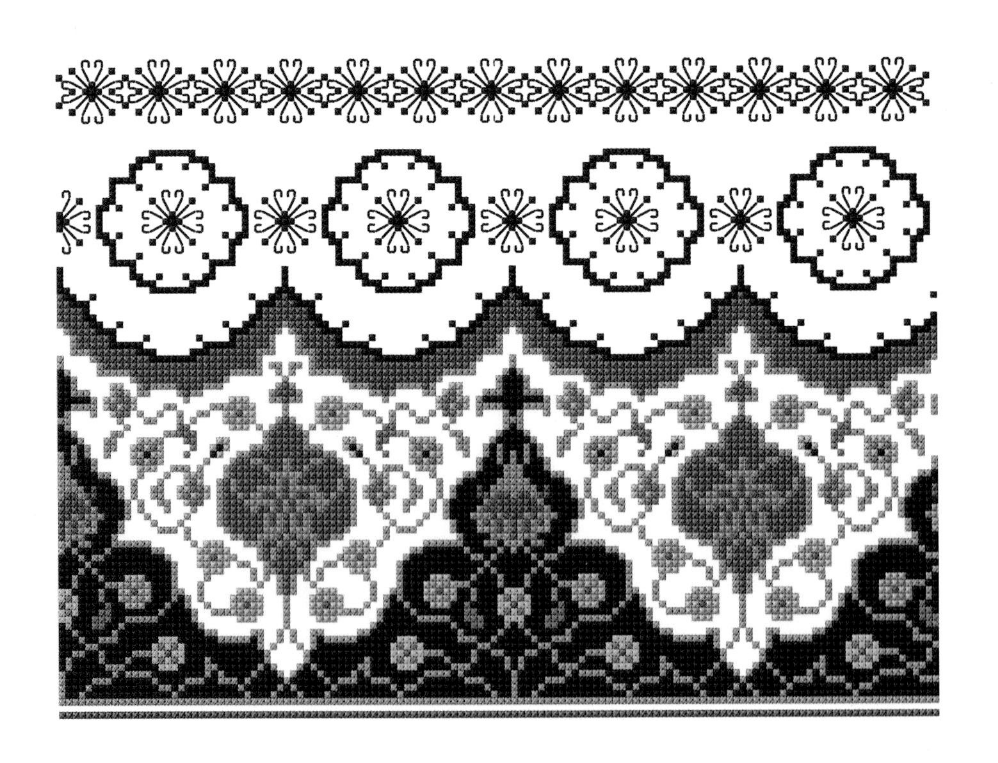

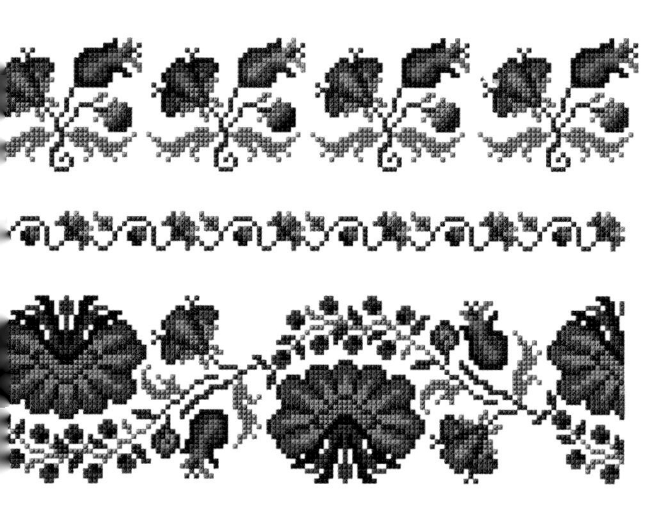
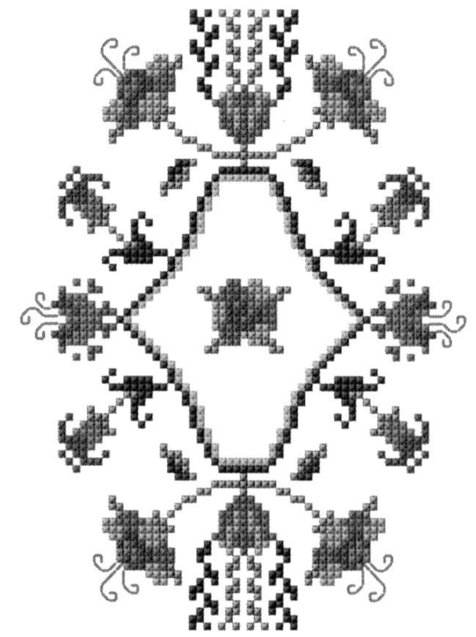
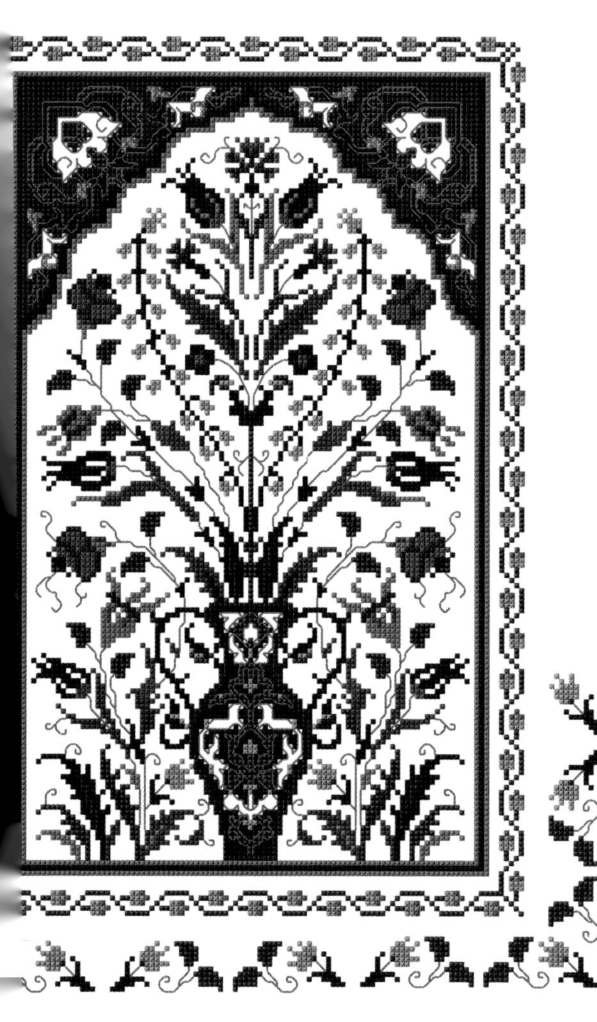

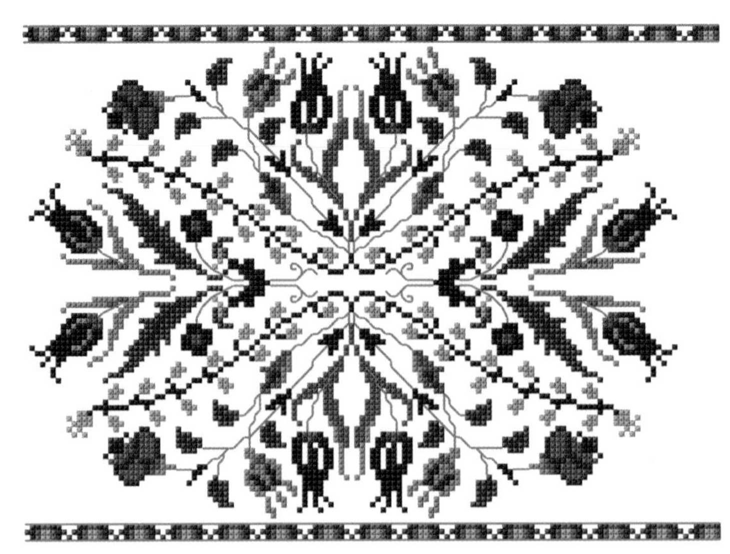
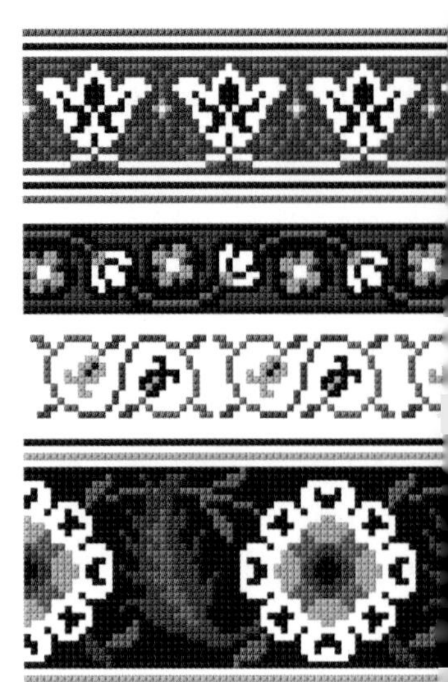
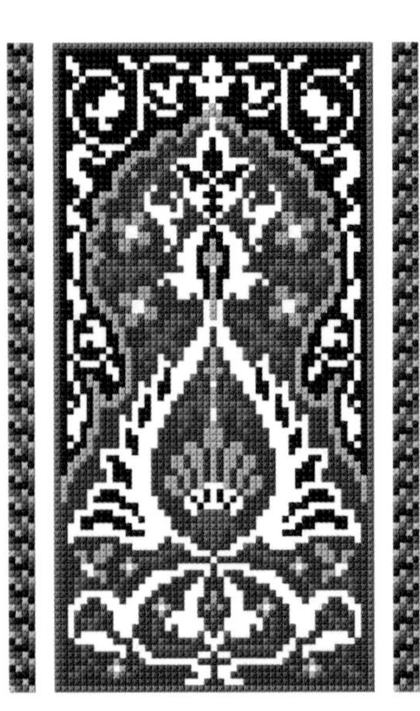
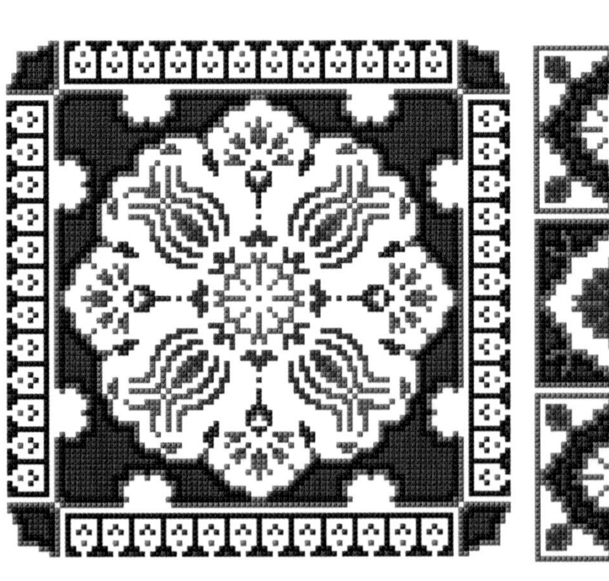
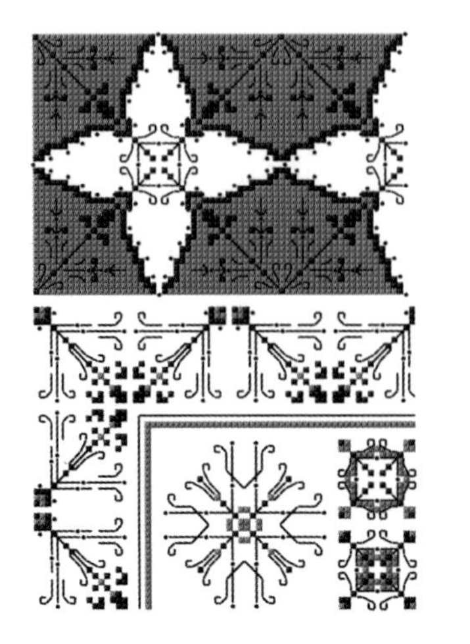
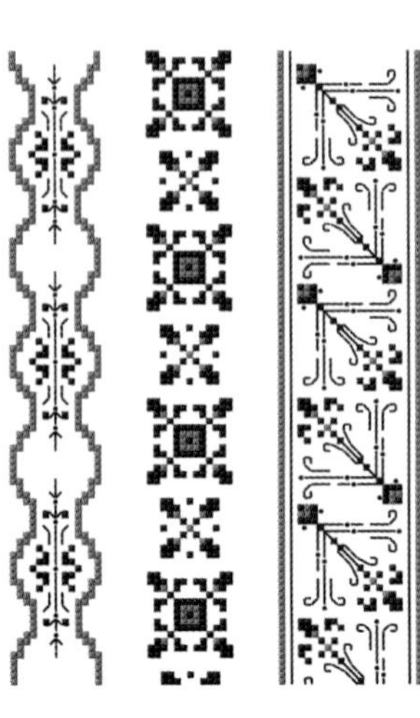

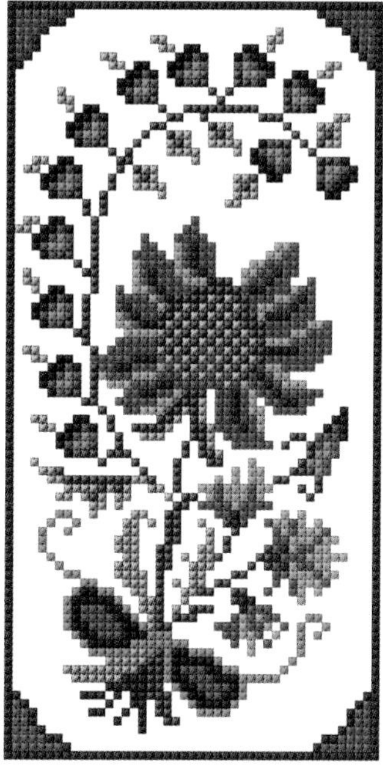

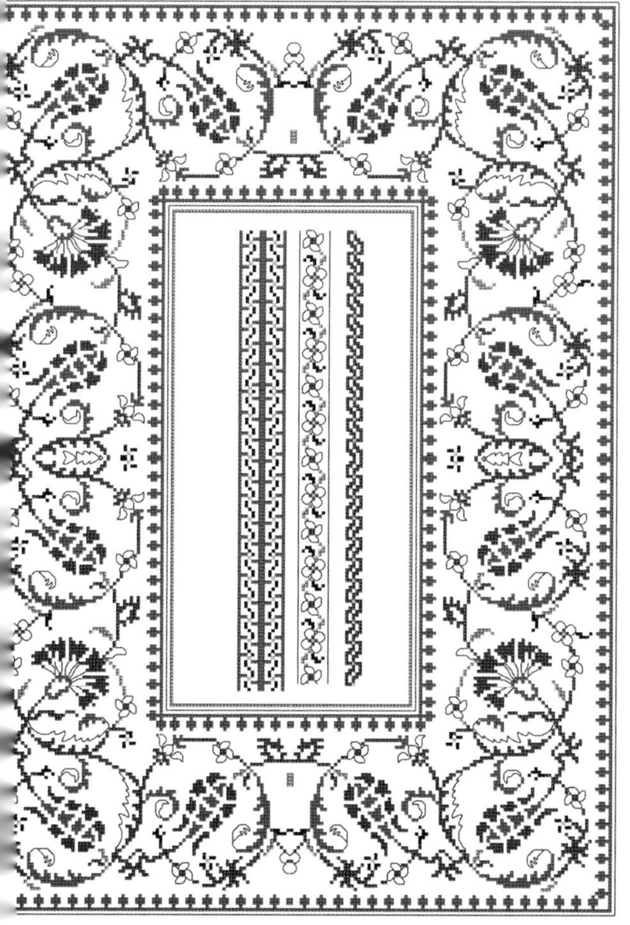

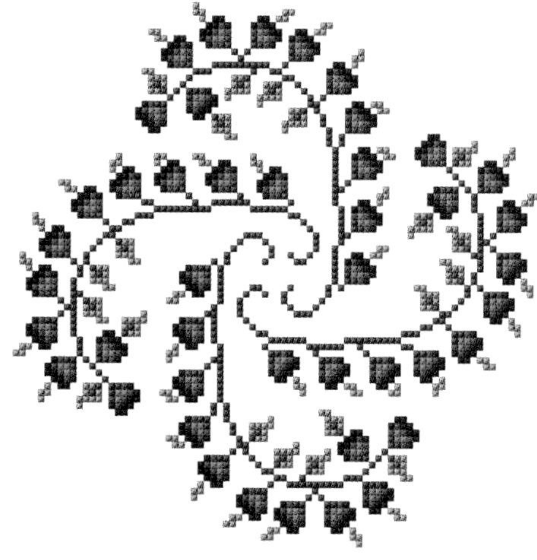

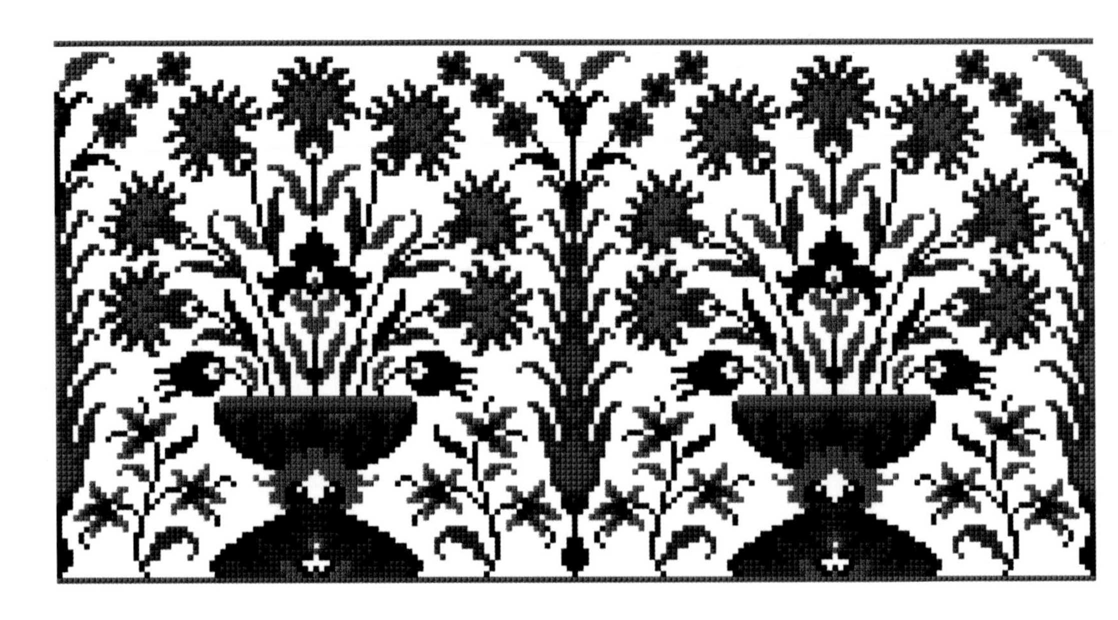

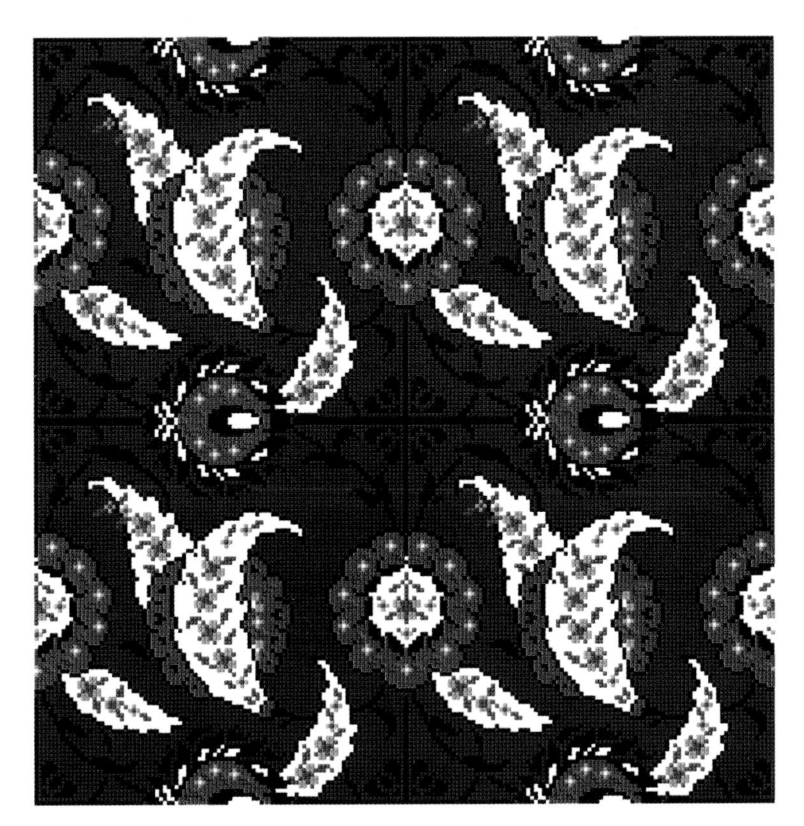

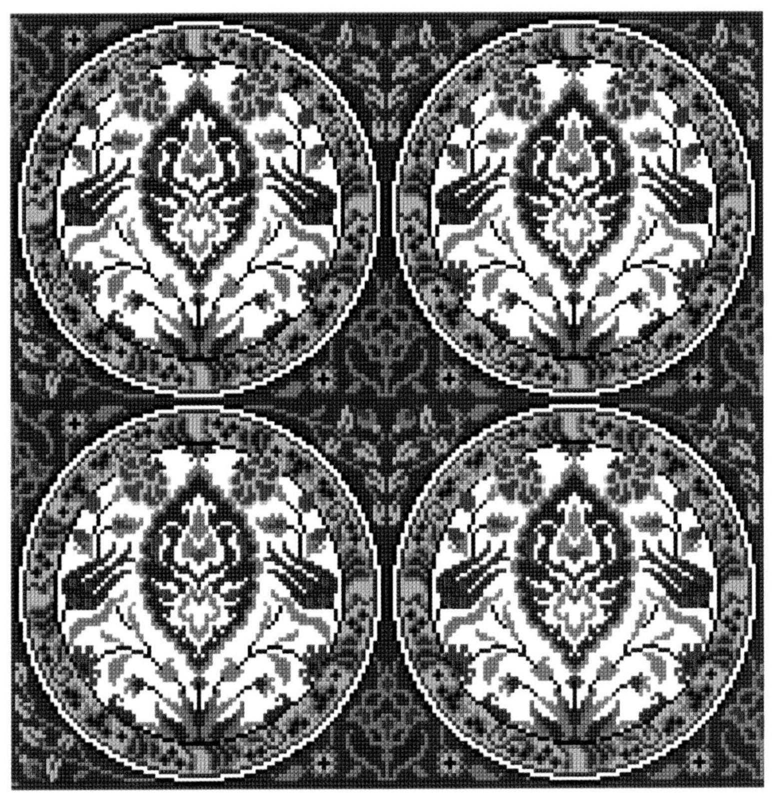

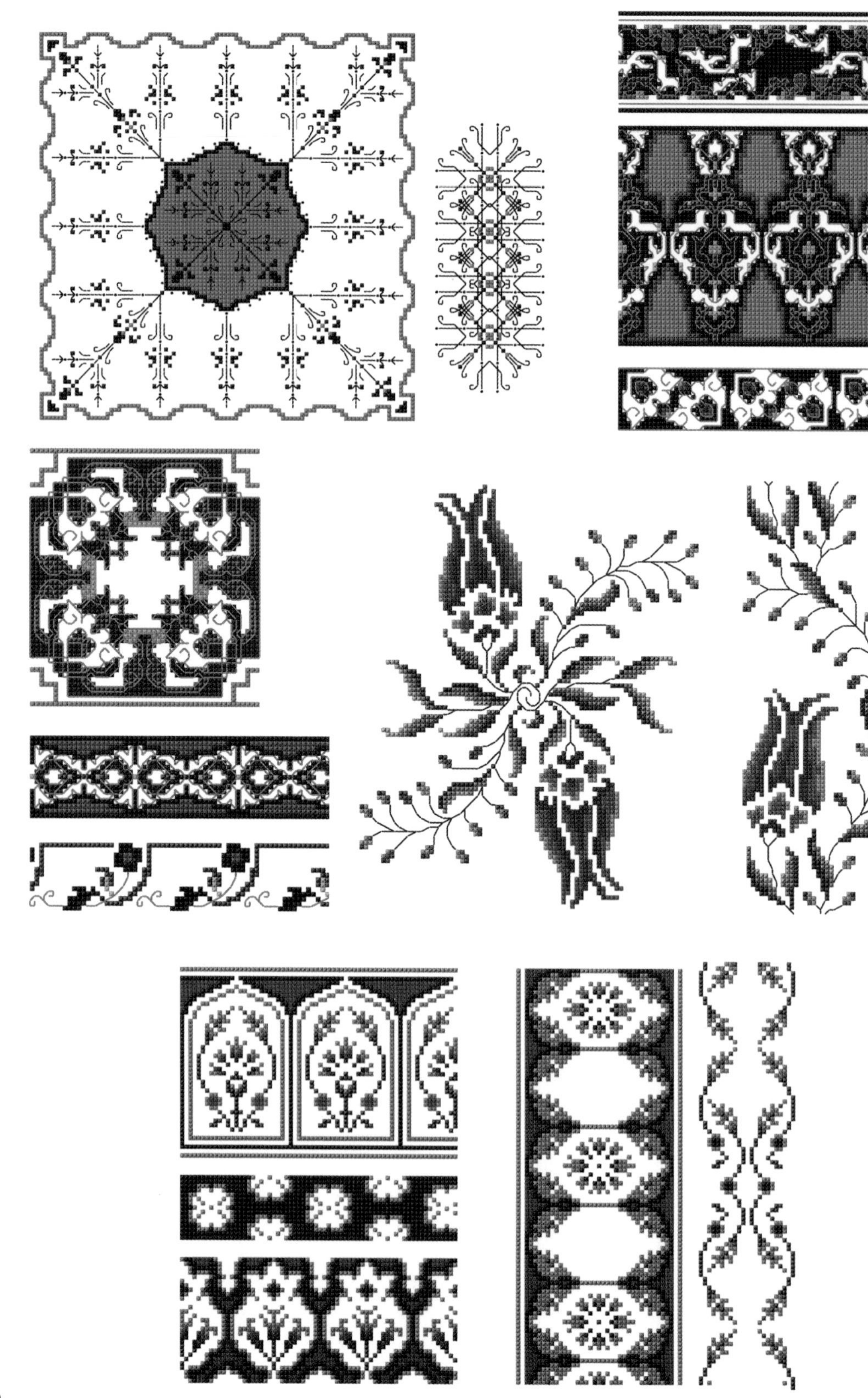

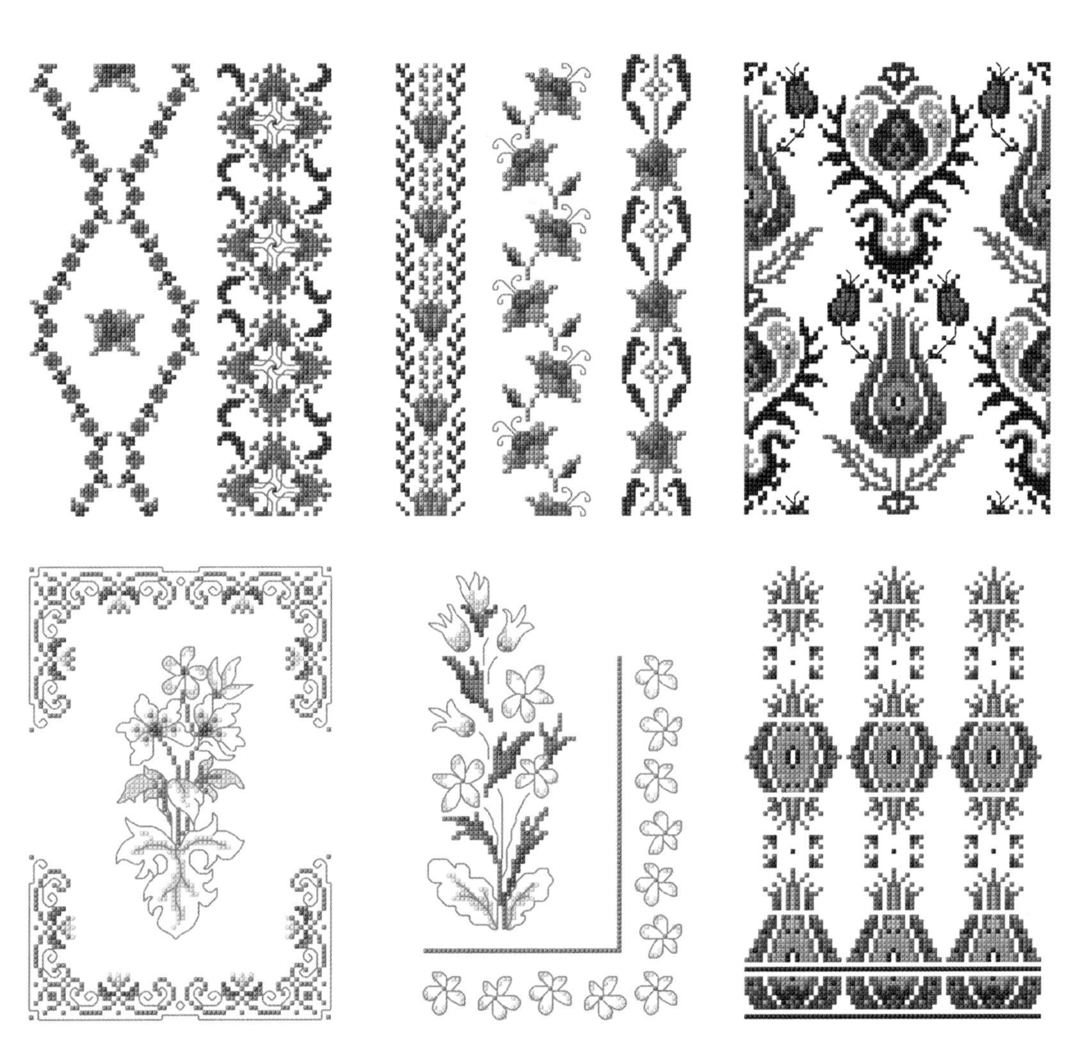

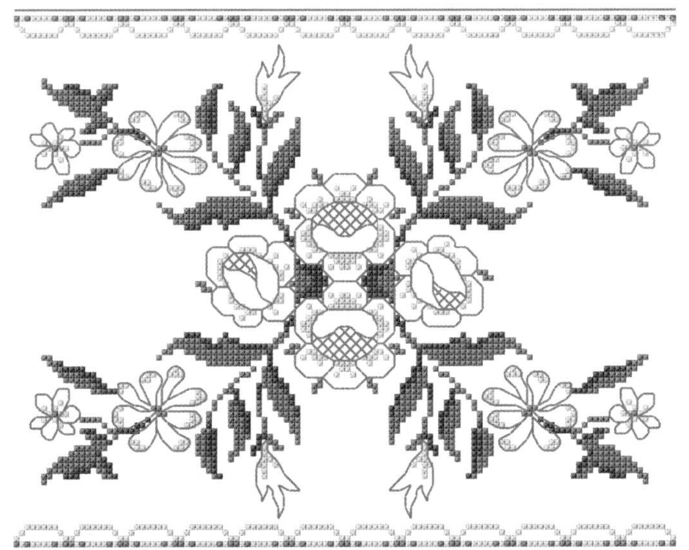

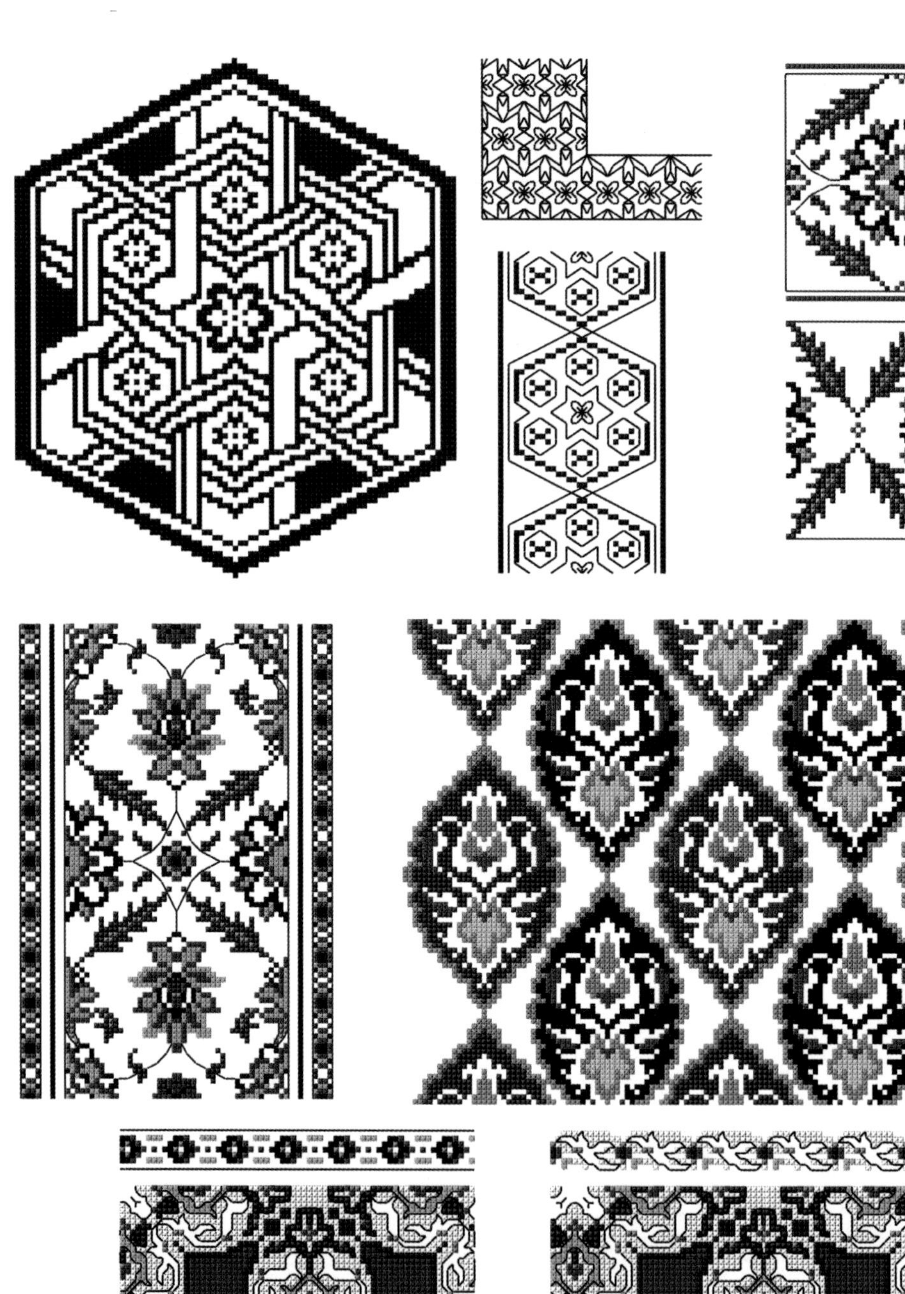

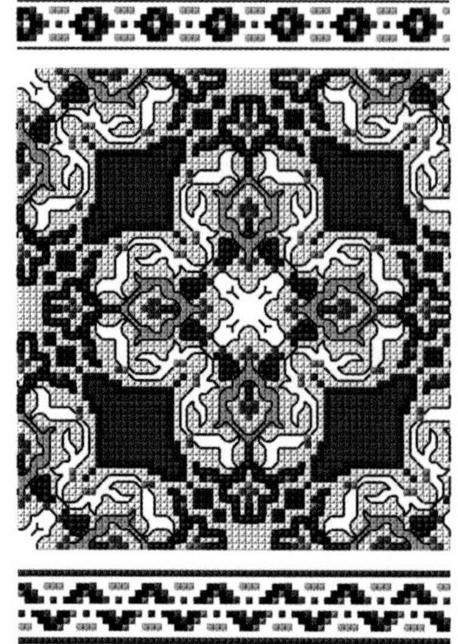

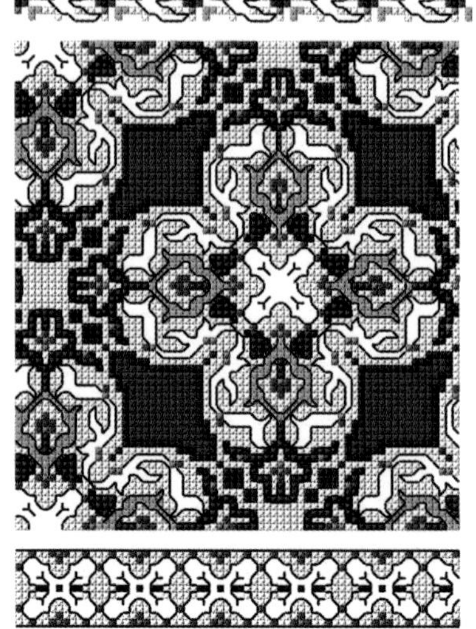

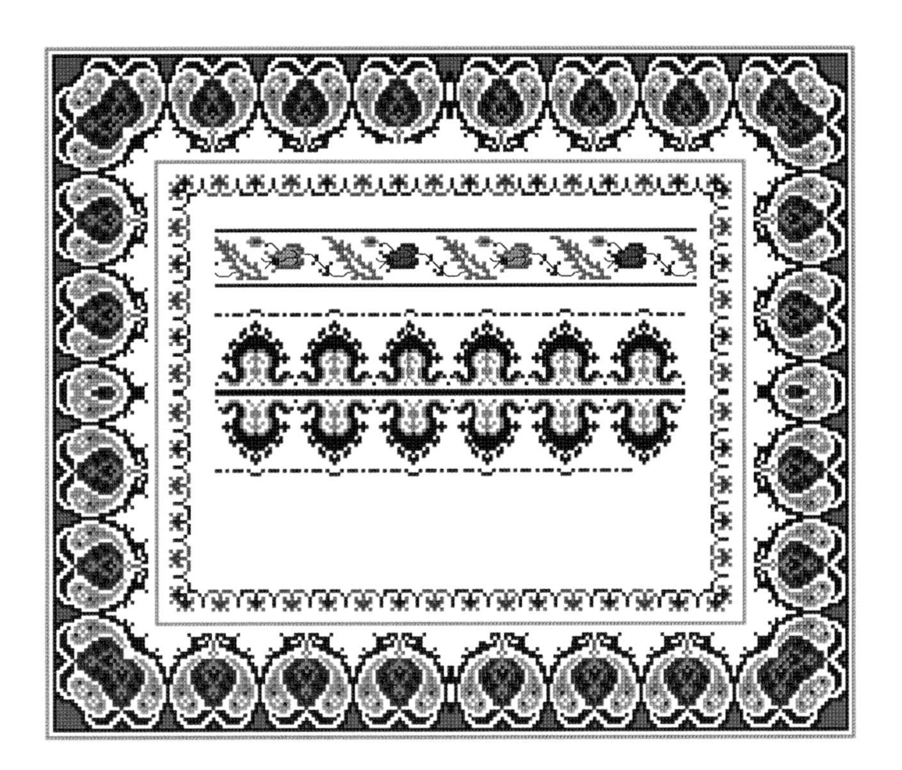

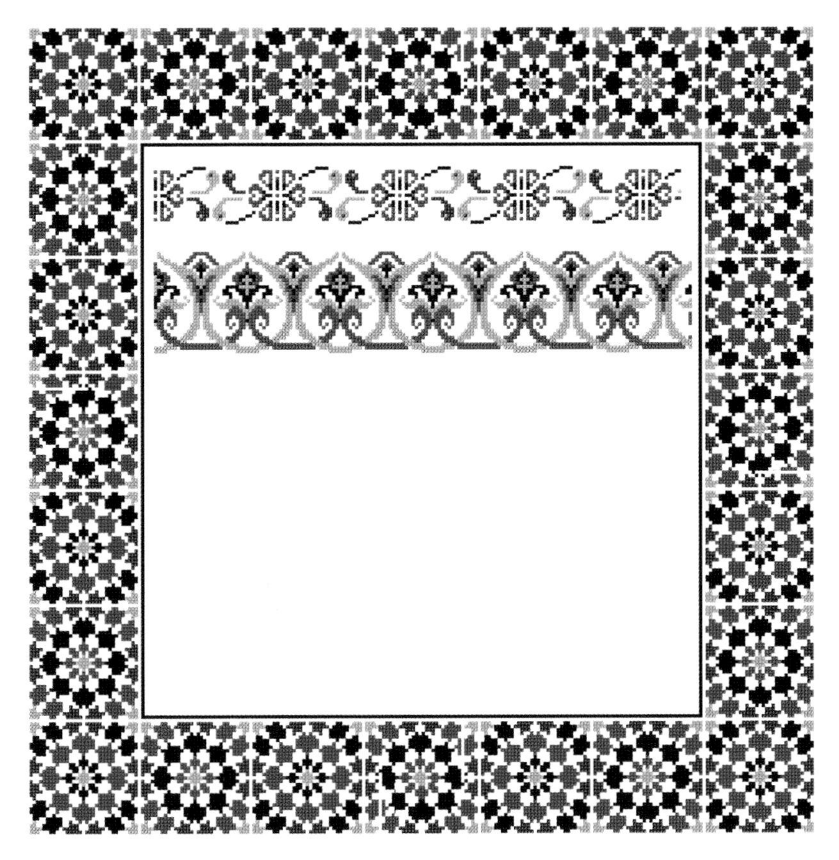

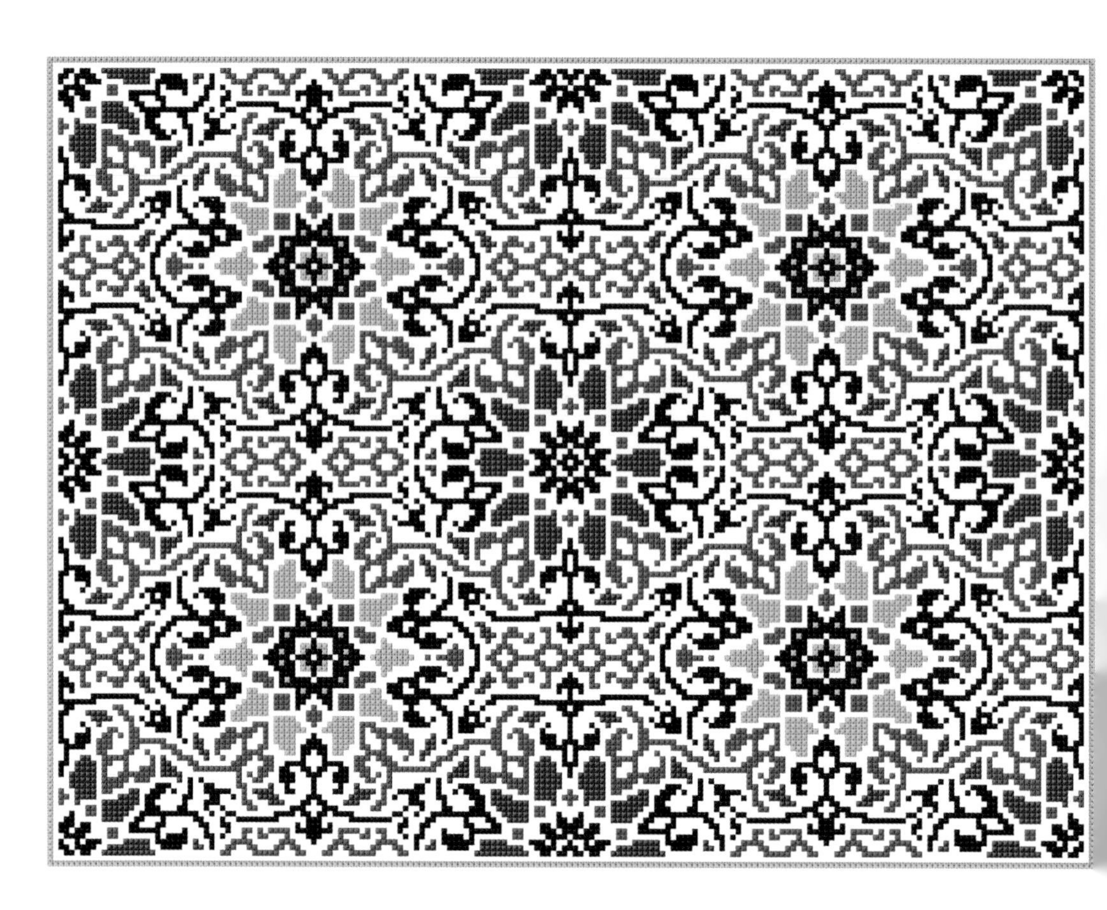

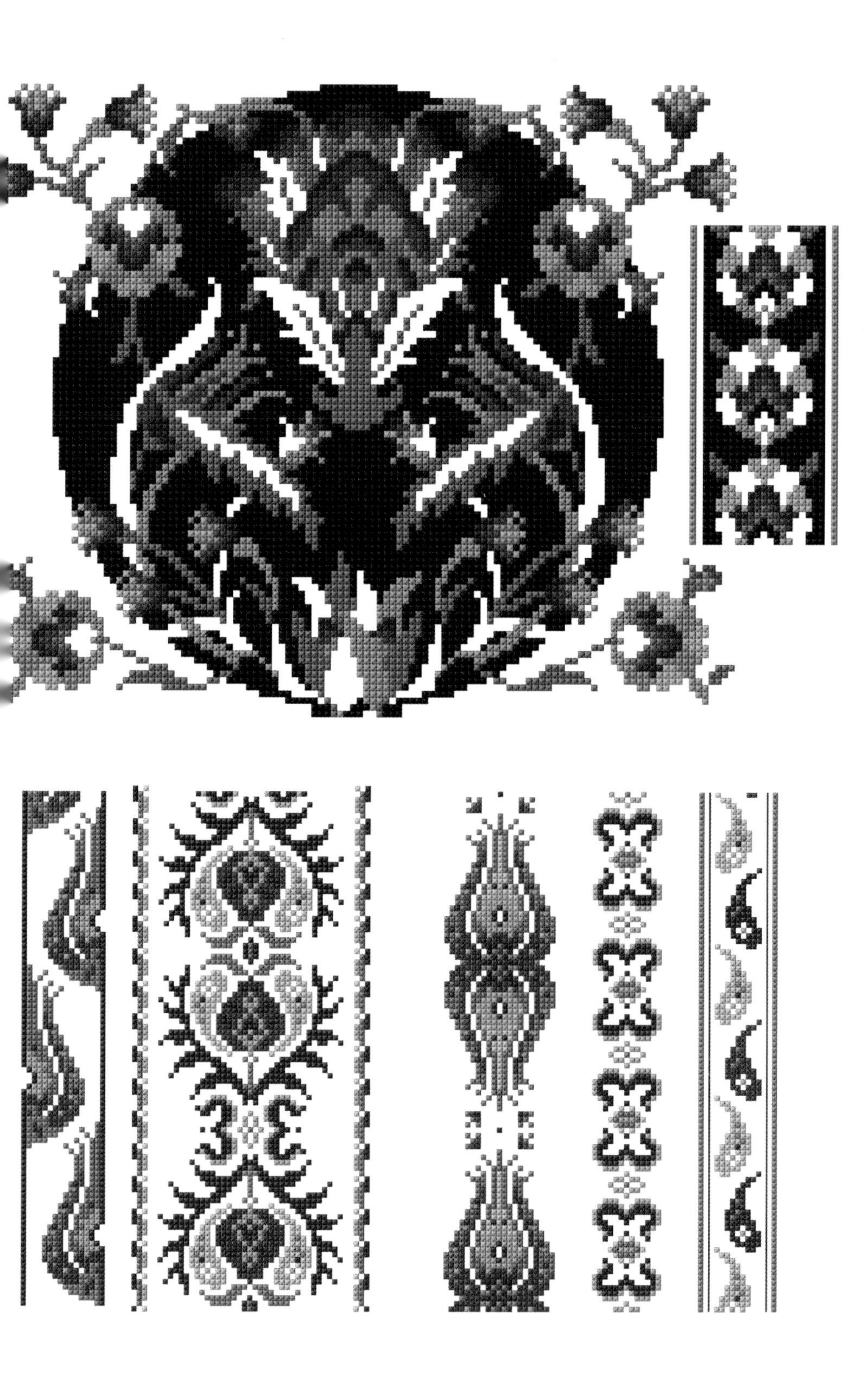

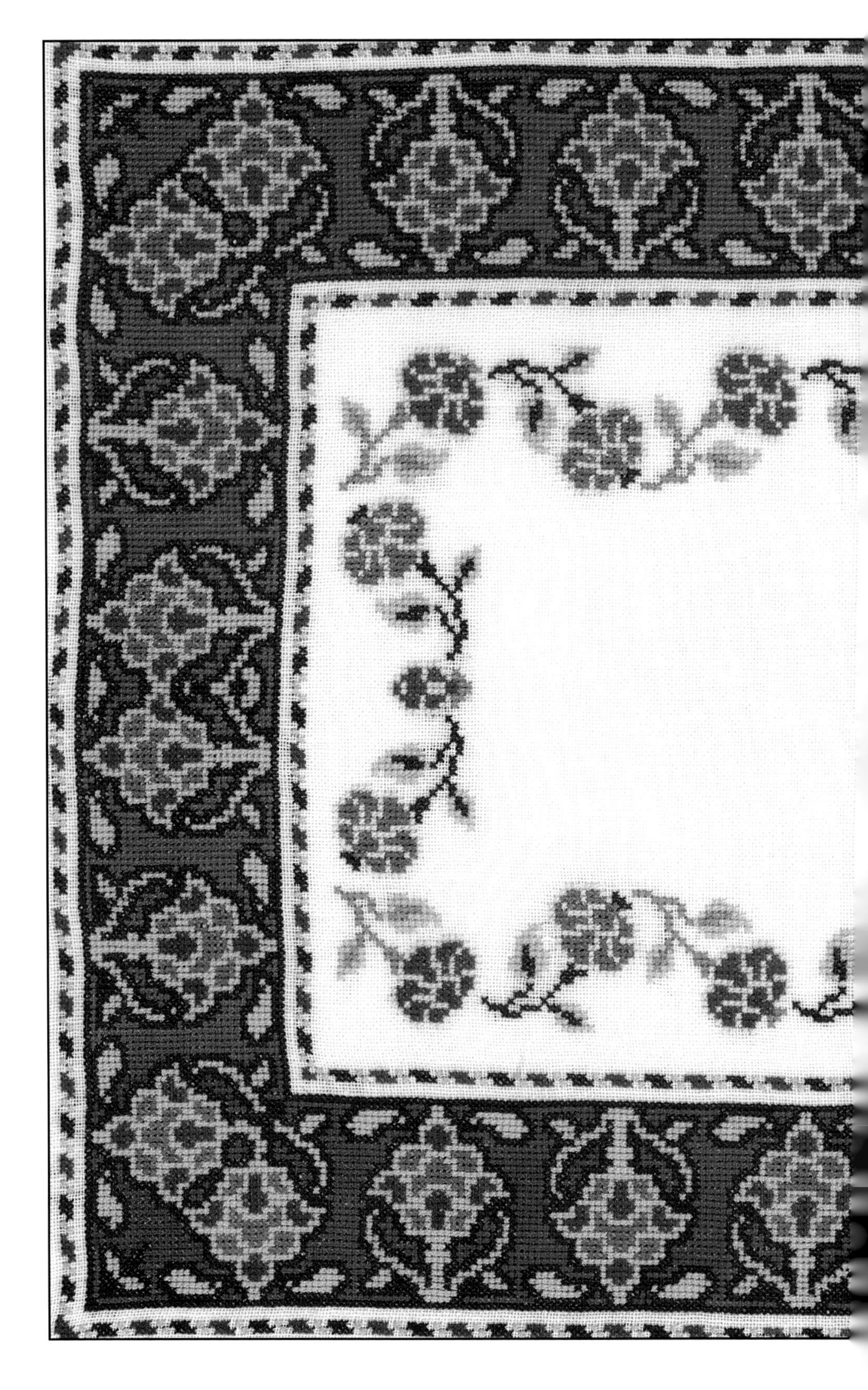

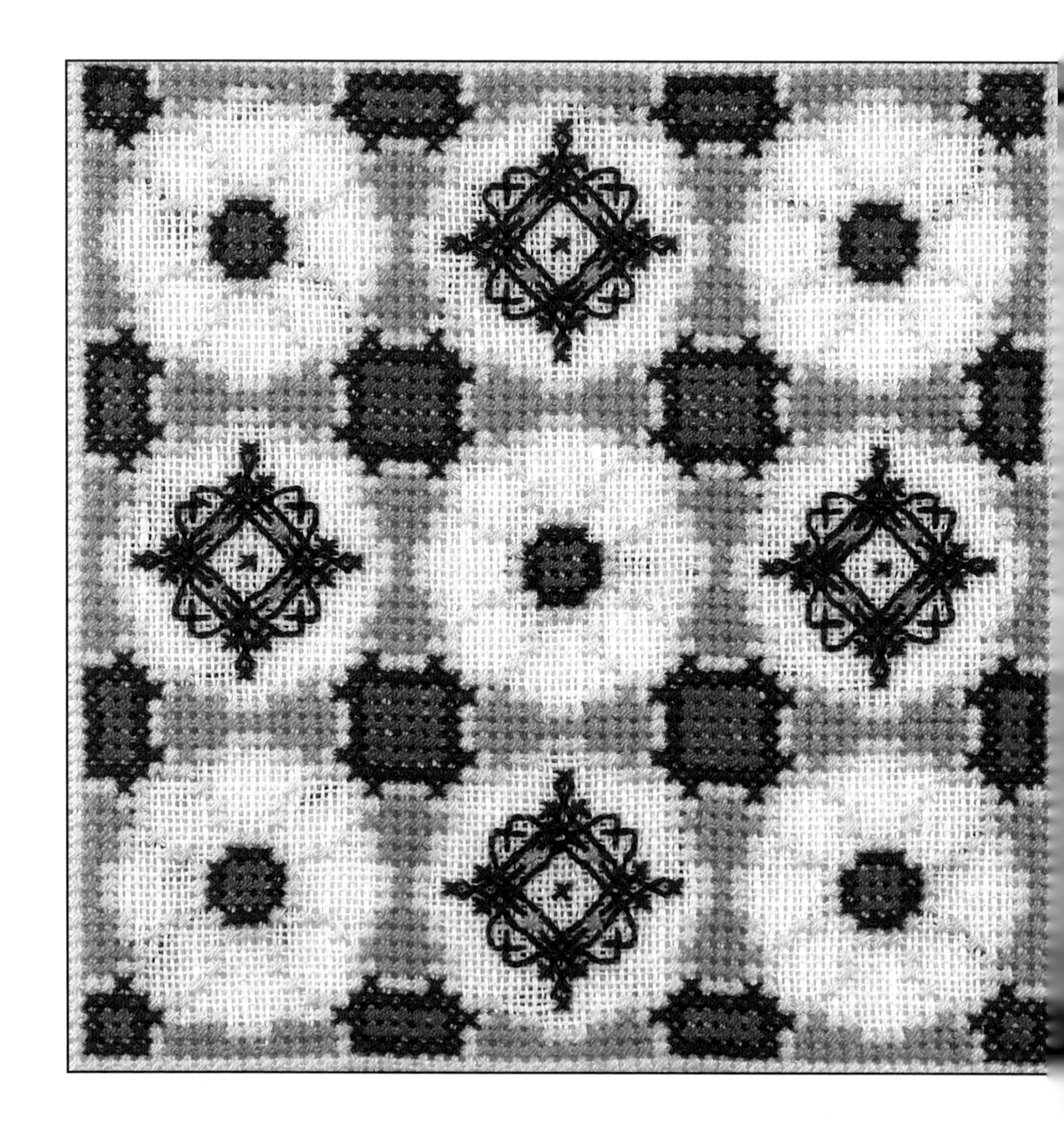

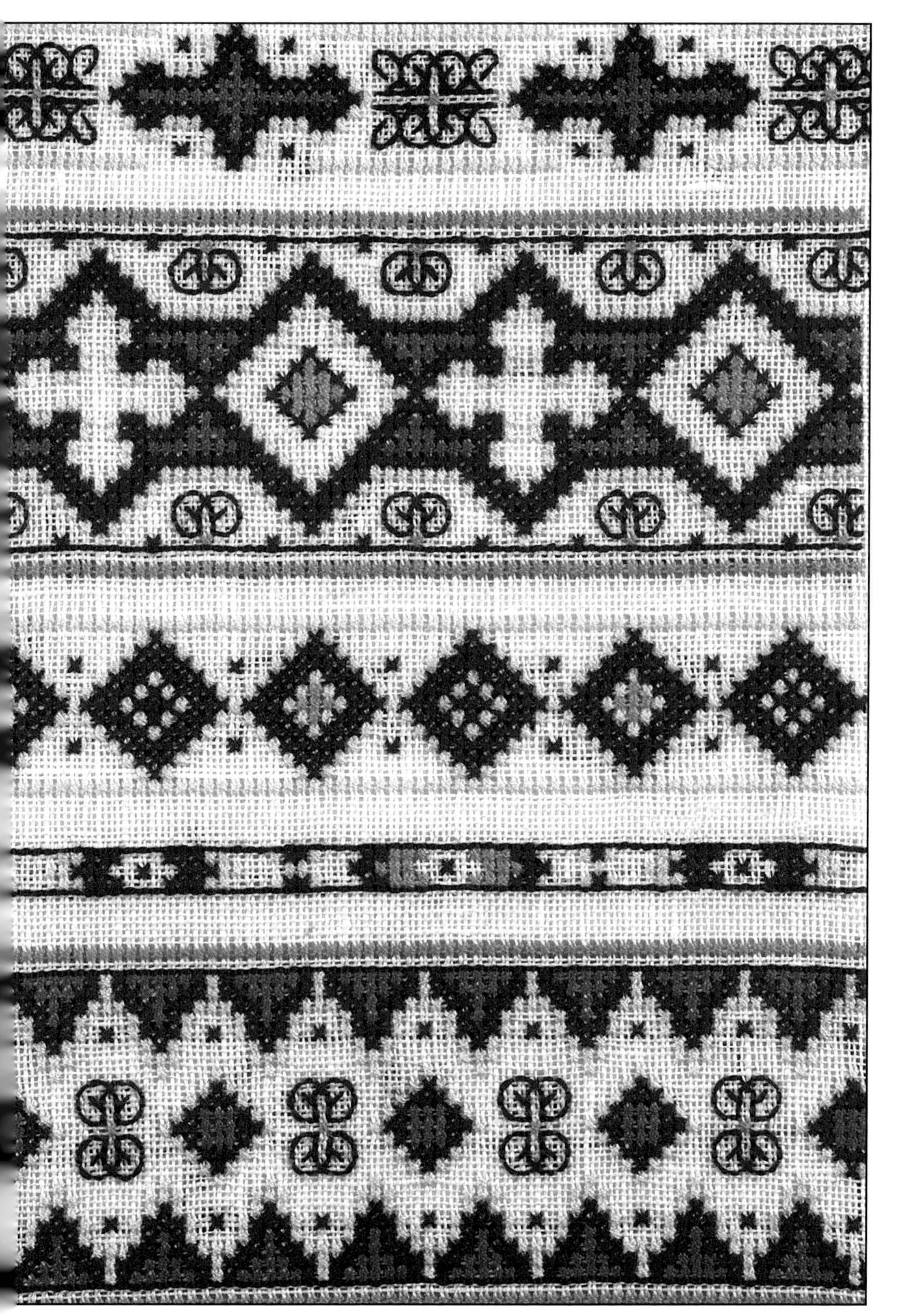

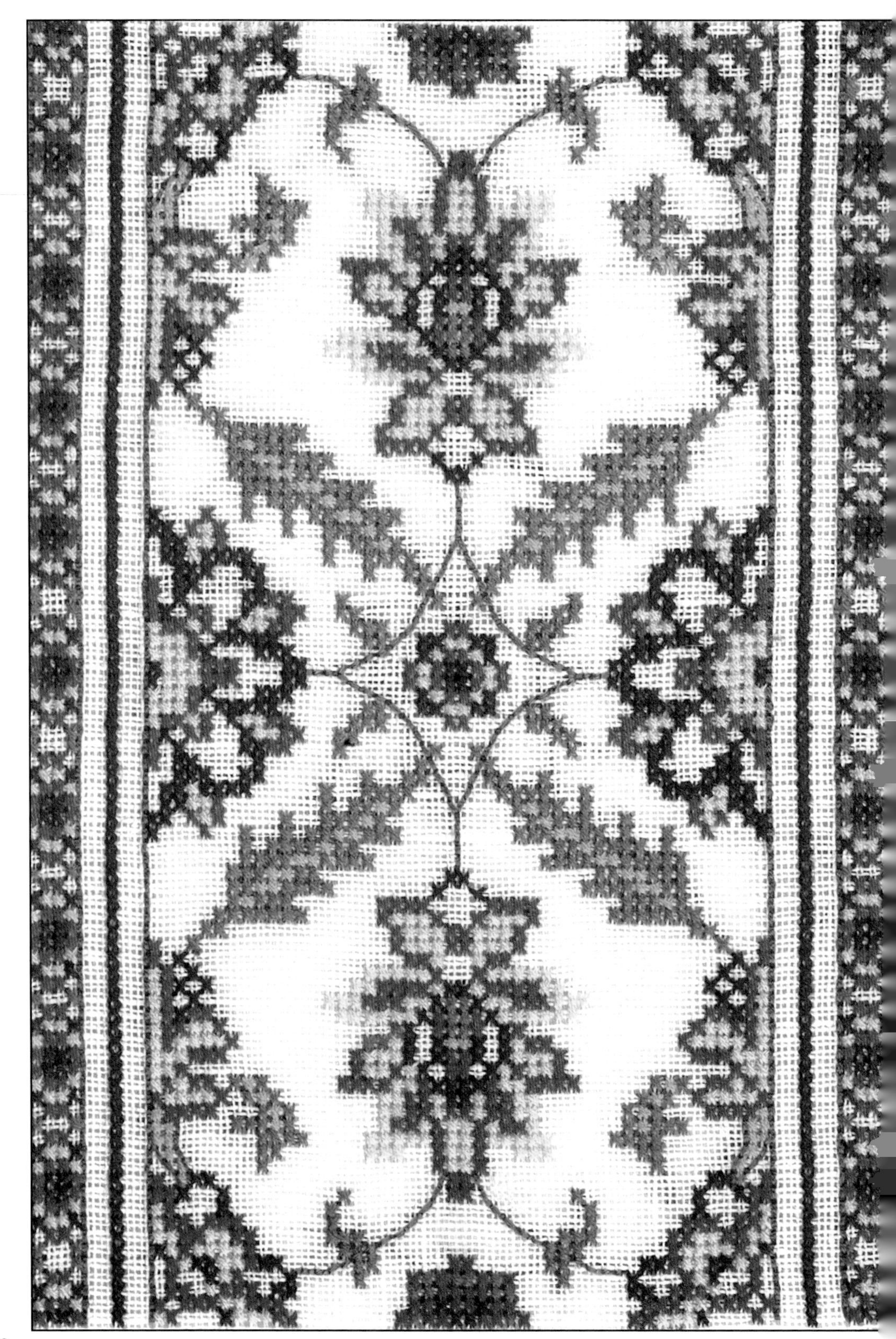

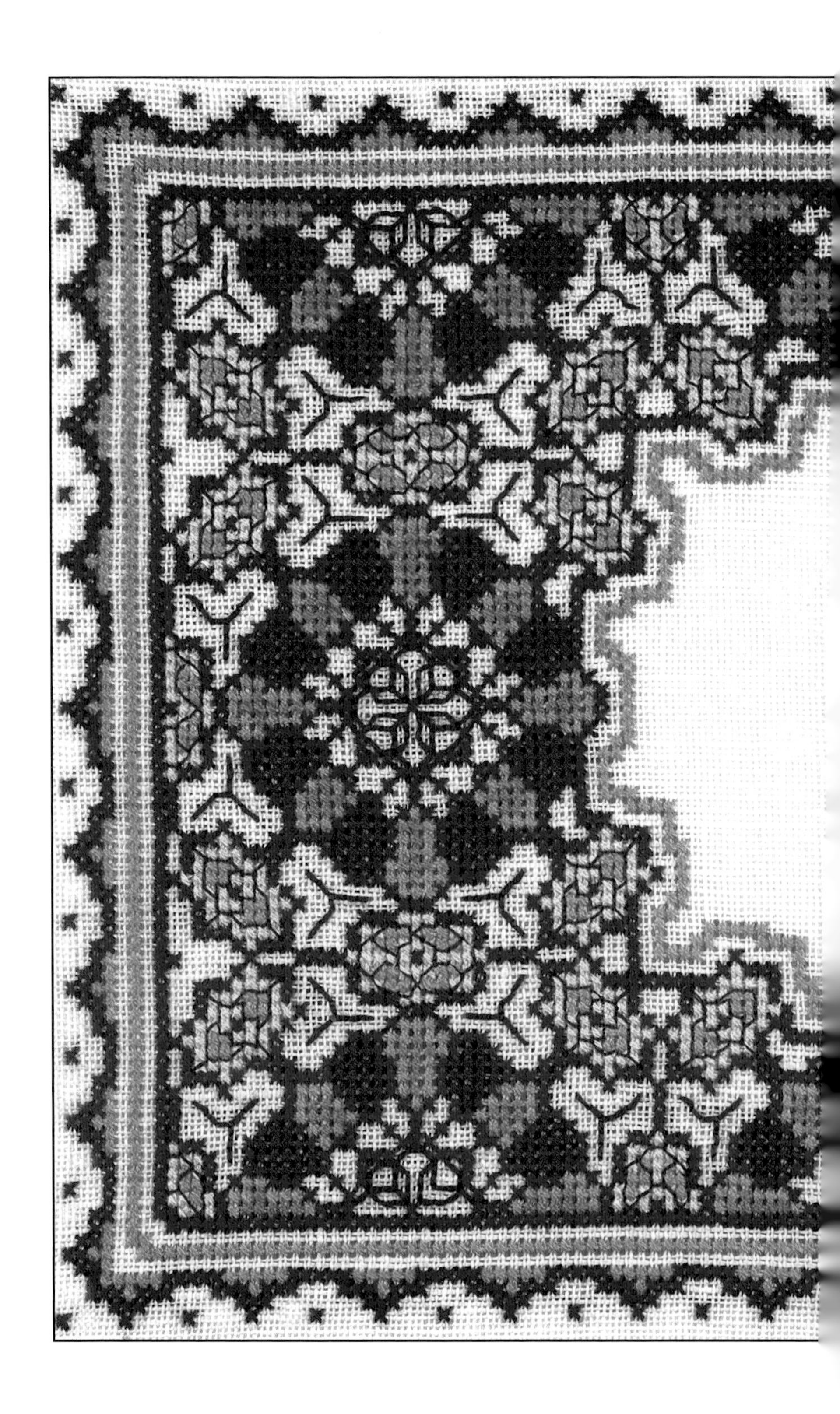

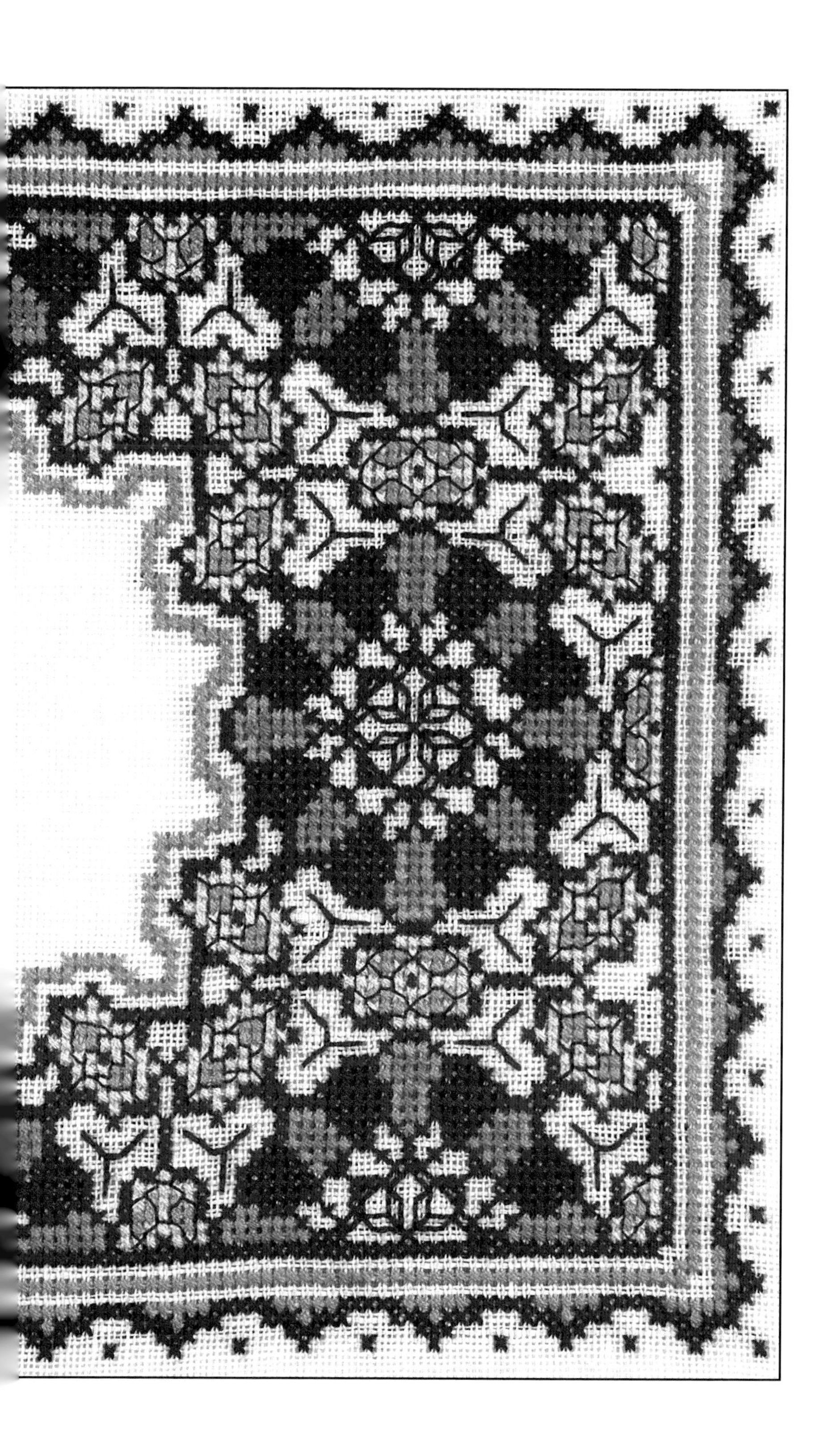

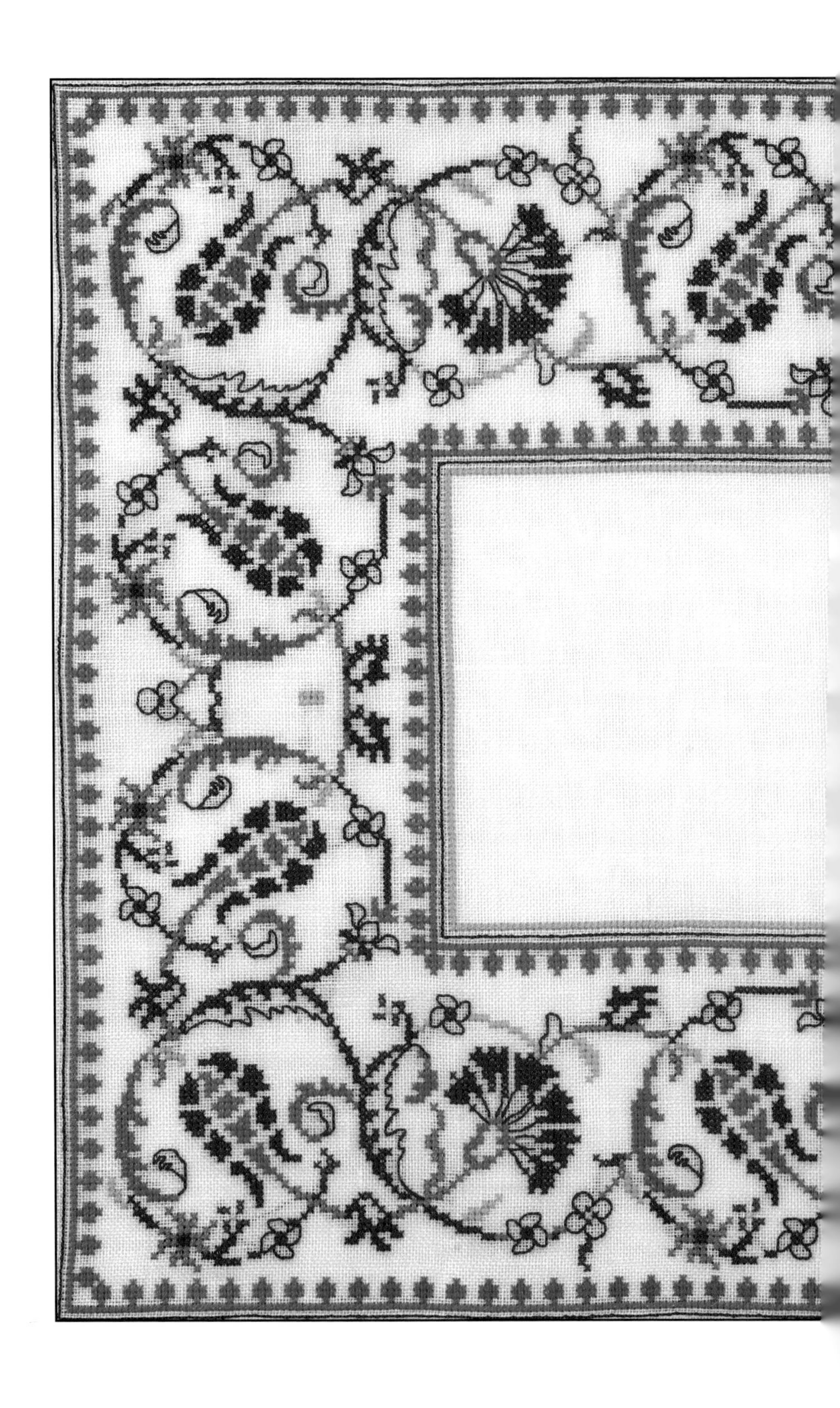

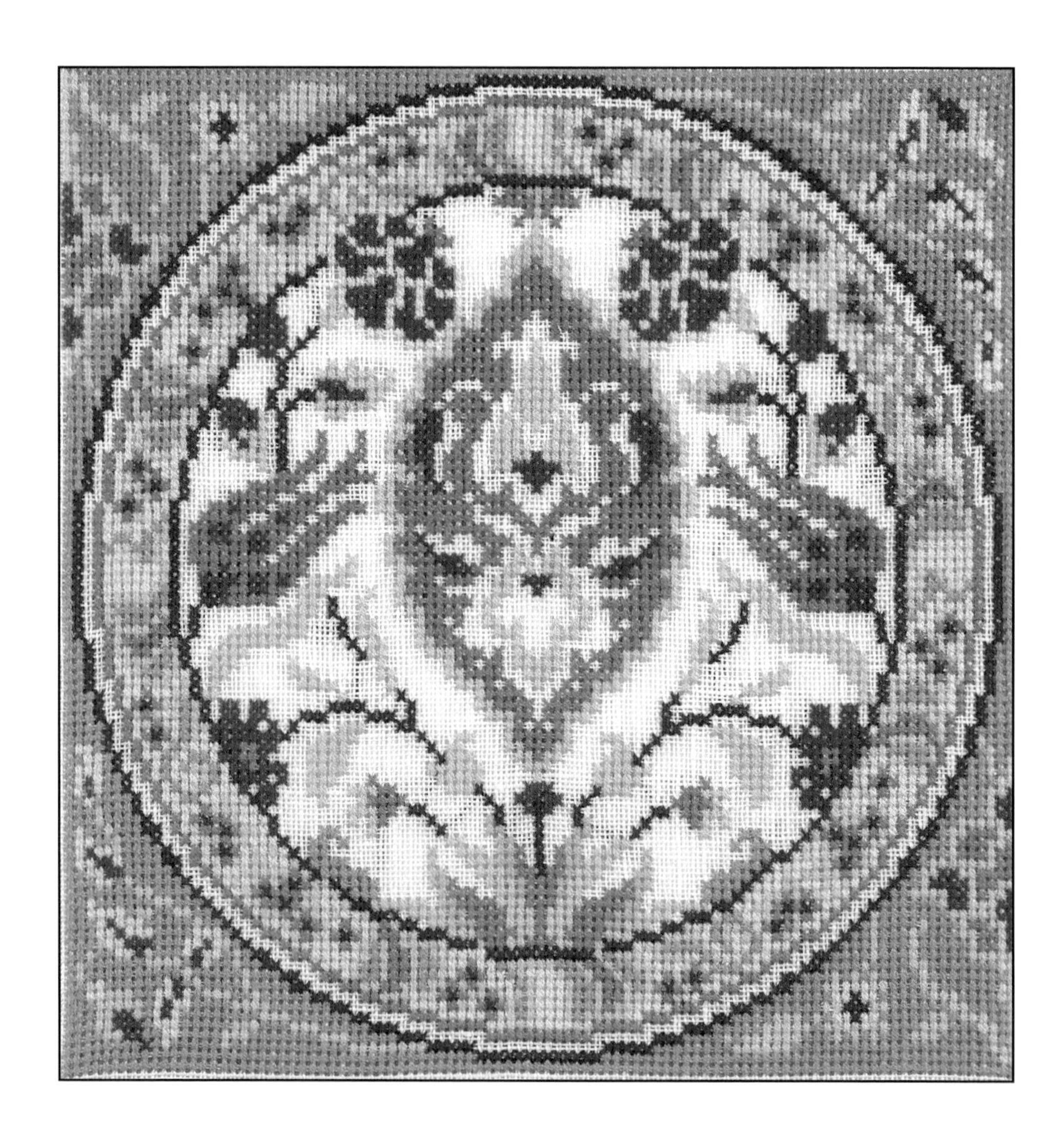

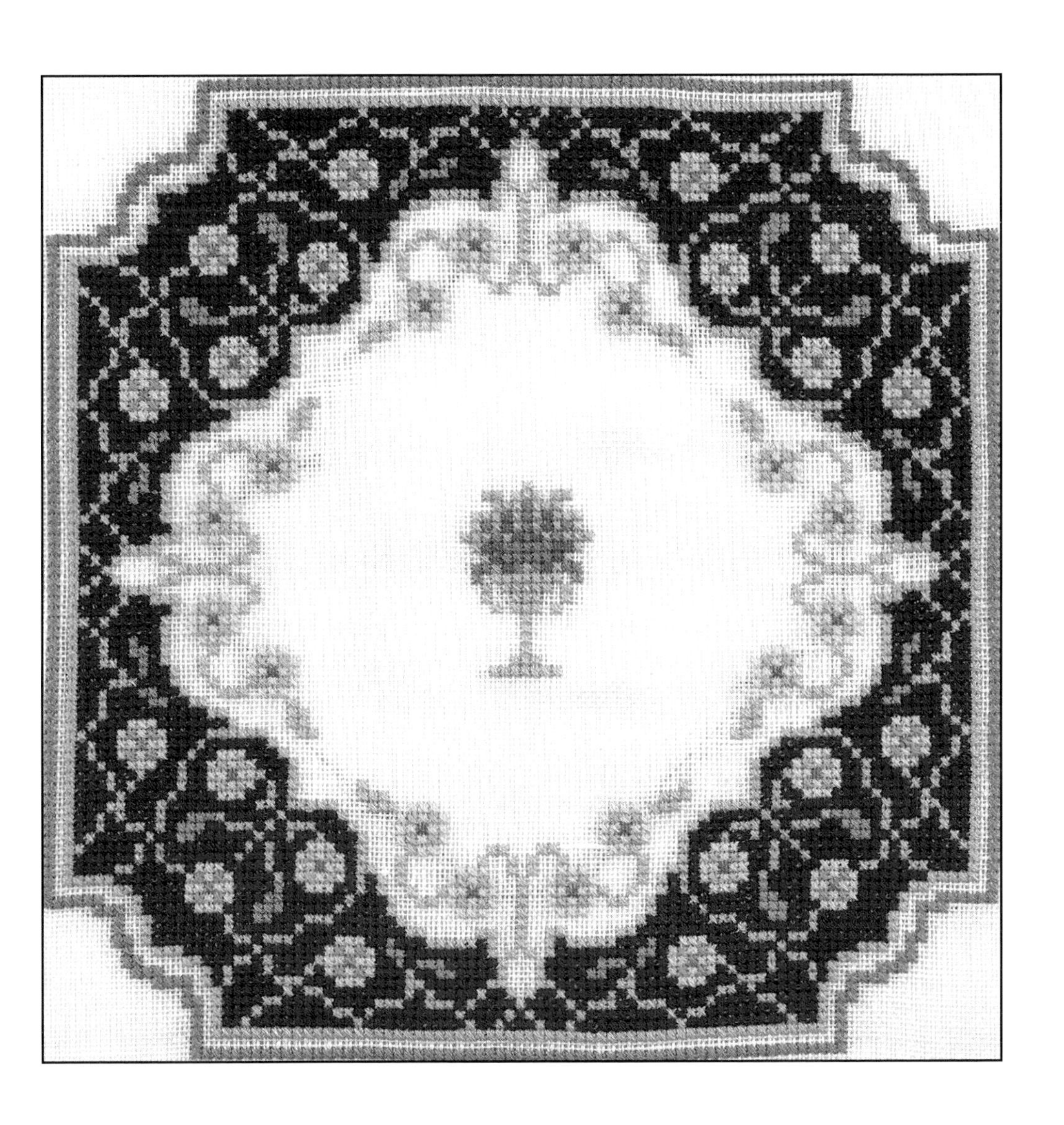

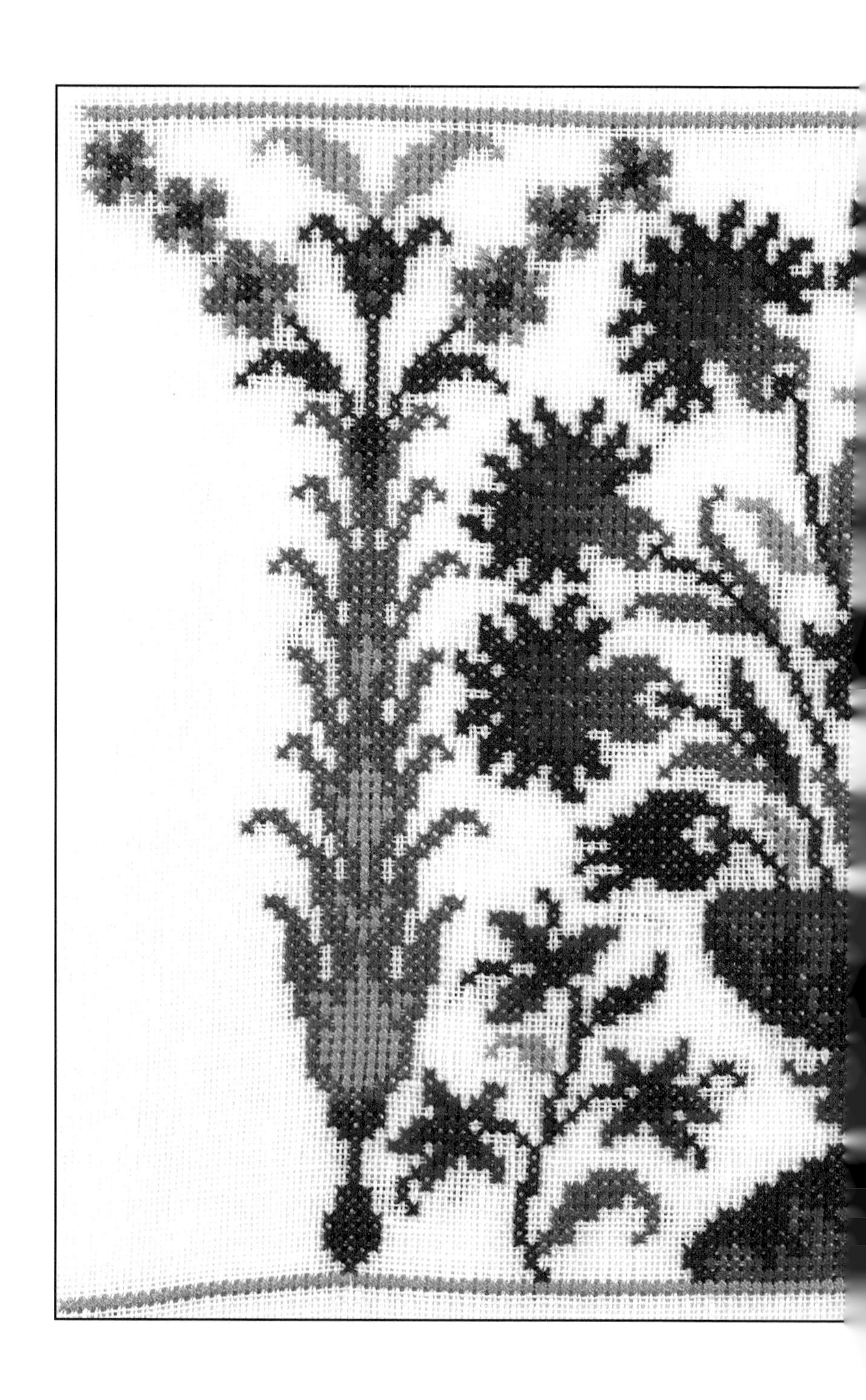

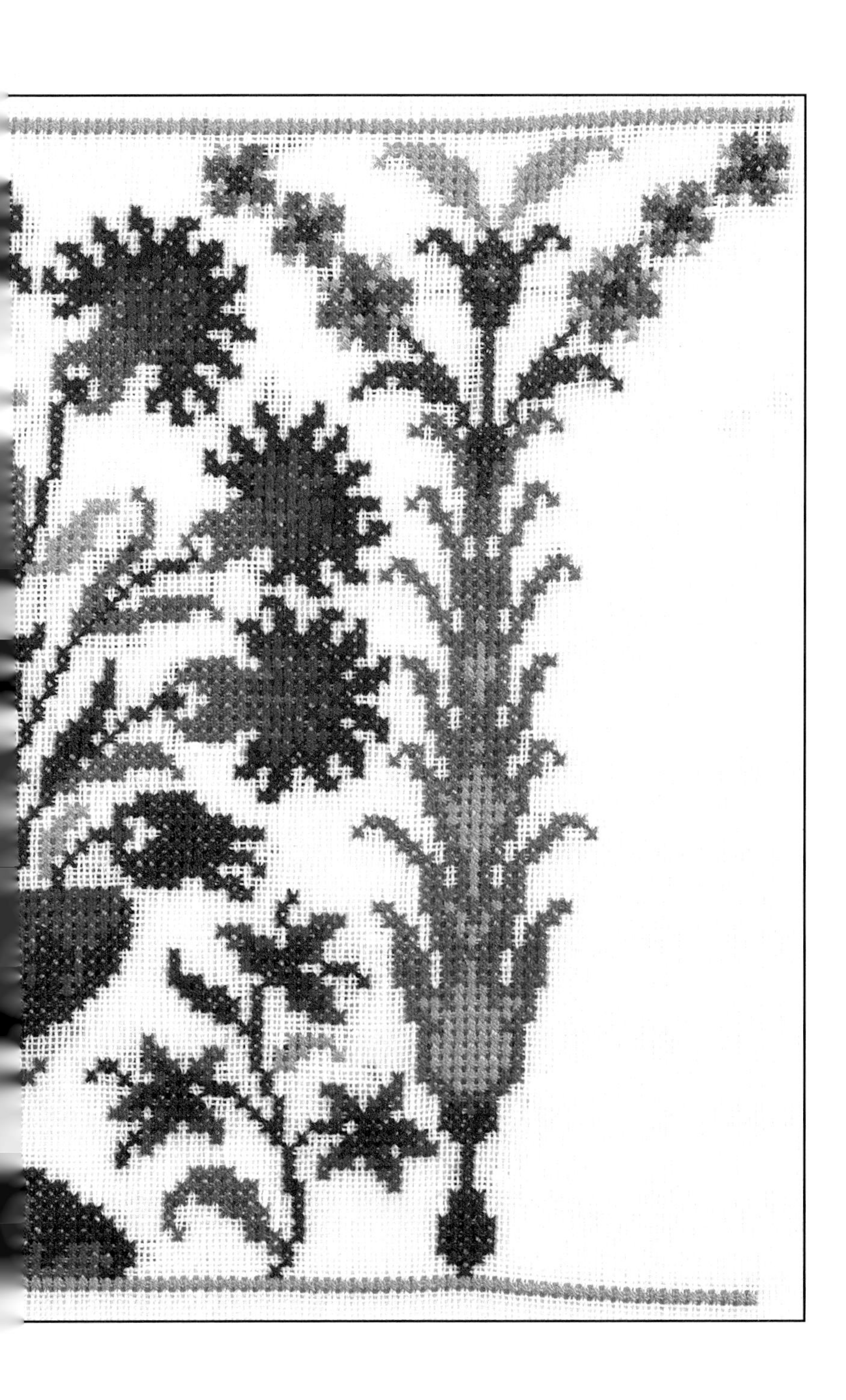

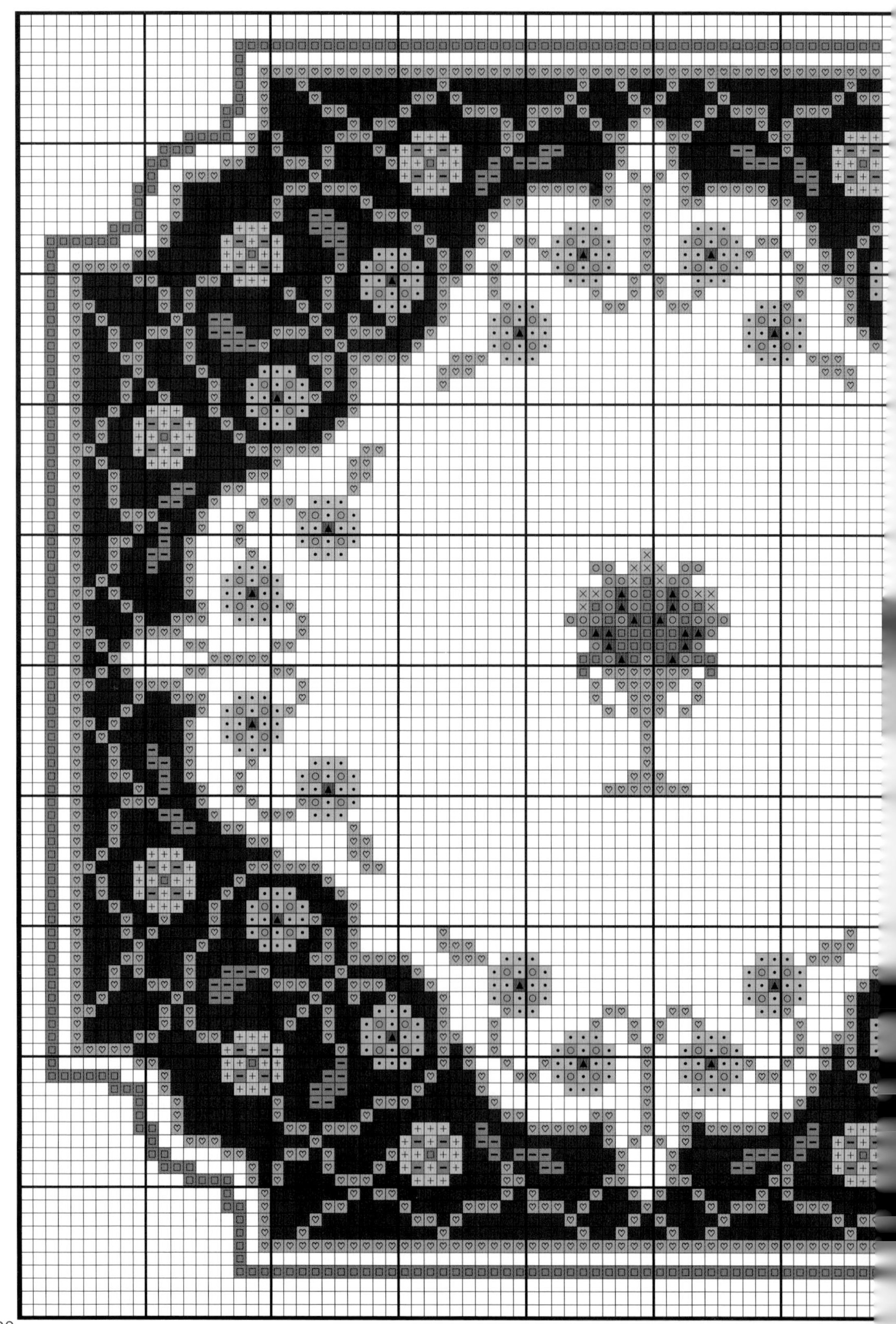

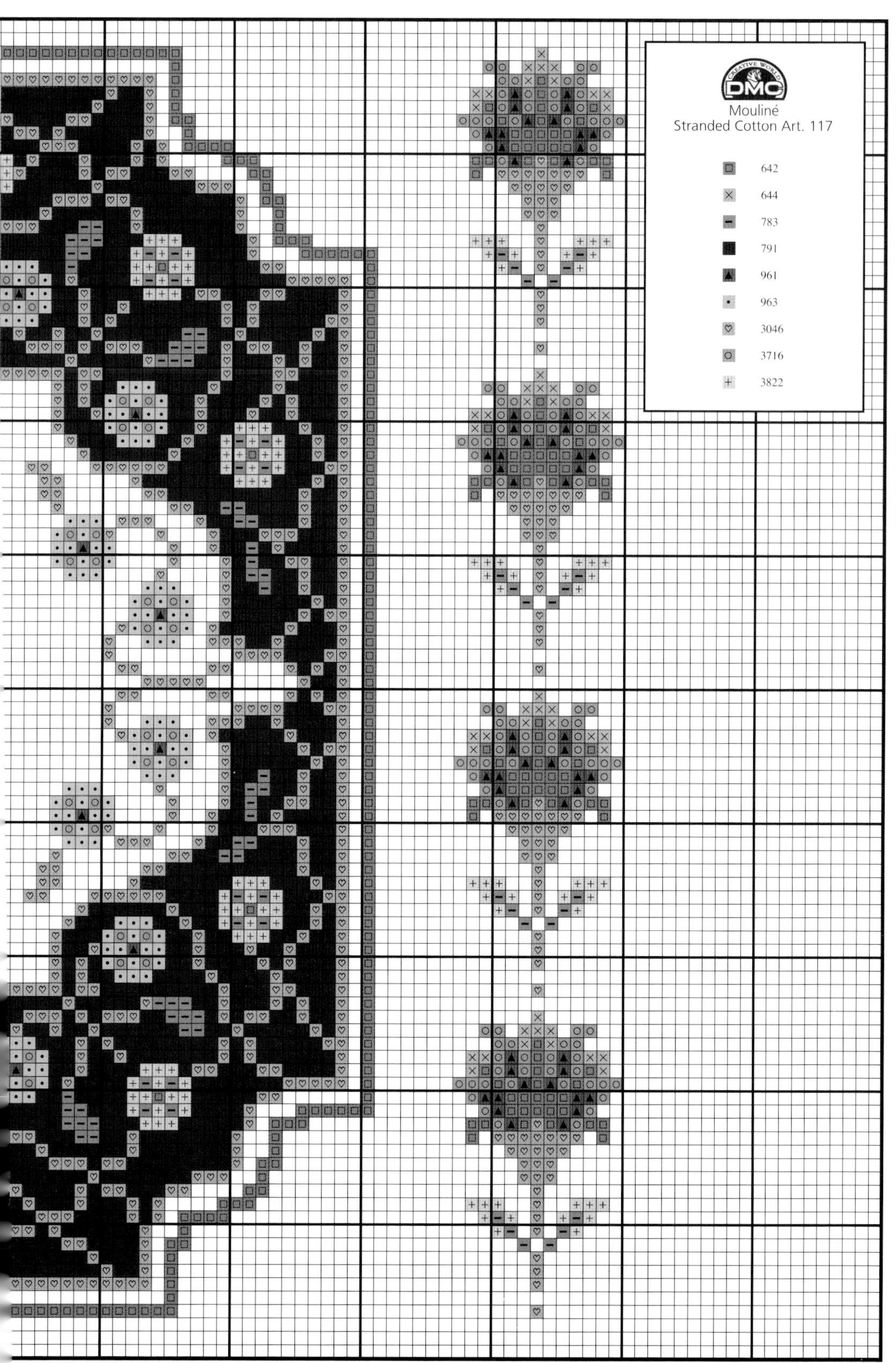
DMC
Mouliné
Stranded Cotton Art. 117
642
644
783
791
961
963
3046
3716
3822

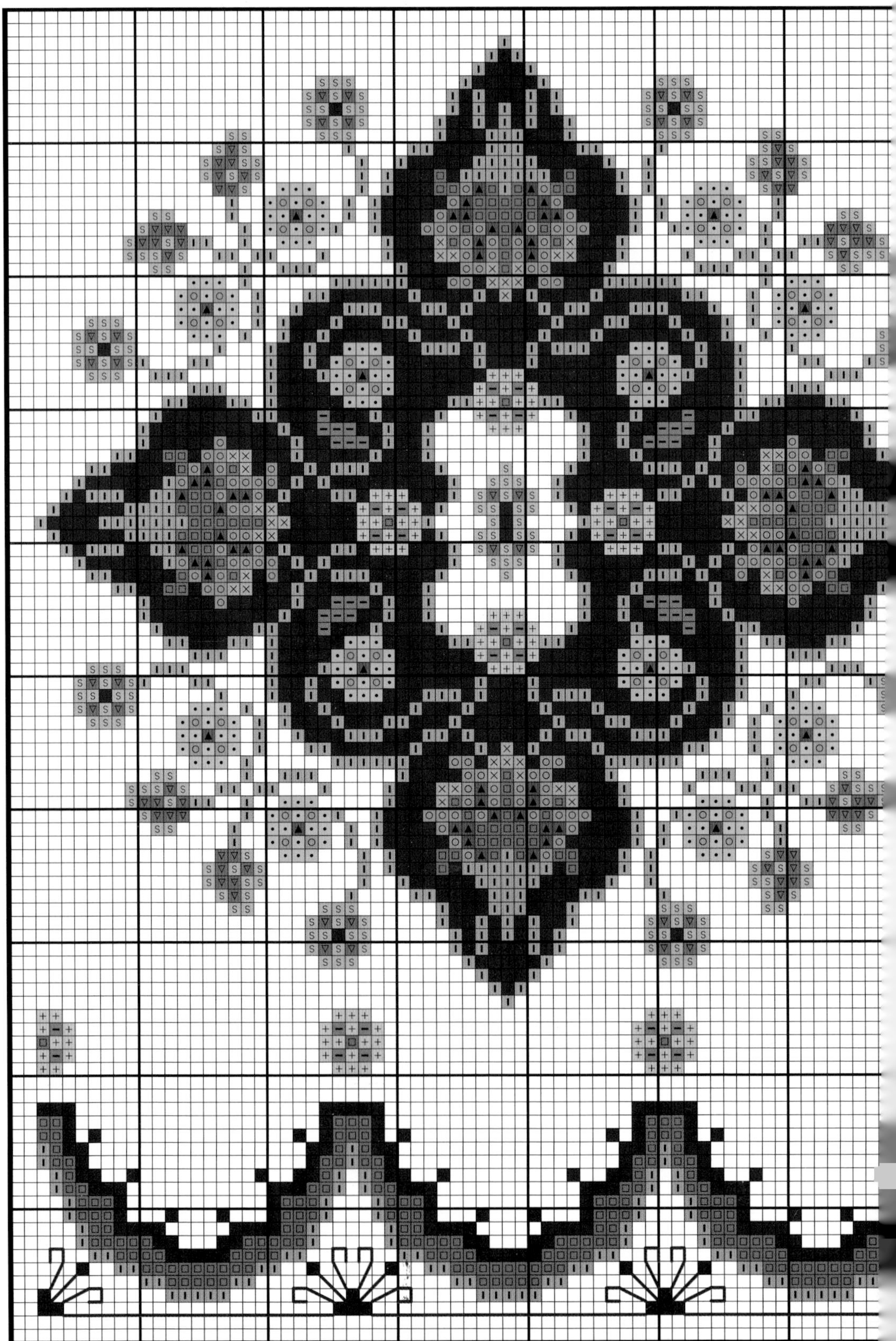

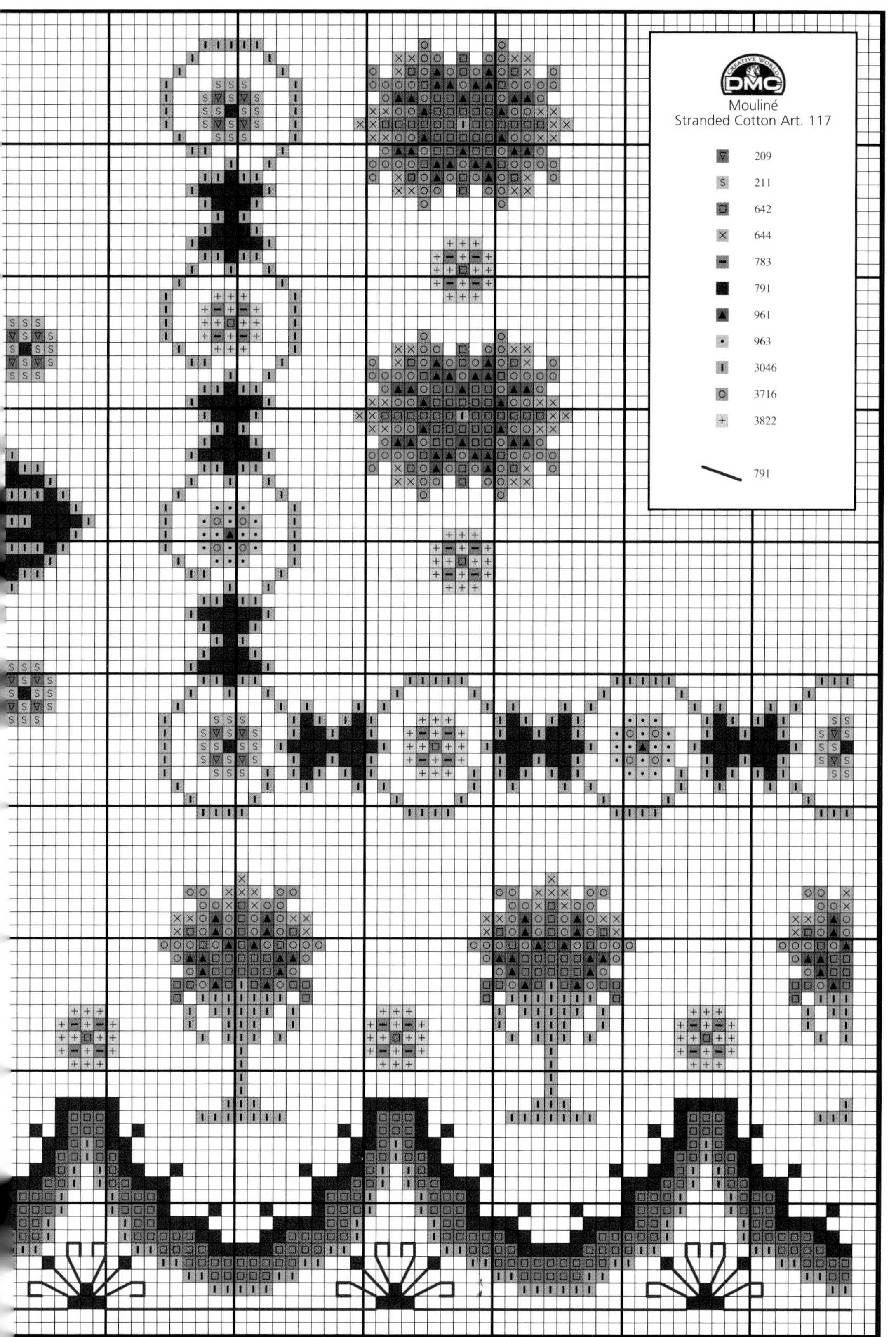

DMC
Mouliné
Stranded Cotton Art. 117
209
211
642
644
783
791
961
963
3046
3716
3822
791

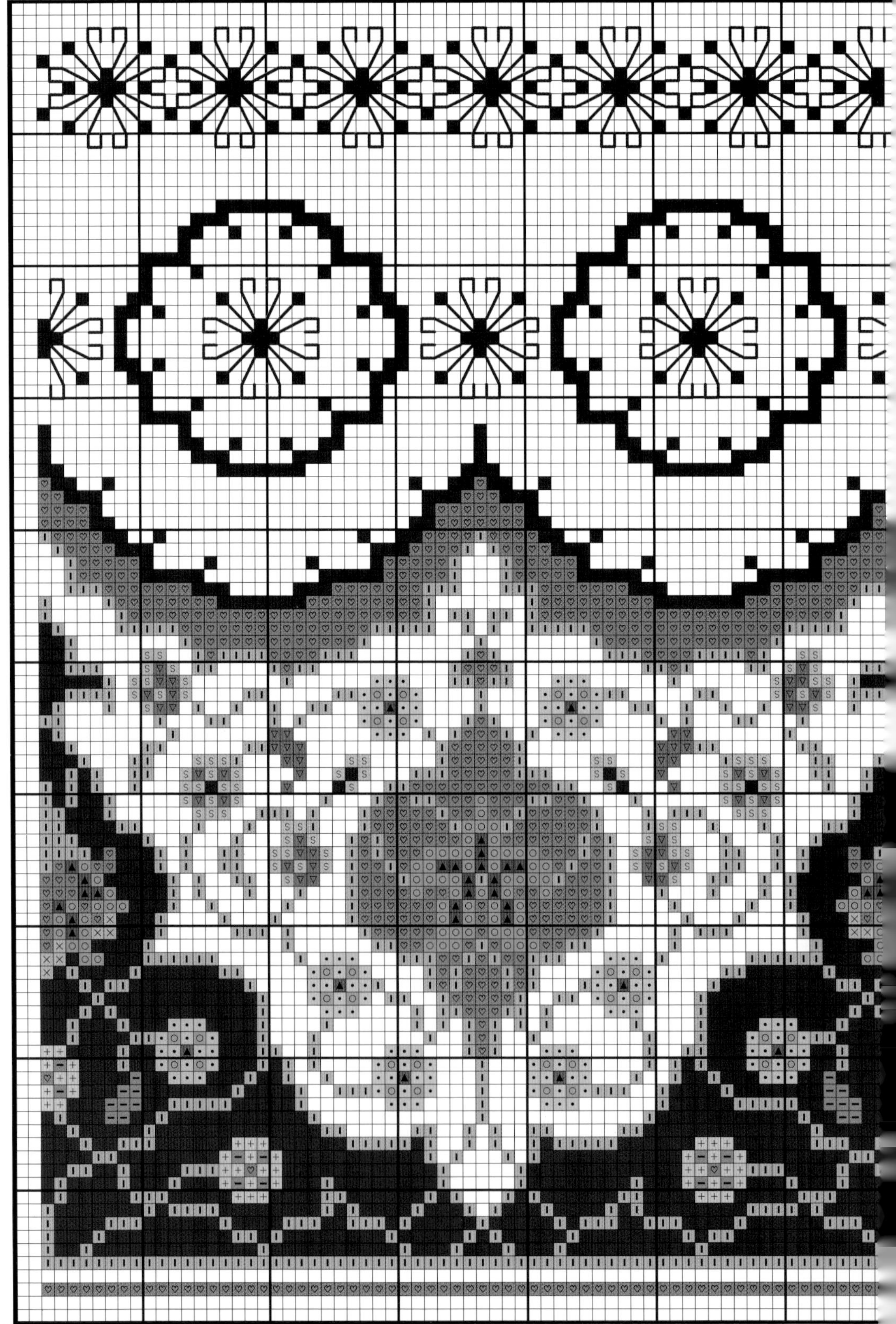

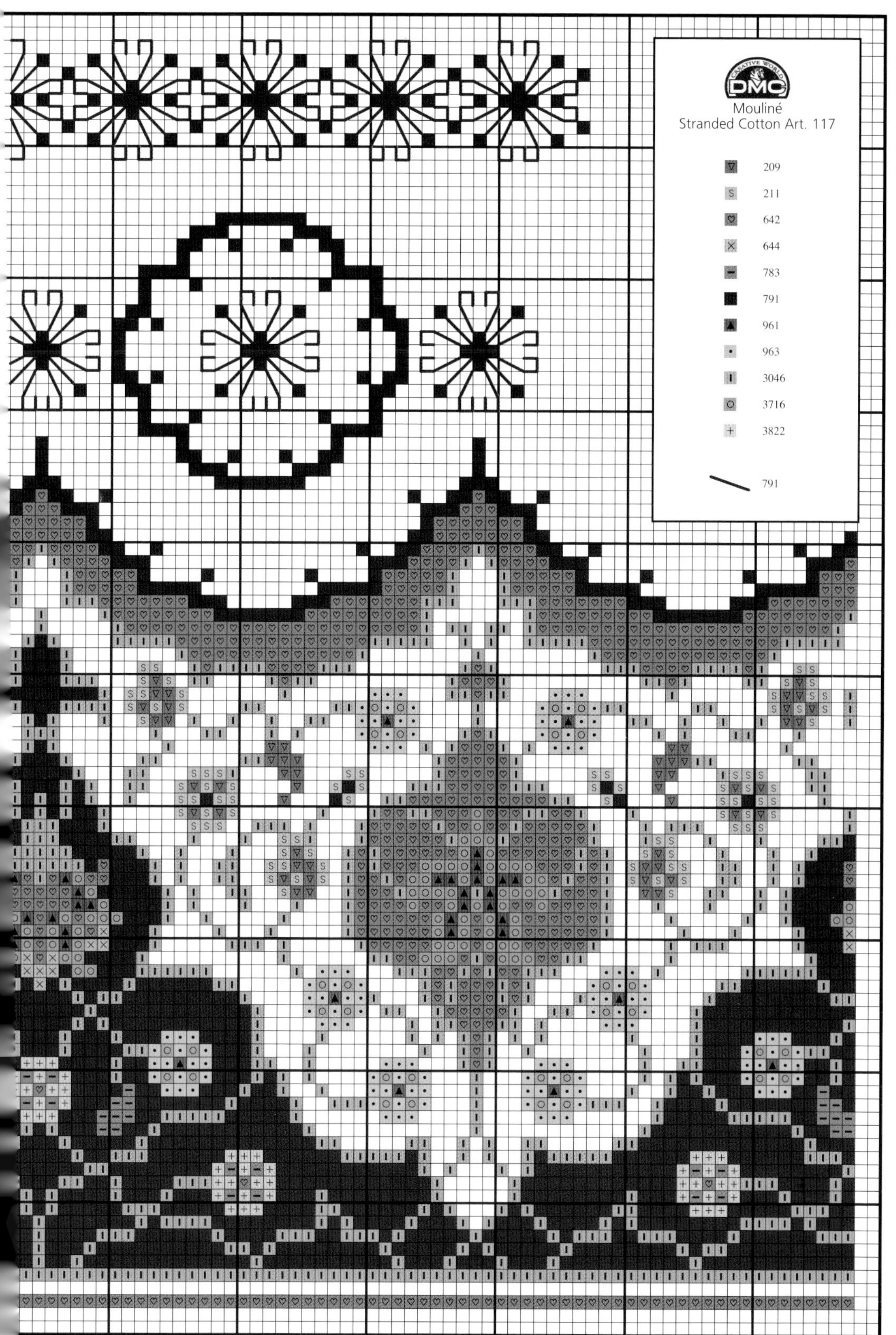
DMC
CREATIVE WORLD
Mouliné
Stranded Cotton Art. 117
209
211
642
644
783
791
961
963
3046
3716
3822
791

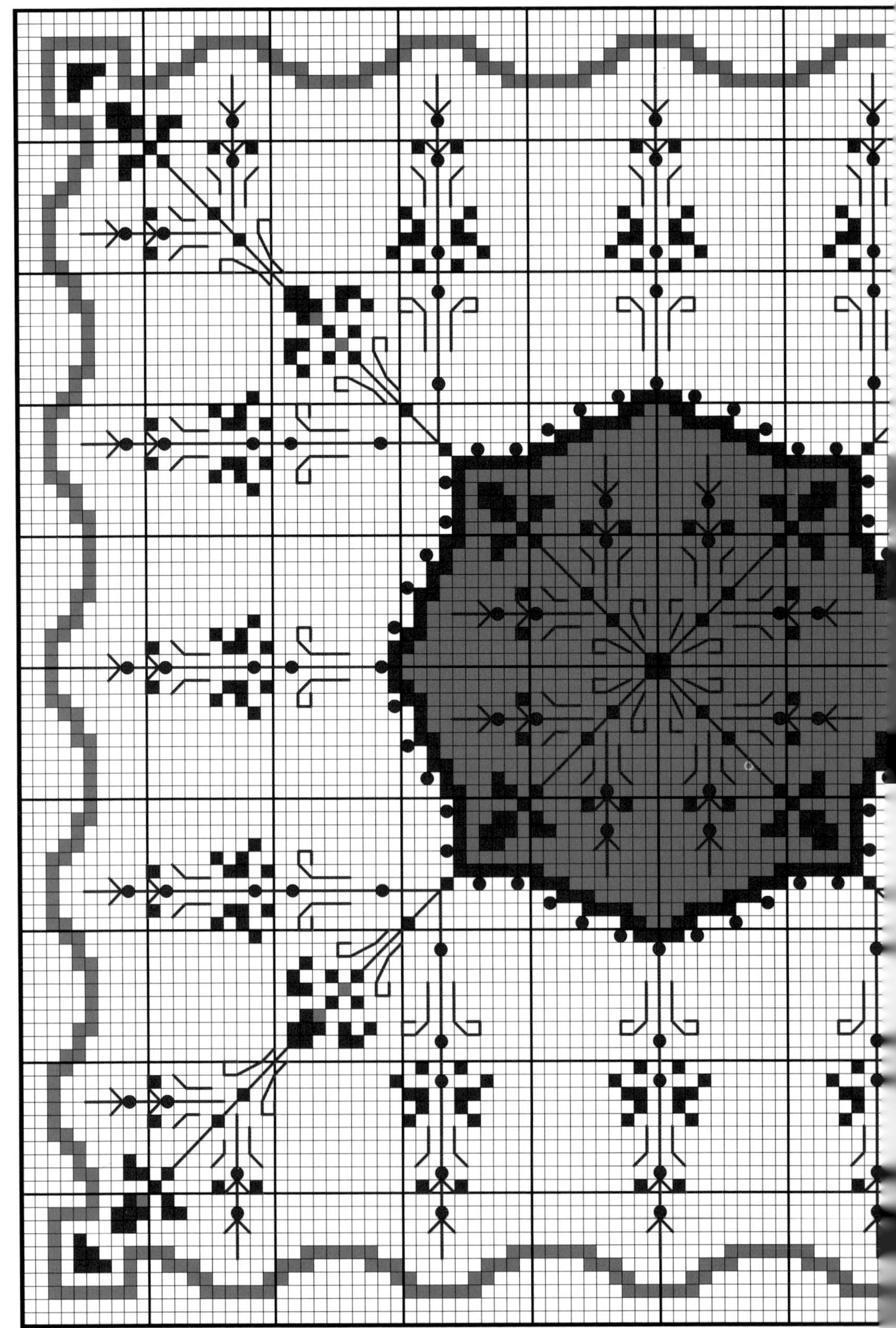

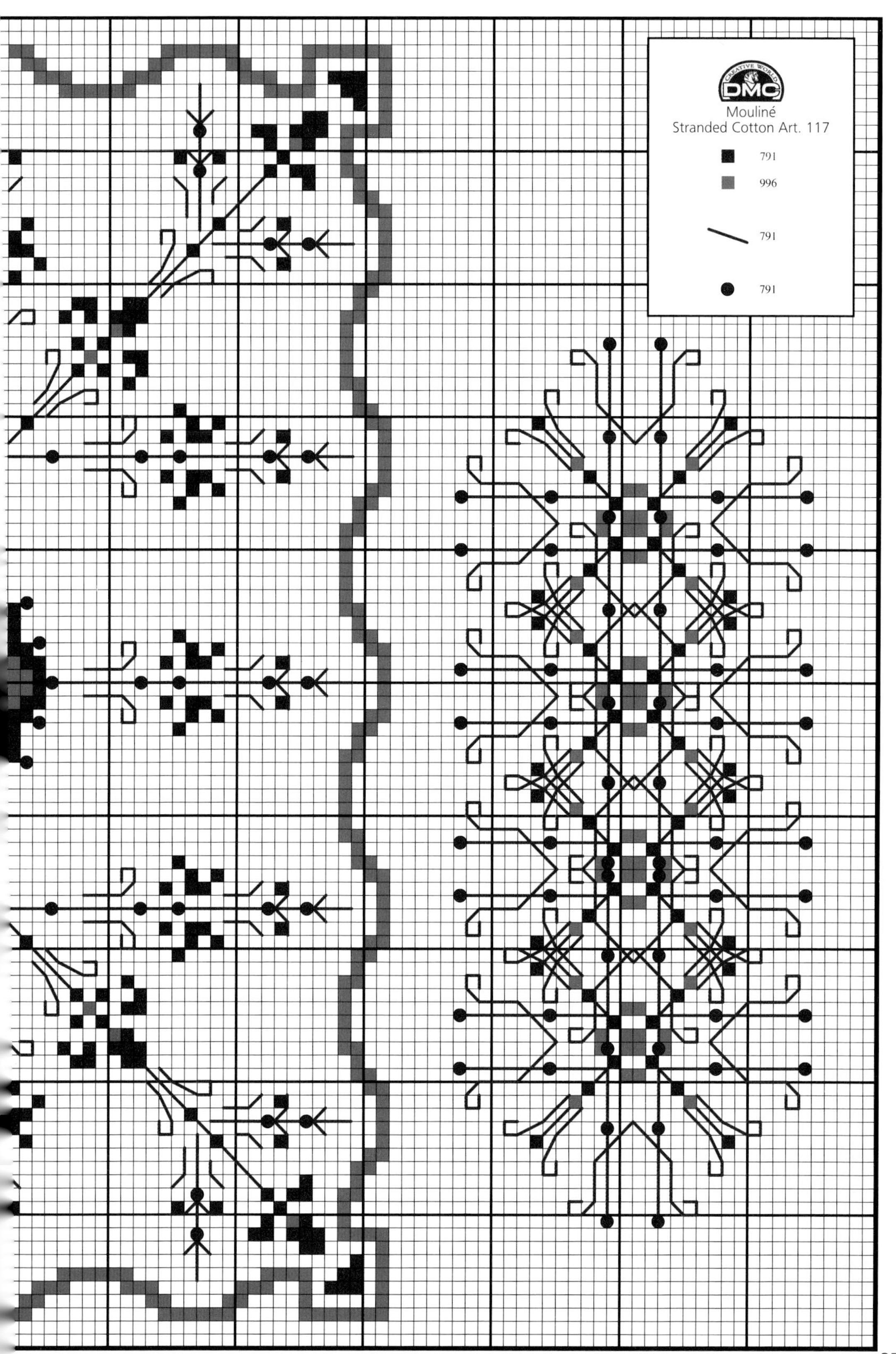
DMC
CREATIVE WORLD
Mouliné
Stranded Cotton Art. 117
791
996
791
791

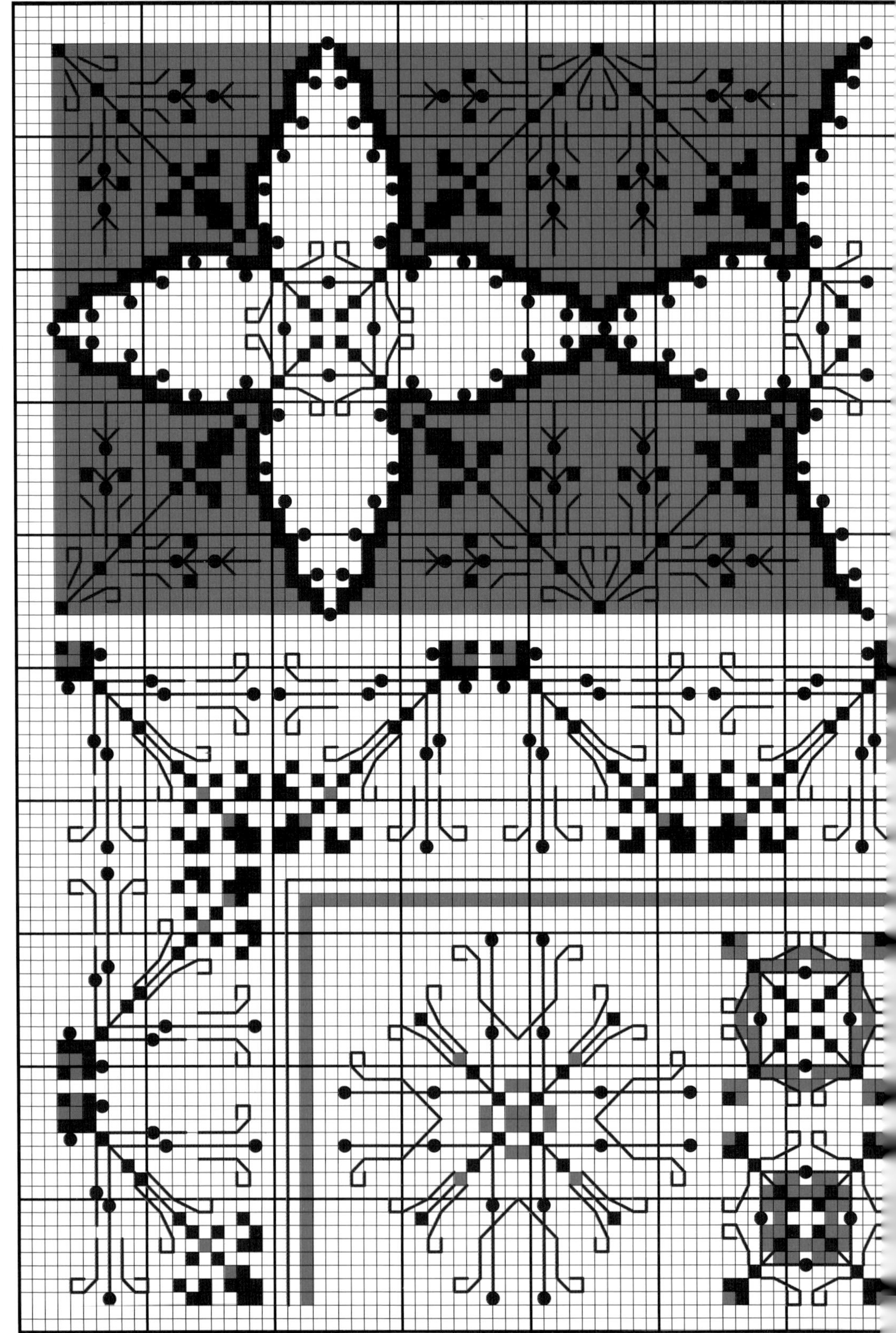

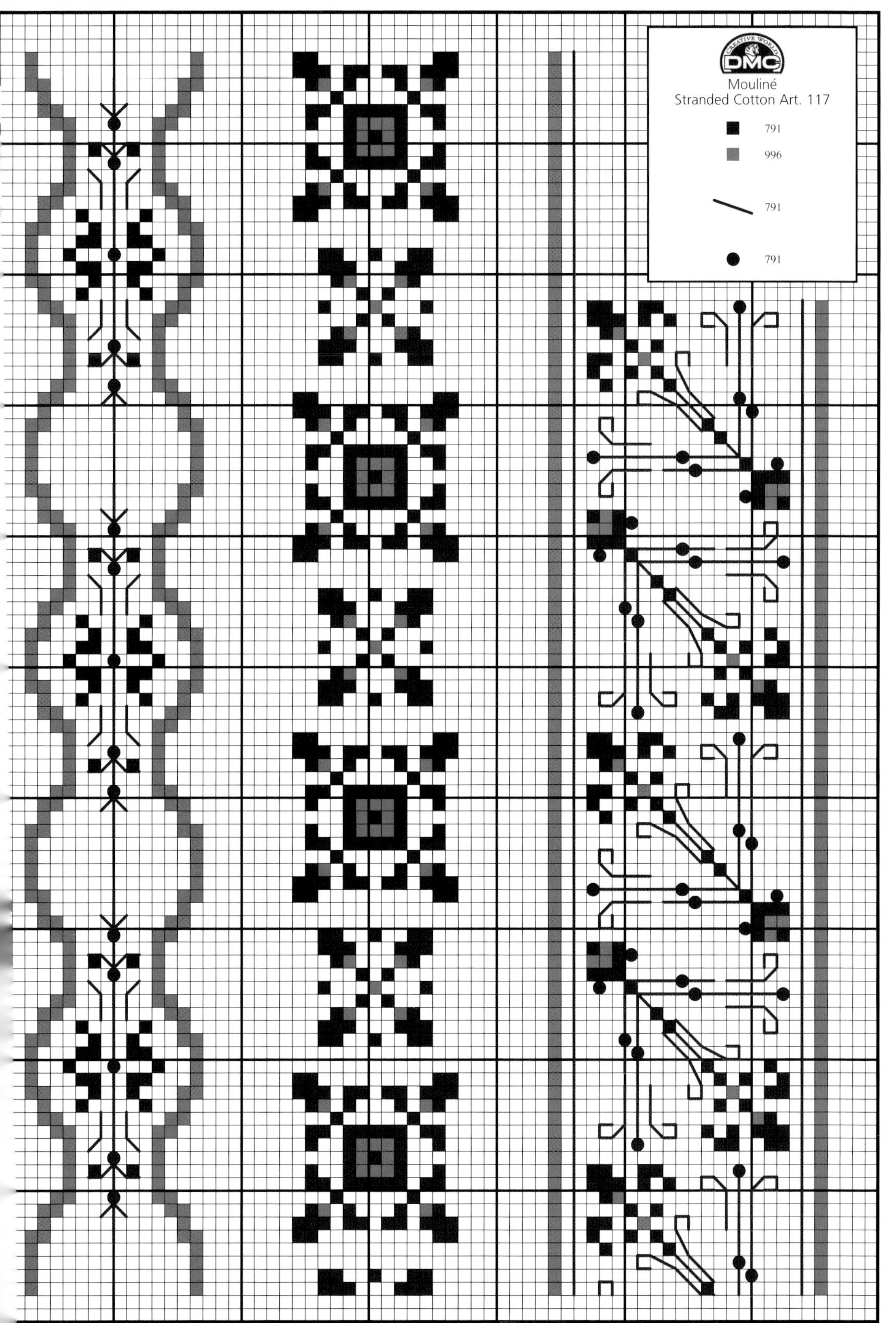
DMC
CREATIVE WORLD
Mouliné
Stranded Cotton Art. 117
791
996
791
791

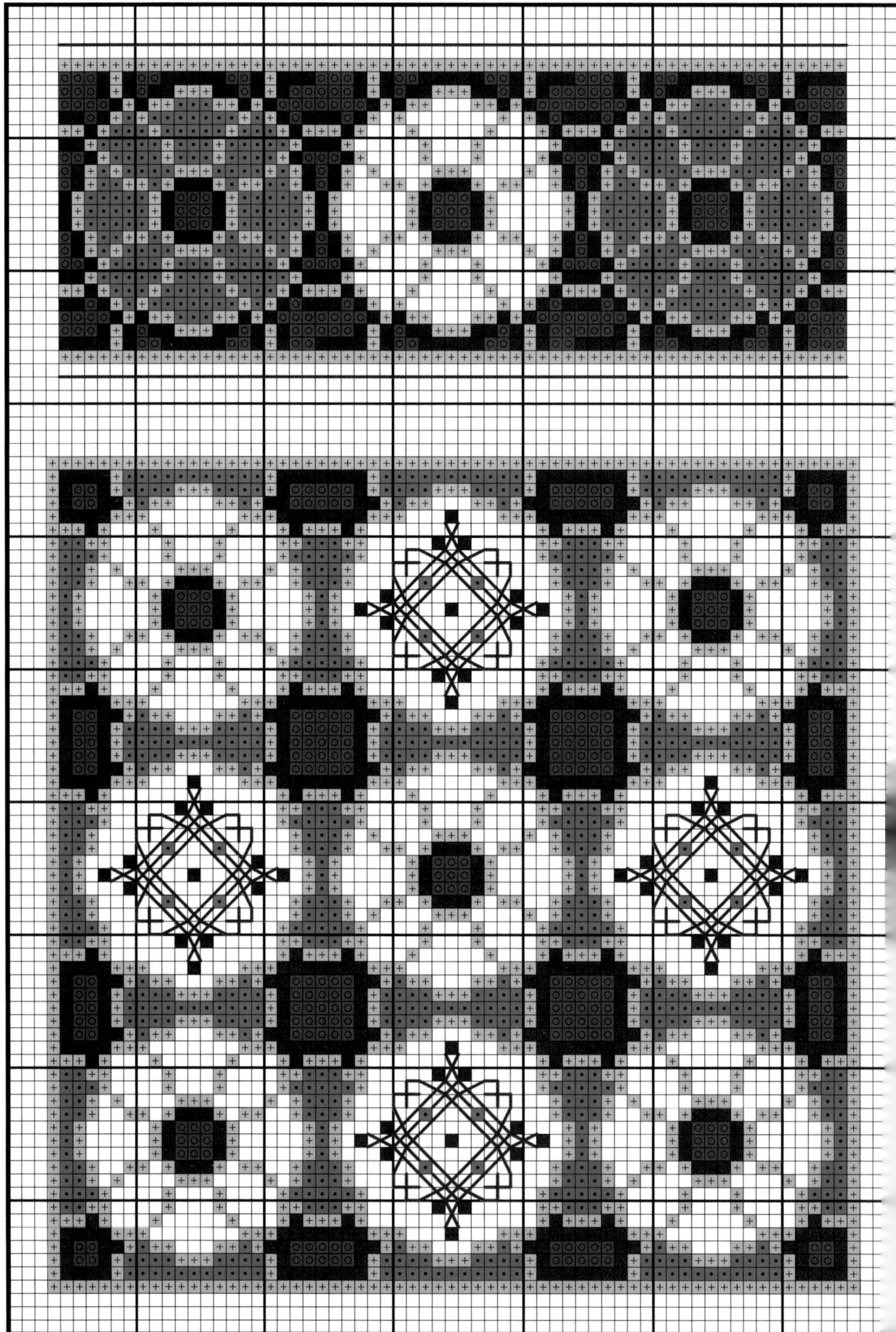

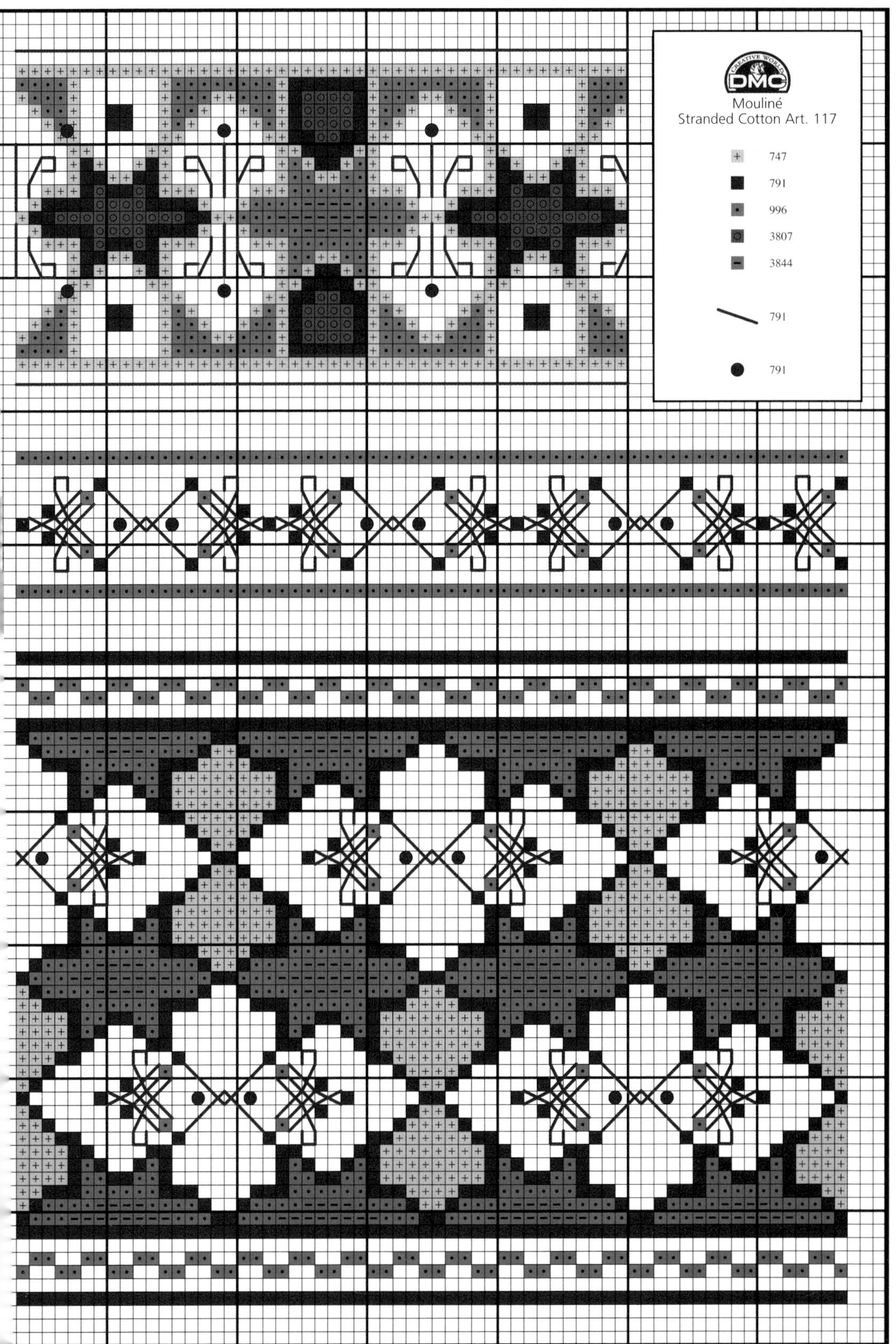
DMC
CREATIVE WORLD
Mouliné
Stranded Cotton Art. 117
747
791
996
3807
3844
791
791

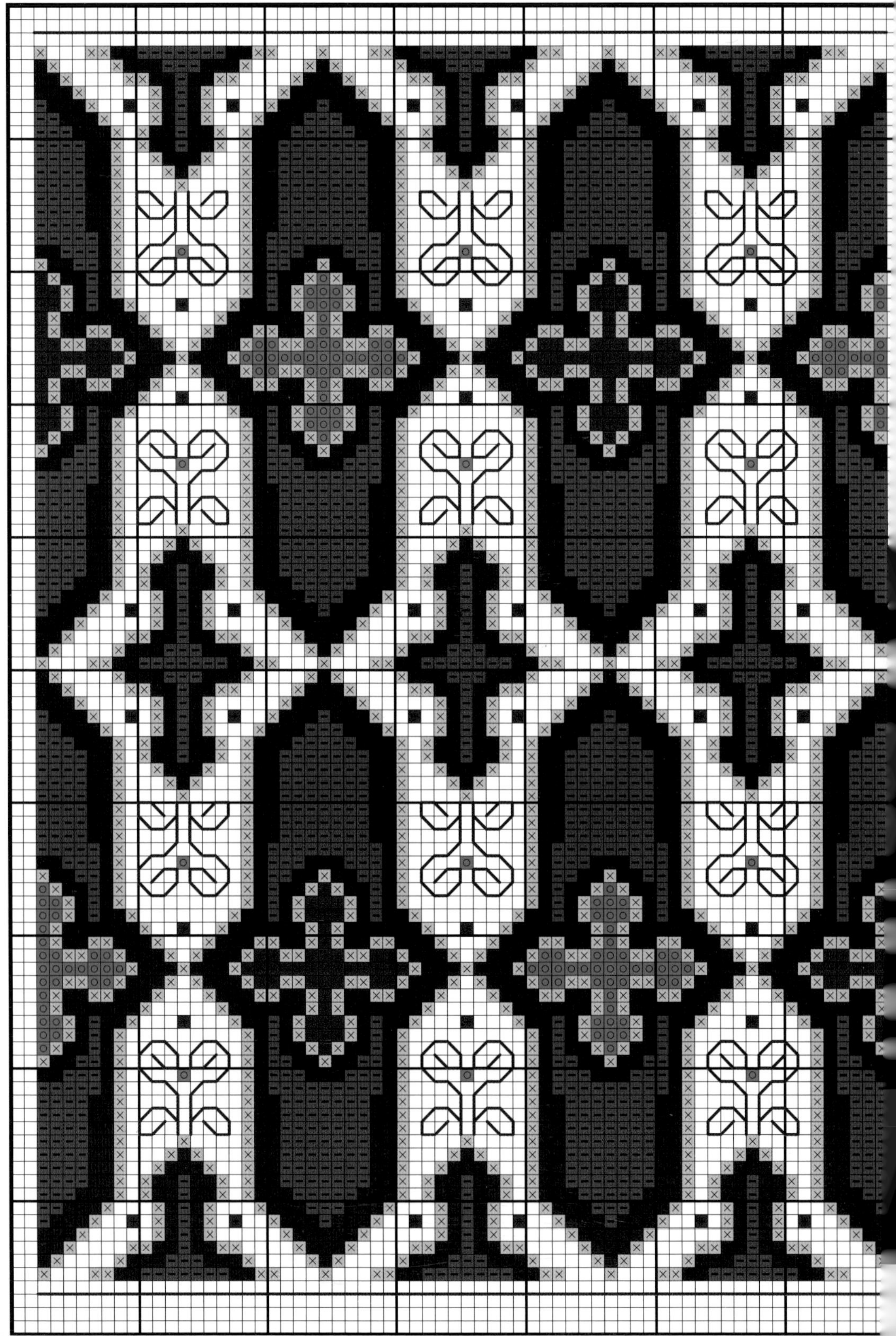

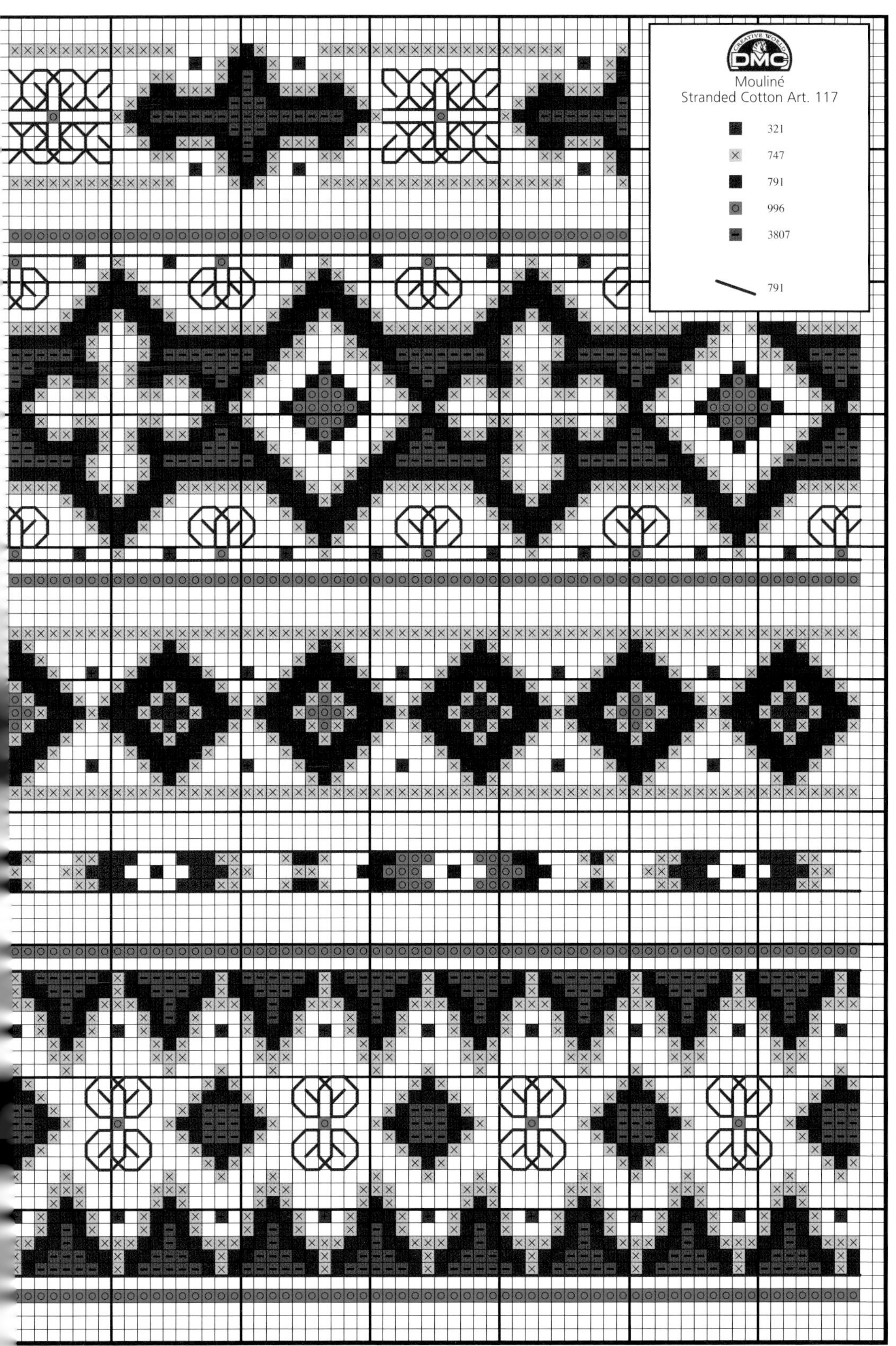
DMC
CREATIVE WORLD
Mouliné
Stranded Cotton Art. 117
321
747
791
996
3807
791

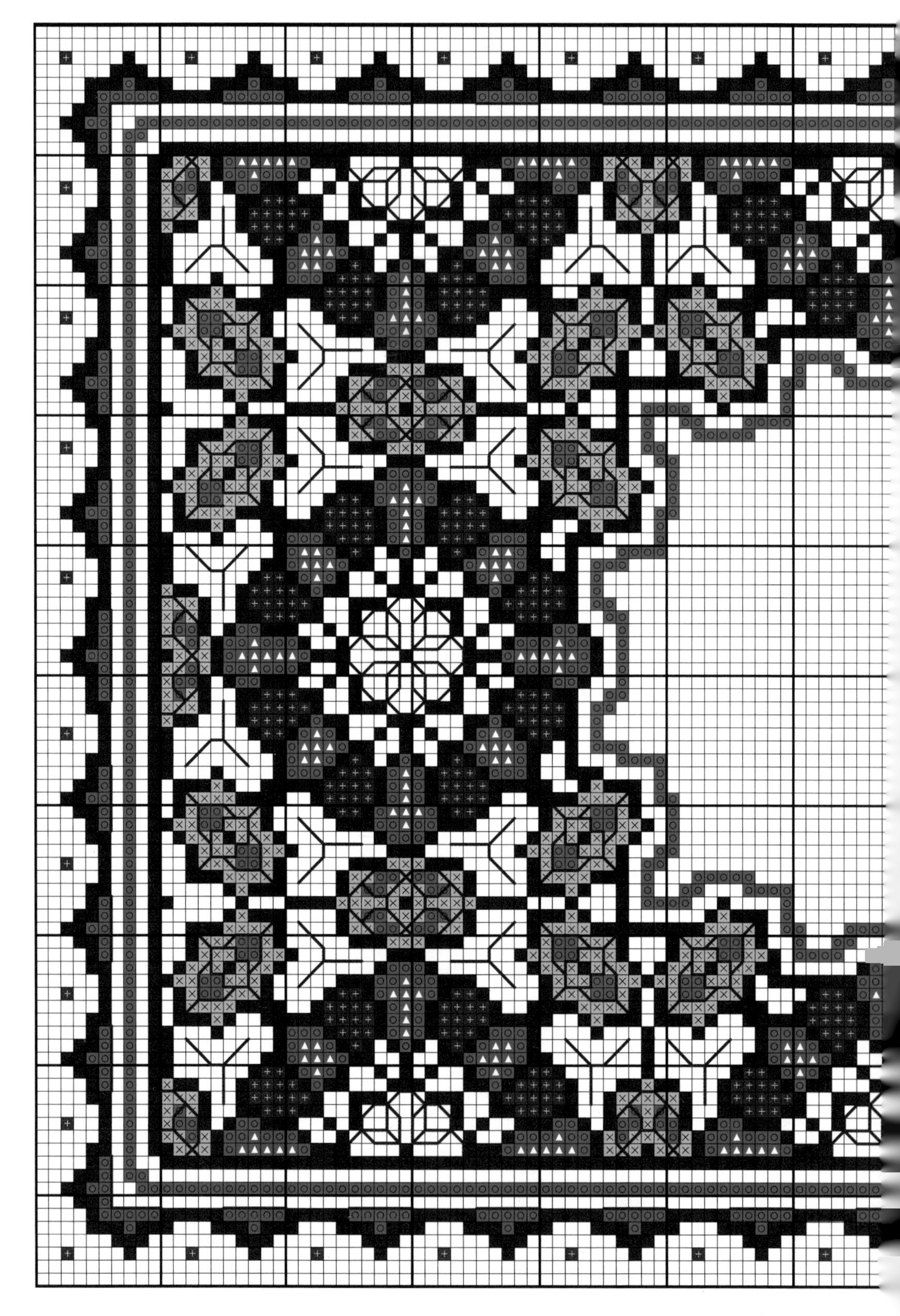

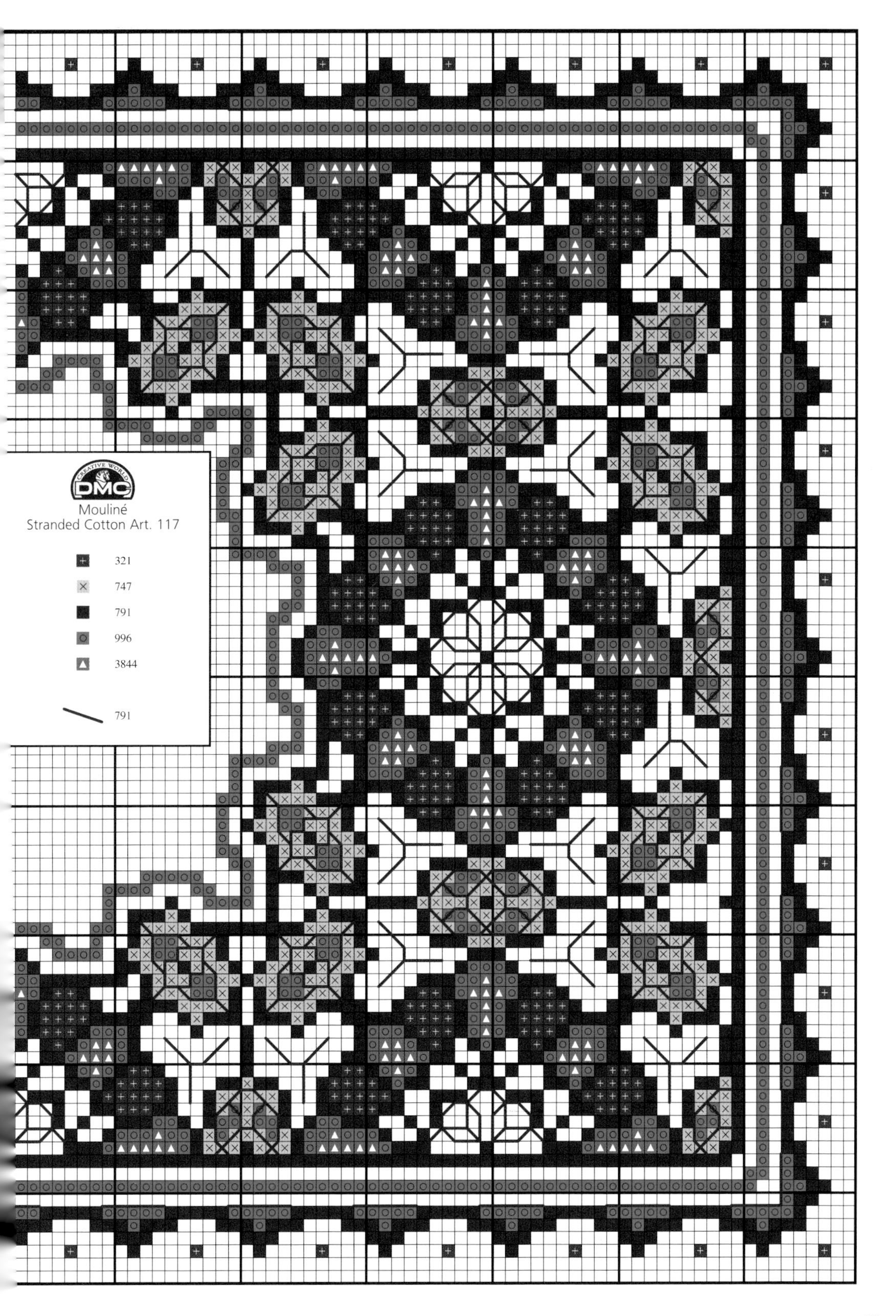
DMC
Mouliné
Stranded Cotton Art. 117
321
747
791
996
3844
791

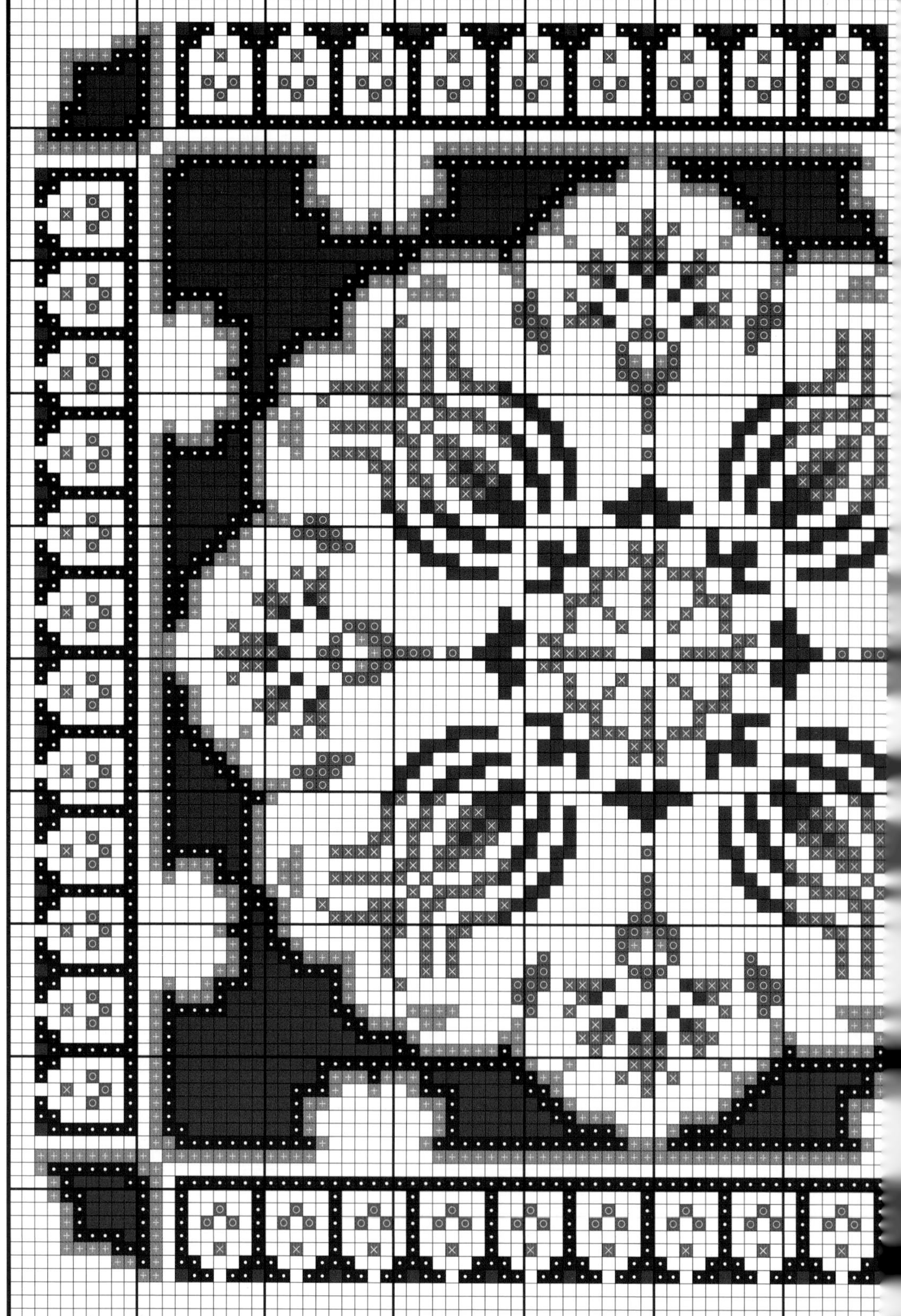

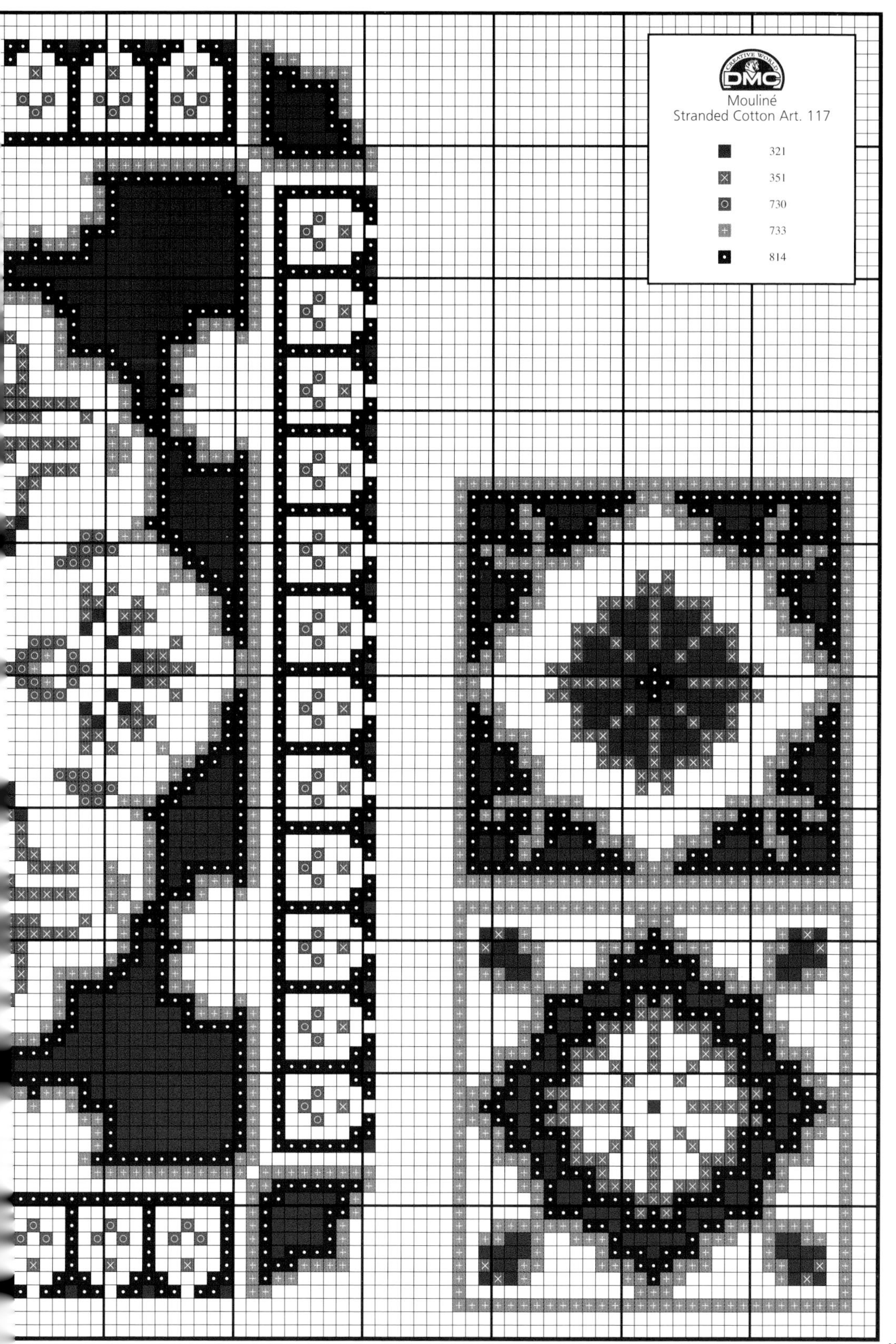
DMC
CREATIVE WORLD
Mouliné
Stranded Cotton Art. 117
321
351
730
733
814

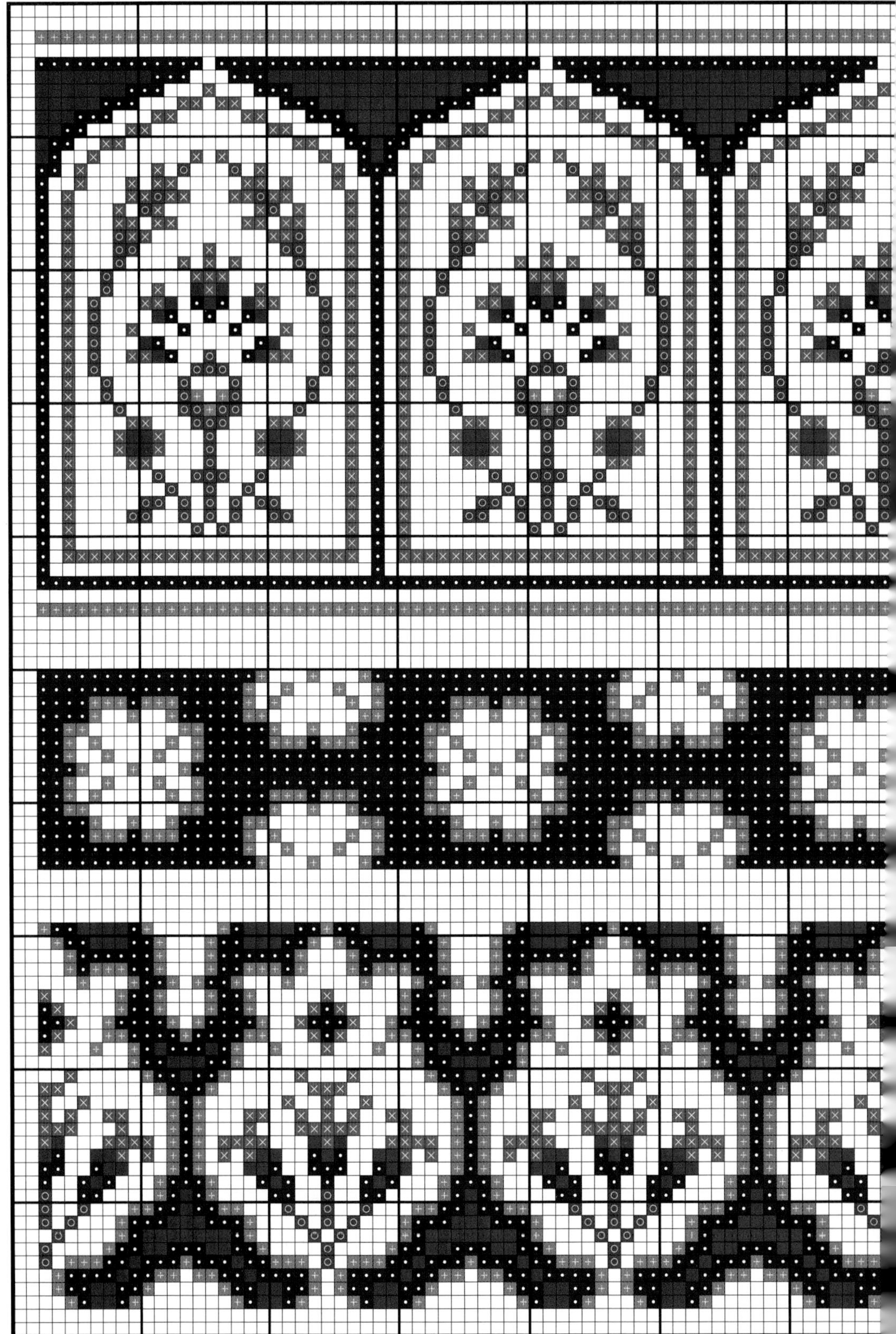

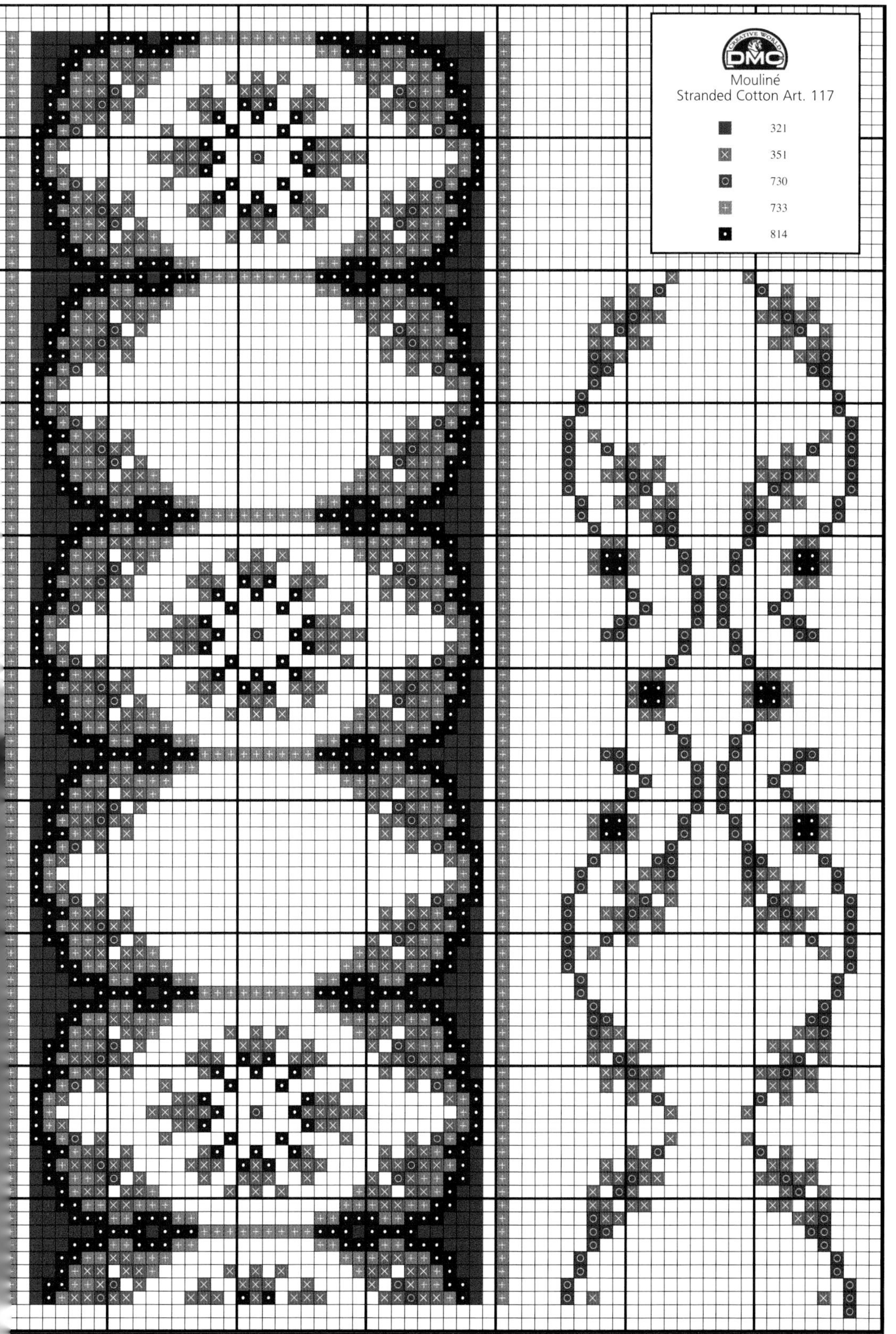
DMC
CREATIVE WORLD
Mouliné
Stranded Cotton Art. 117
321
351
730
733
814

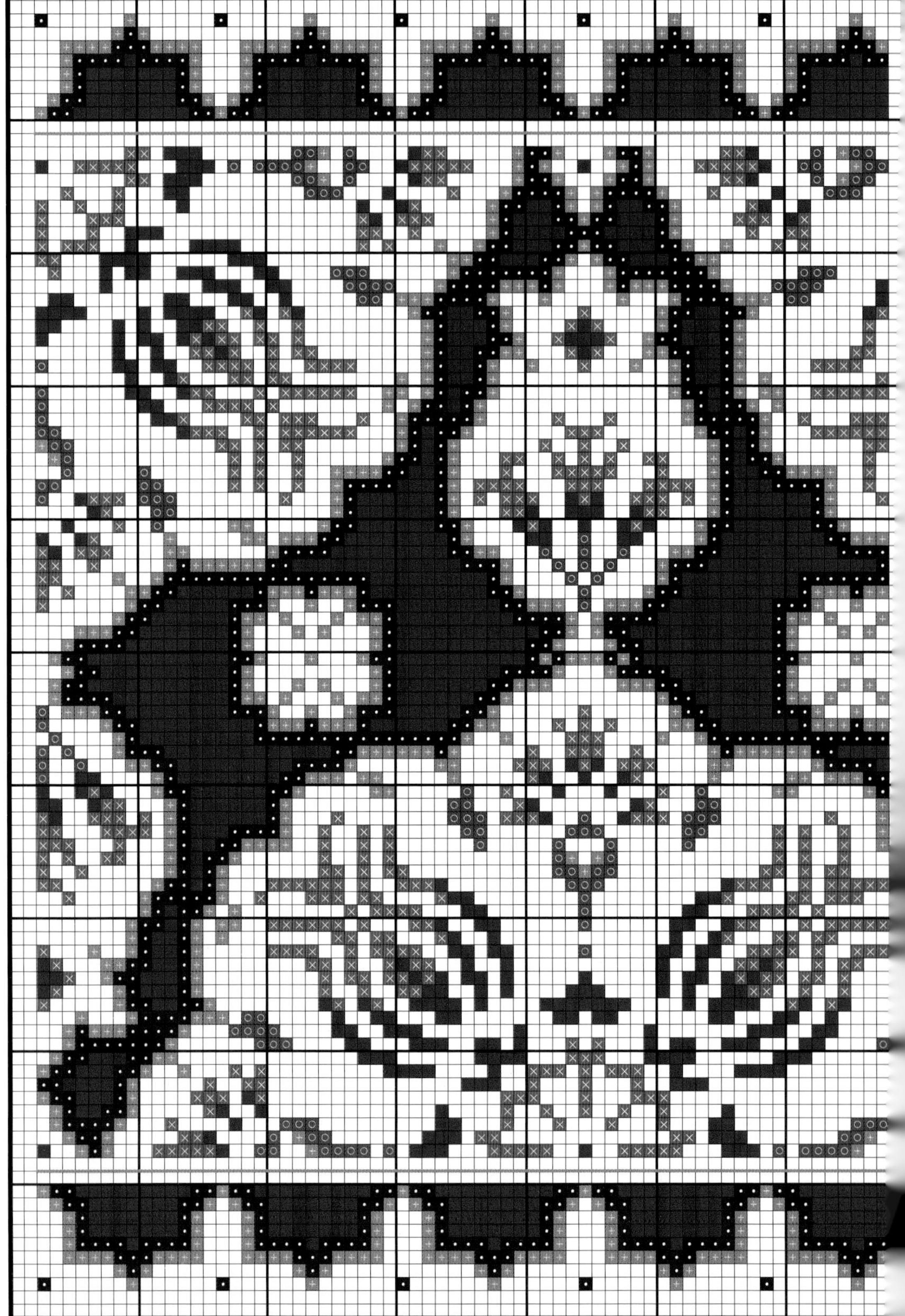

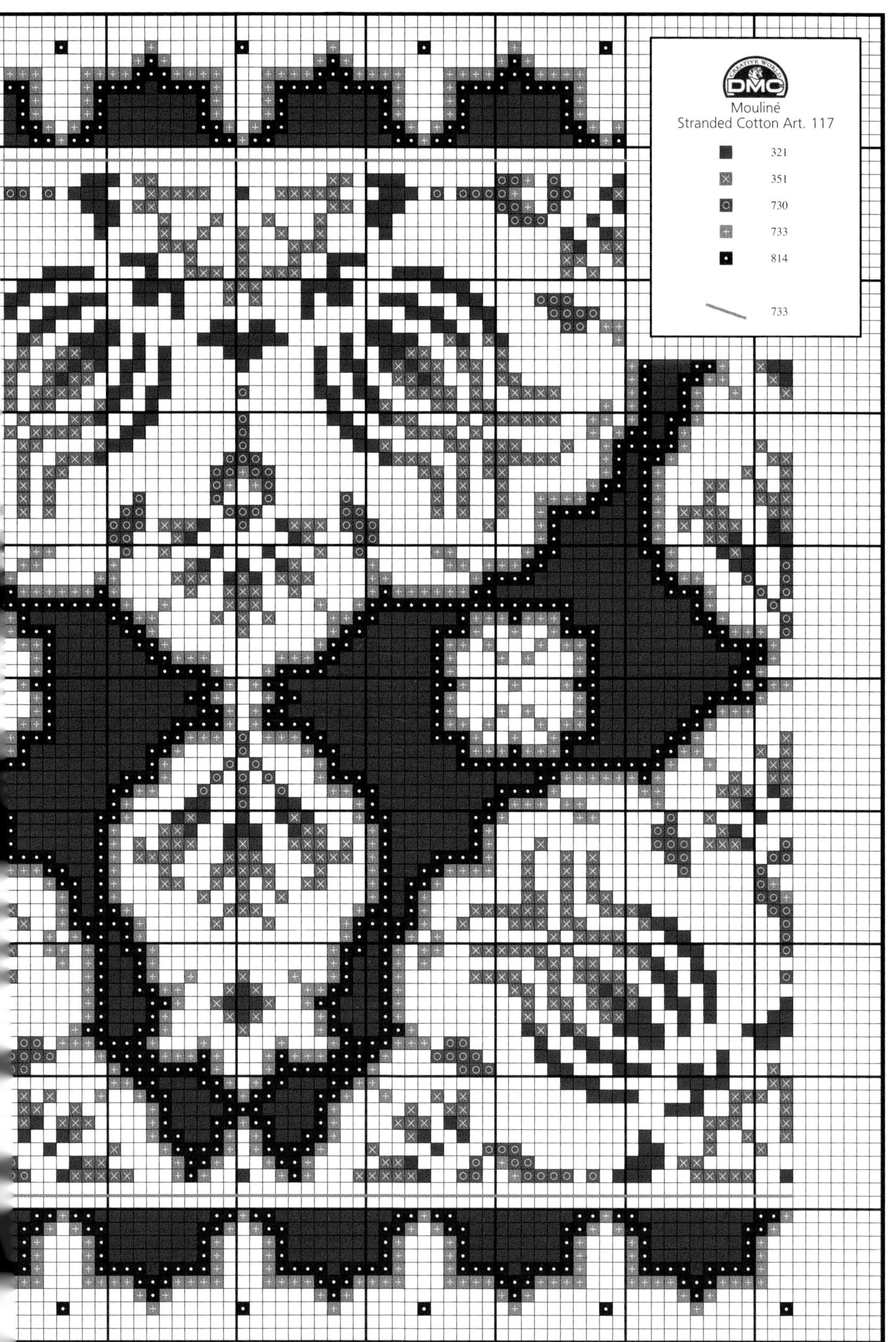
DMC
CREATIVE WORLD
Mouliné
Stranded Cotton Art. 117
321
351
730
733
814
733

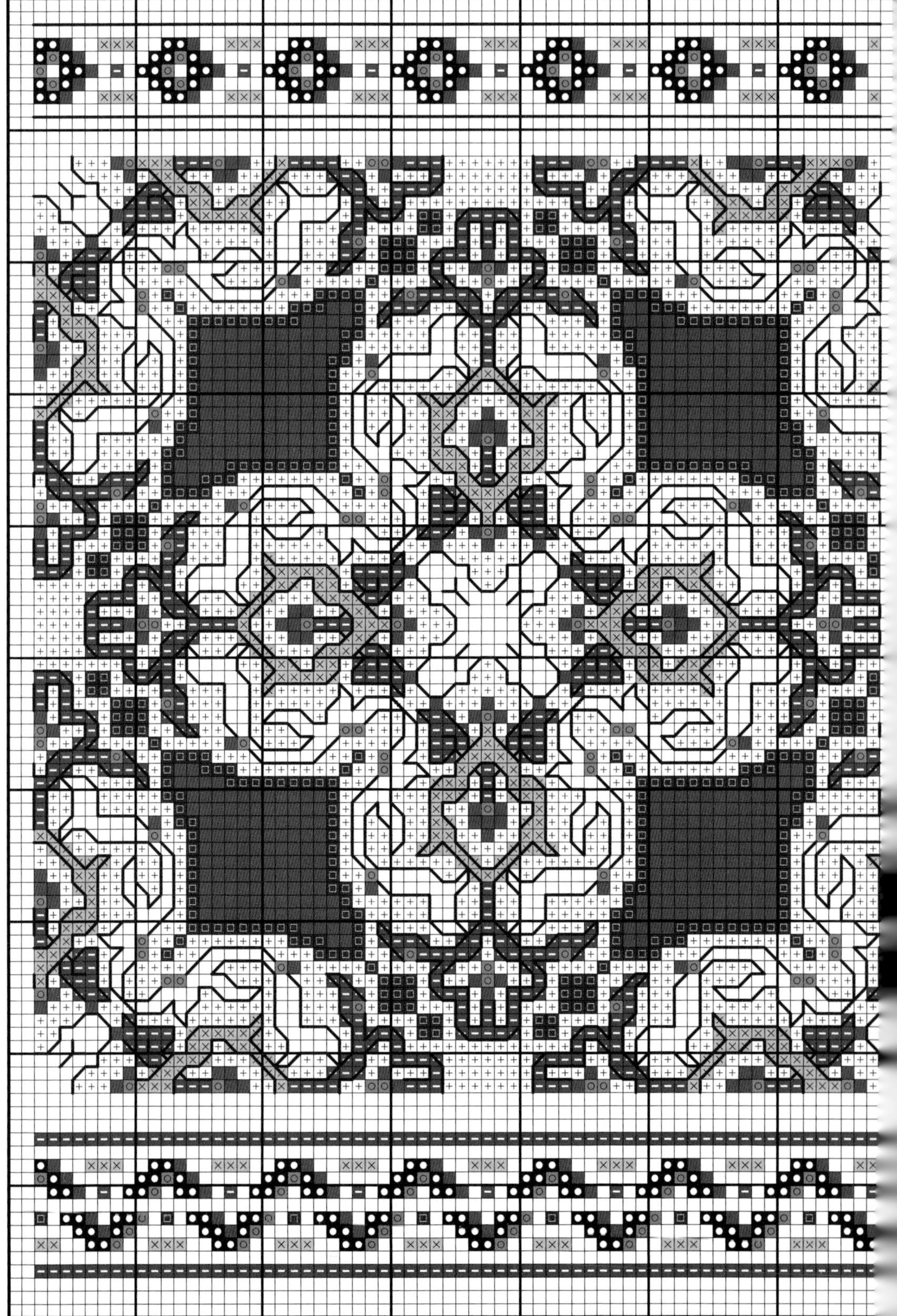

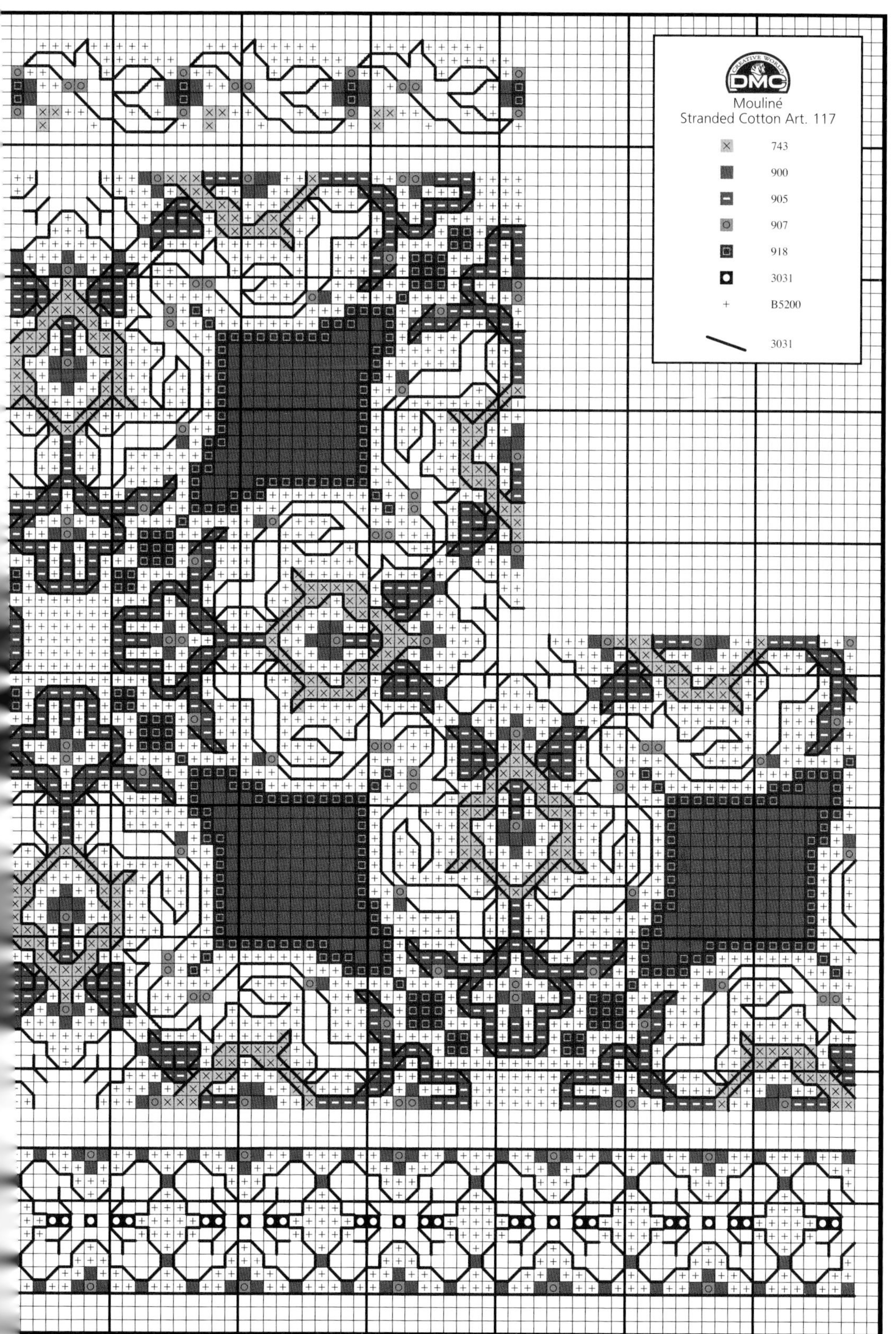
DMC
Mouliné
Stranded Cotton Art. 117
743
900
905
907
918
3031
B5200
3031

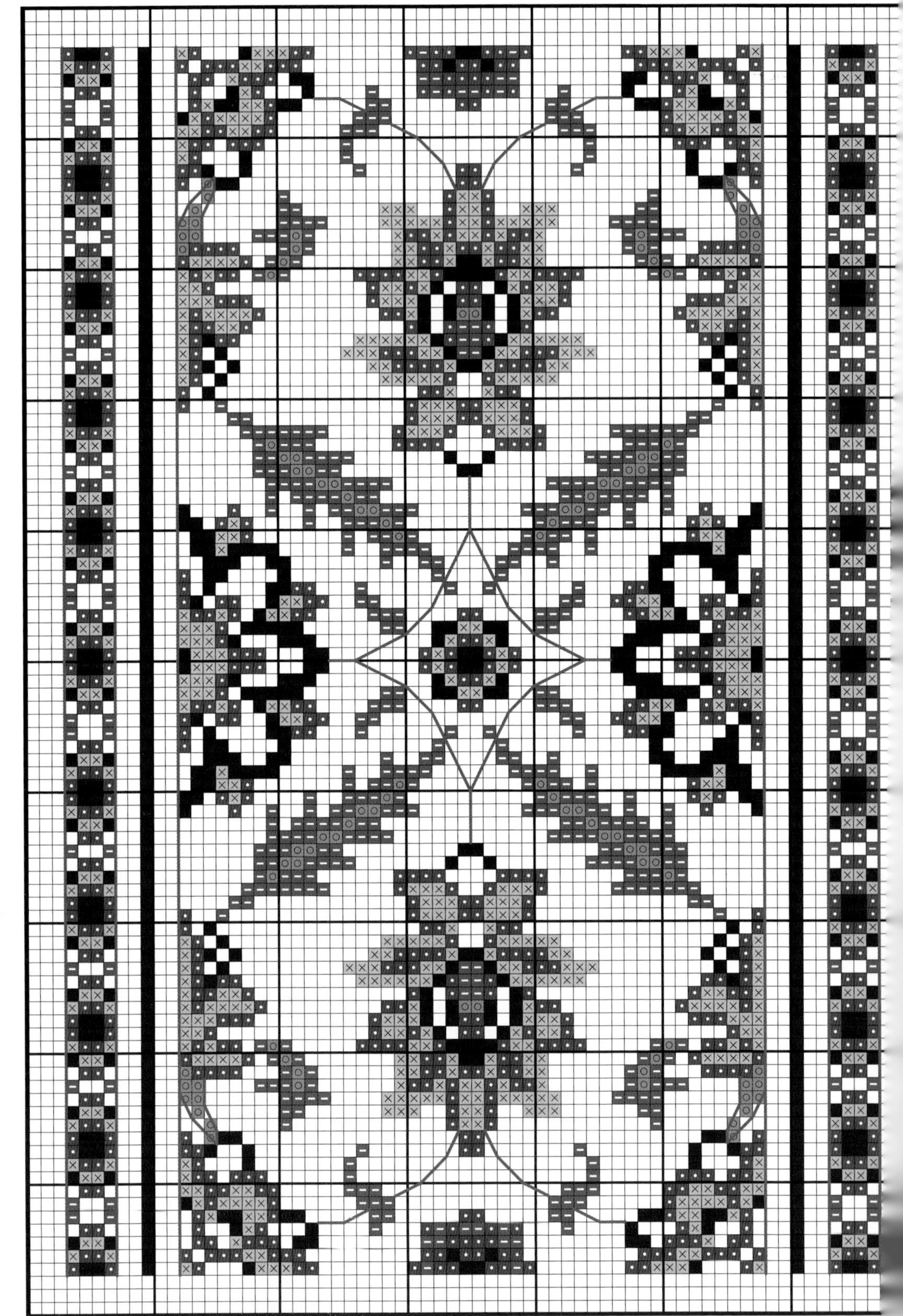

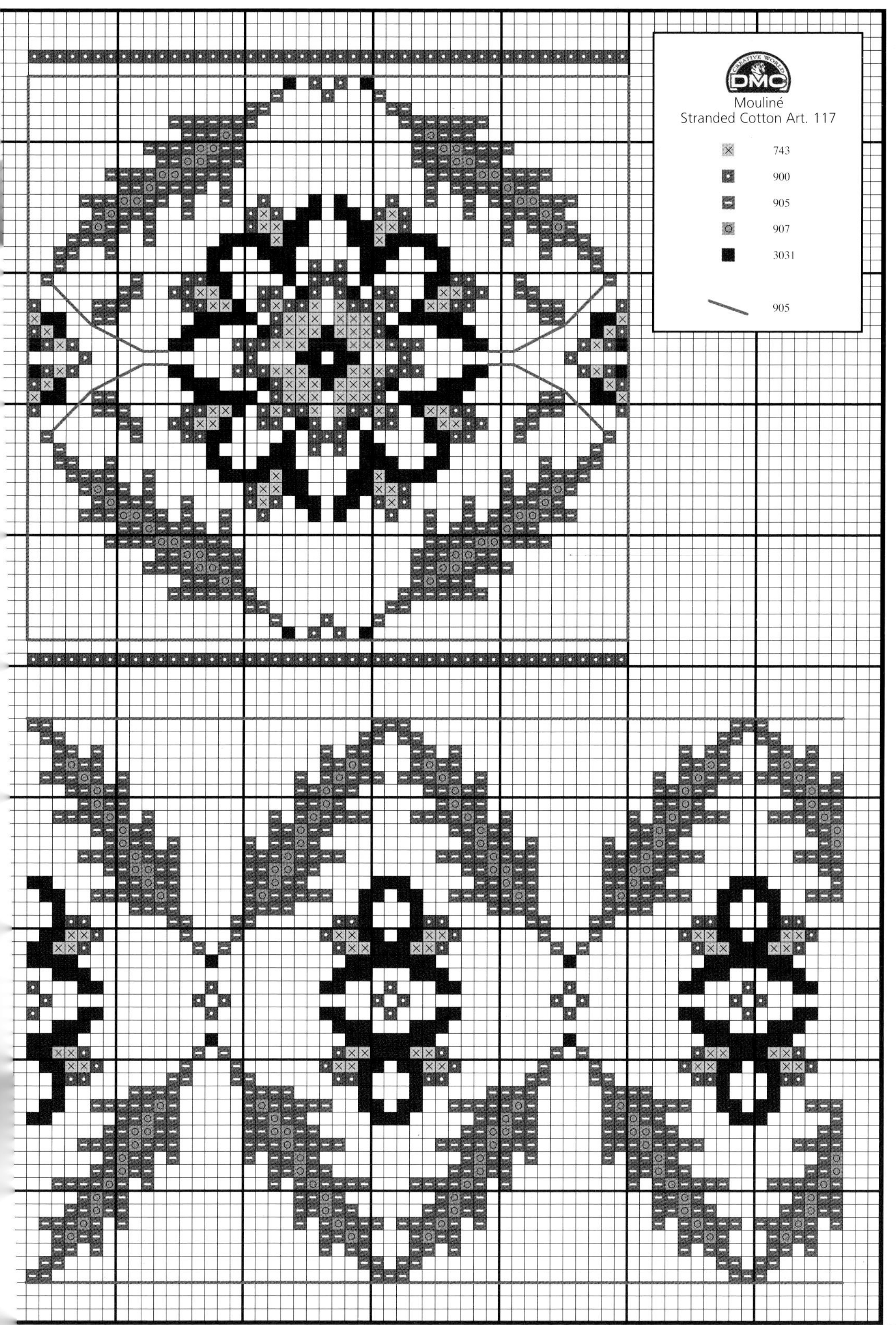
DMC
CREATIVE WORLD
Mouliné
Stranded Cotton Art. 117
743
900
905
907
3031
905

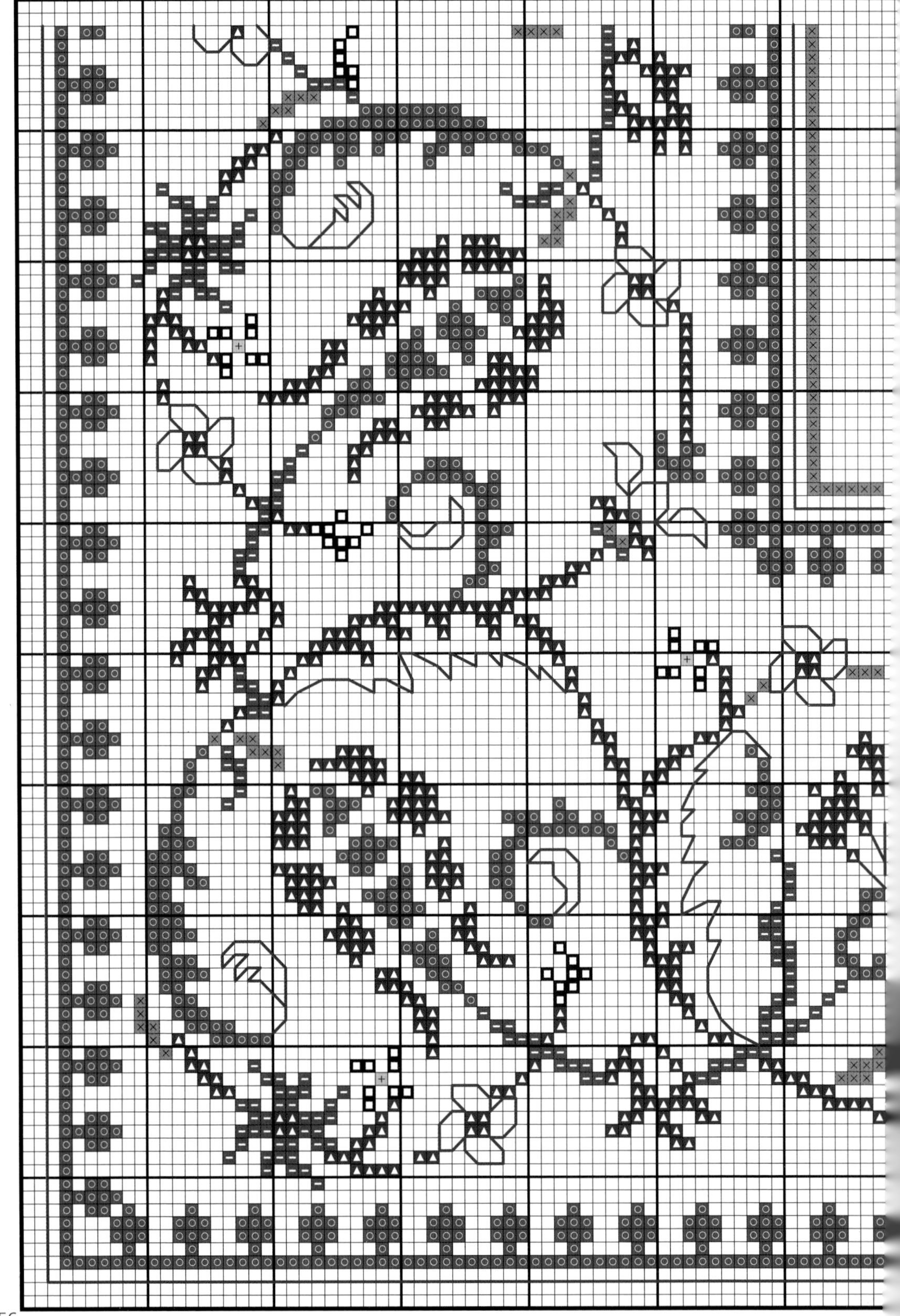

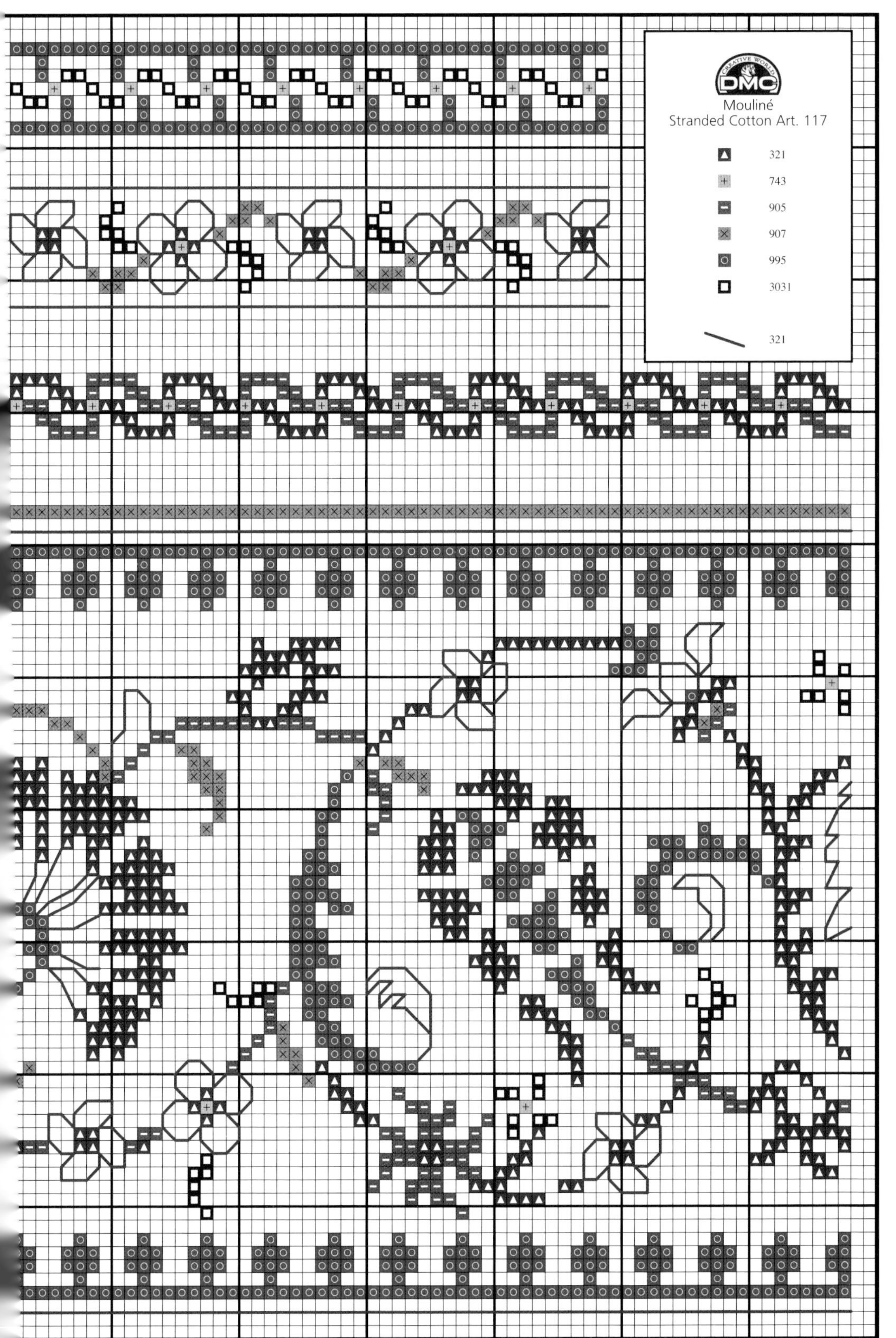
DMC
Mouliné
Stranded Cotton Art. 117
321
743
905
907
995
3031
321

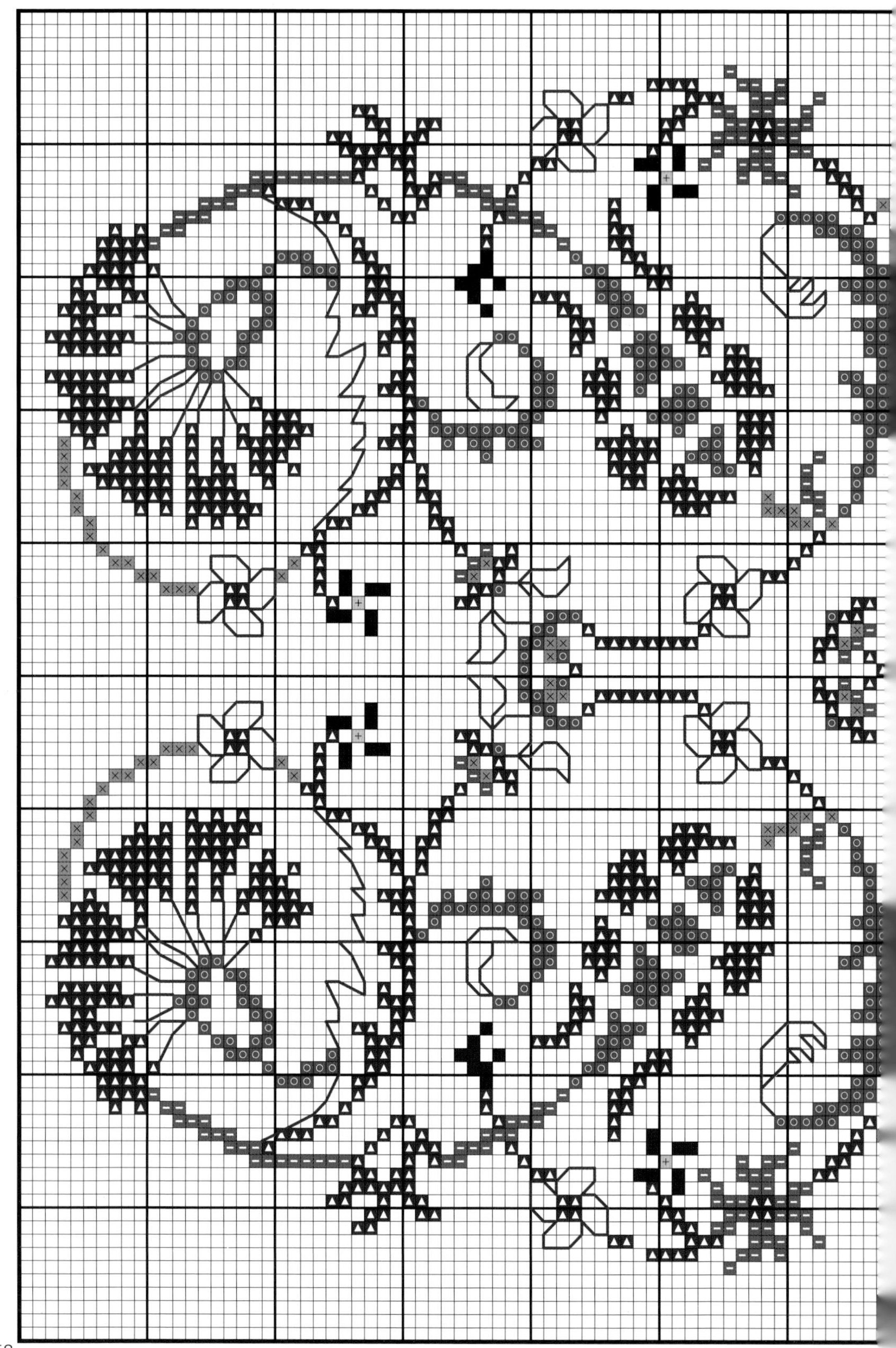

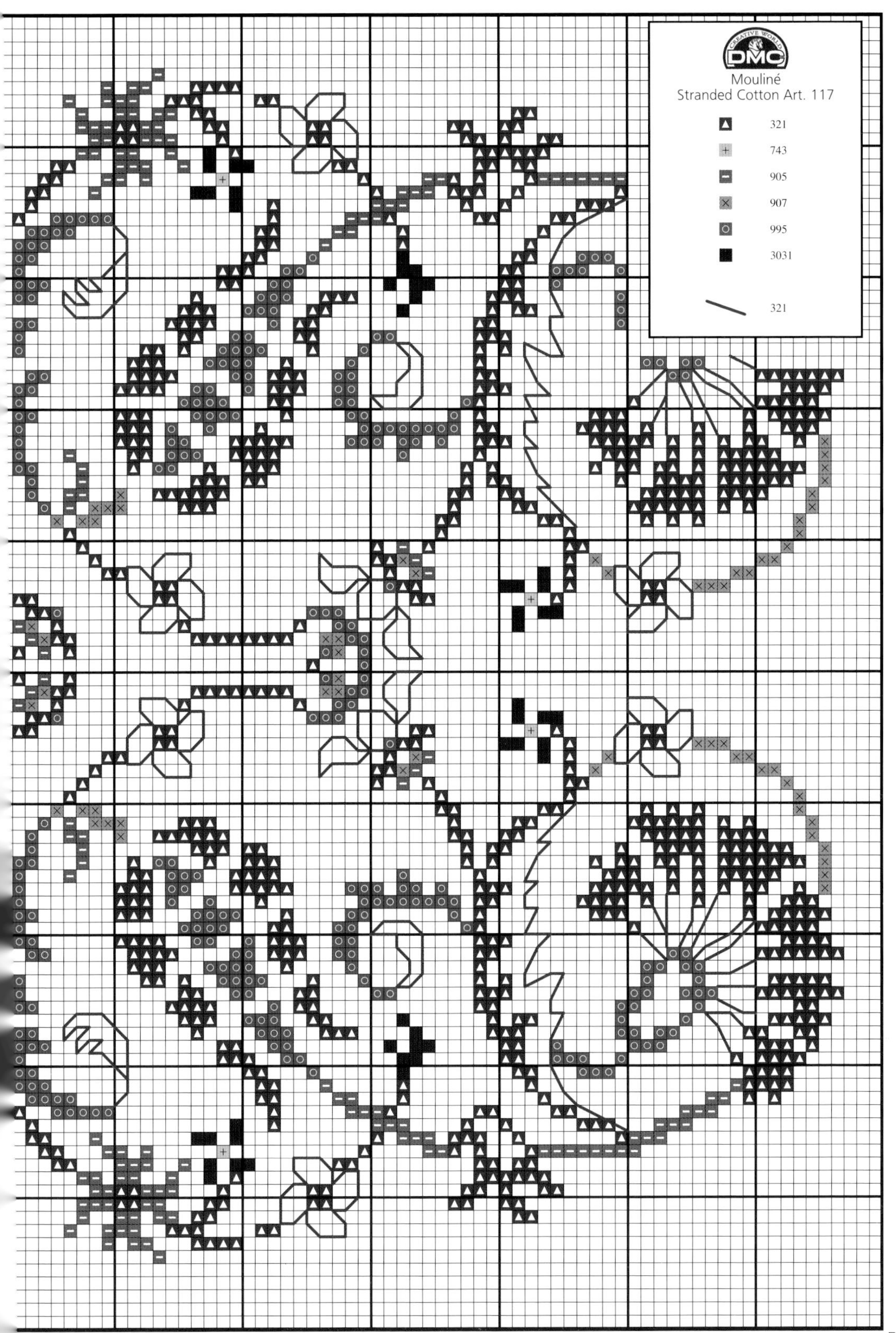
DMC
CREATIVE WORLD
Mouliné
Stranded Cotton Art. 117
321
743
905
907
995
3031
321

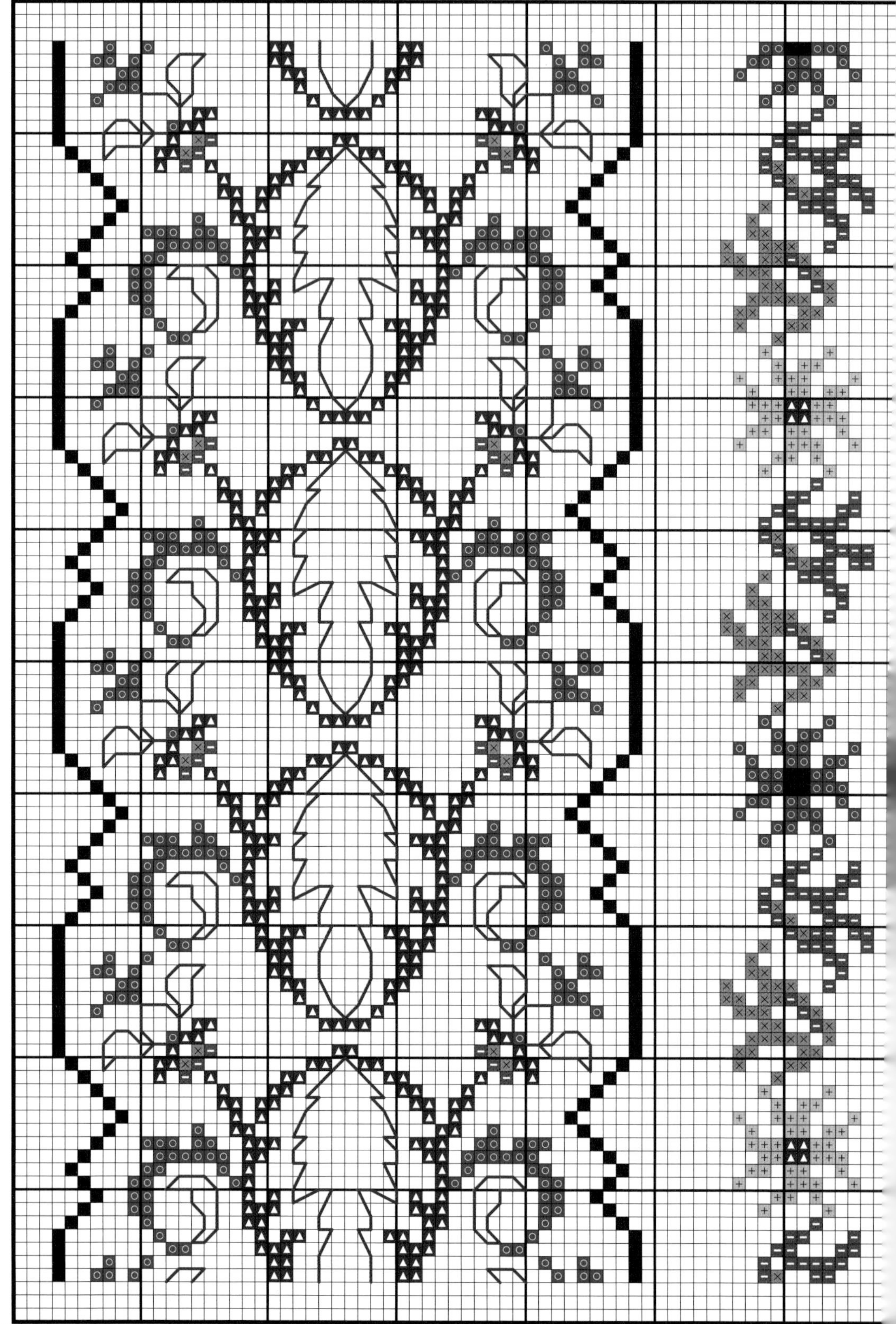

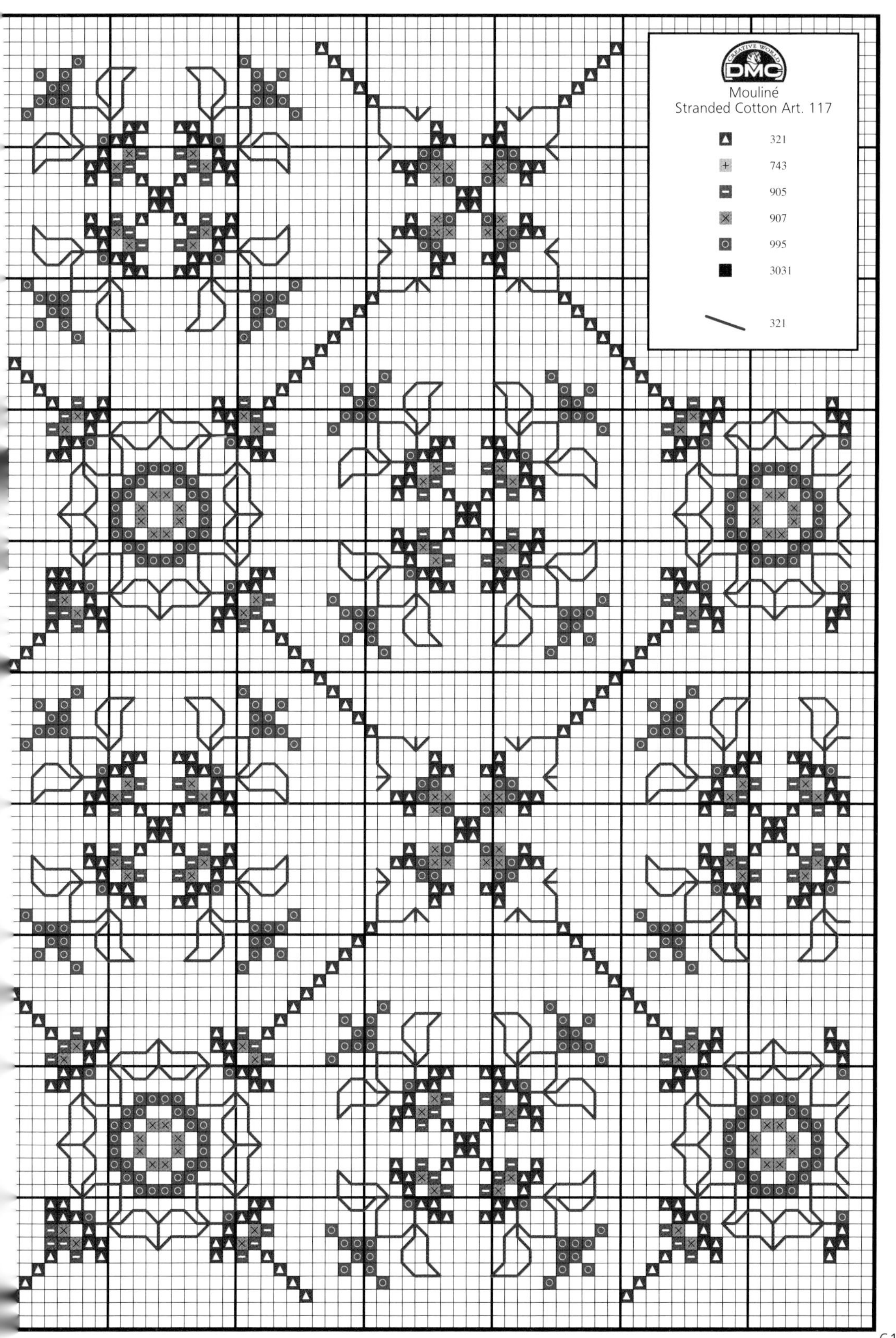
DMC
CREATIVE WORLD
Mouliné
Stranded Cotton Art. 117
321
743
905
907
995
3031
321

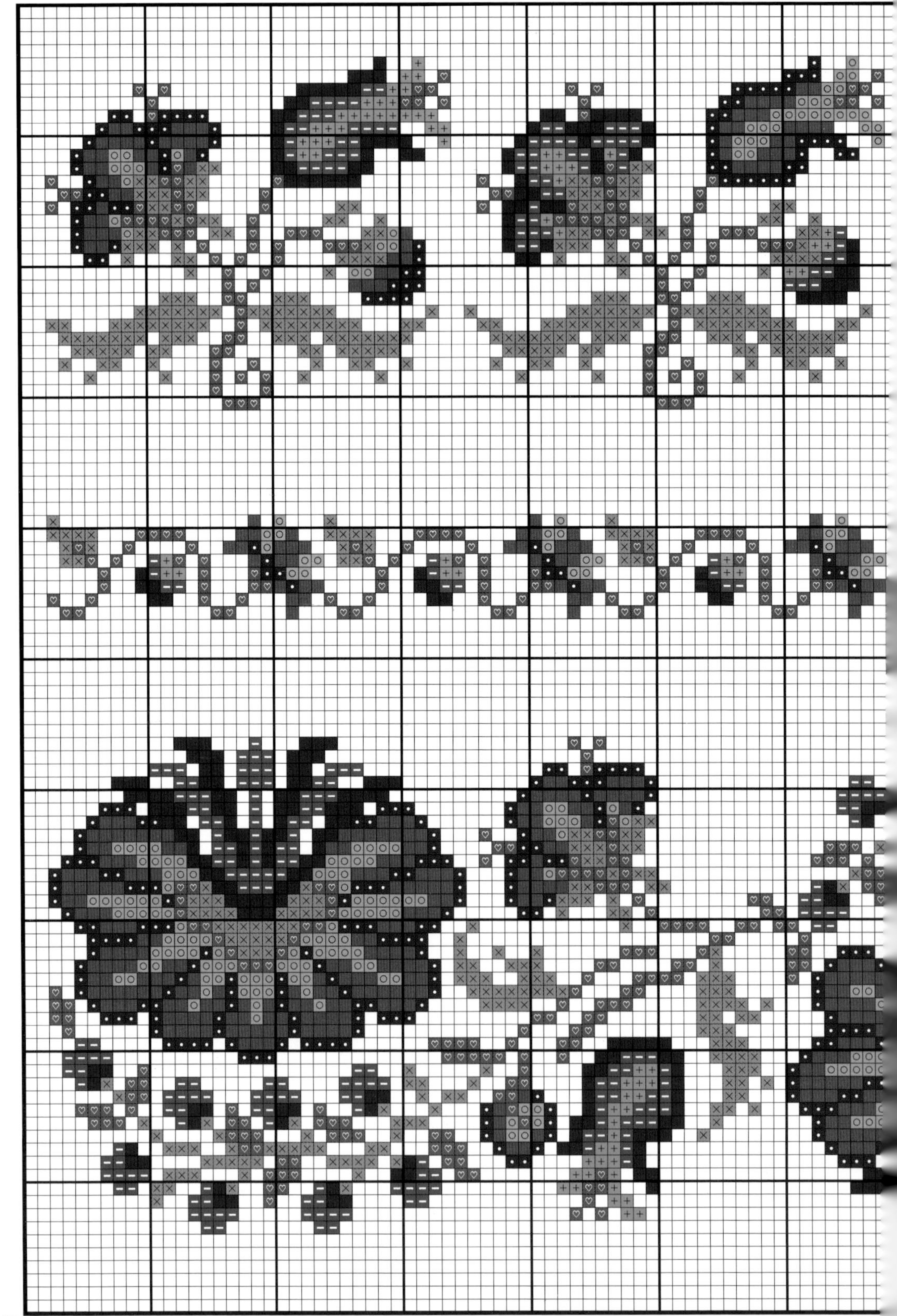

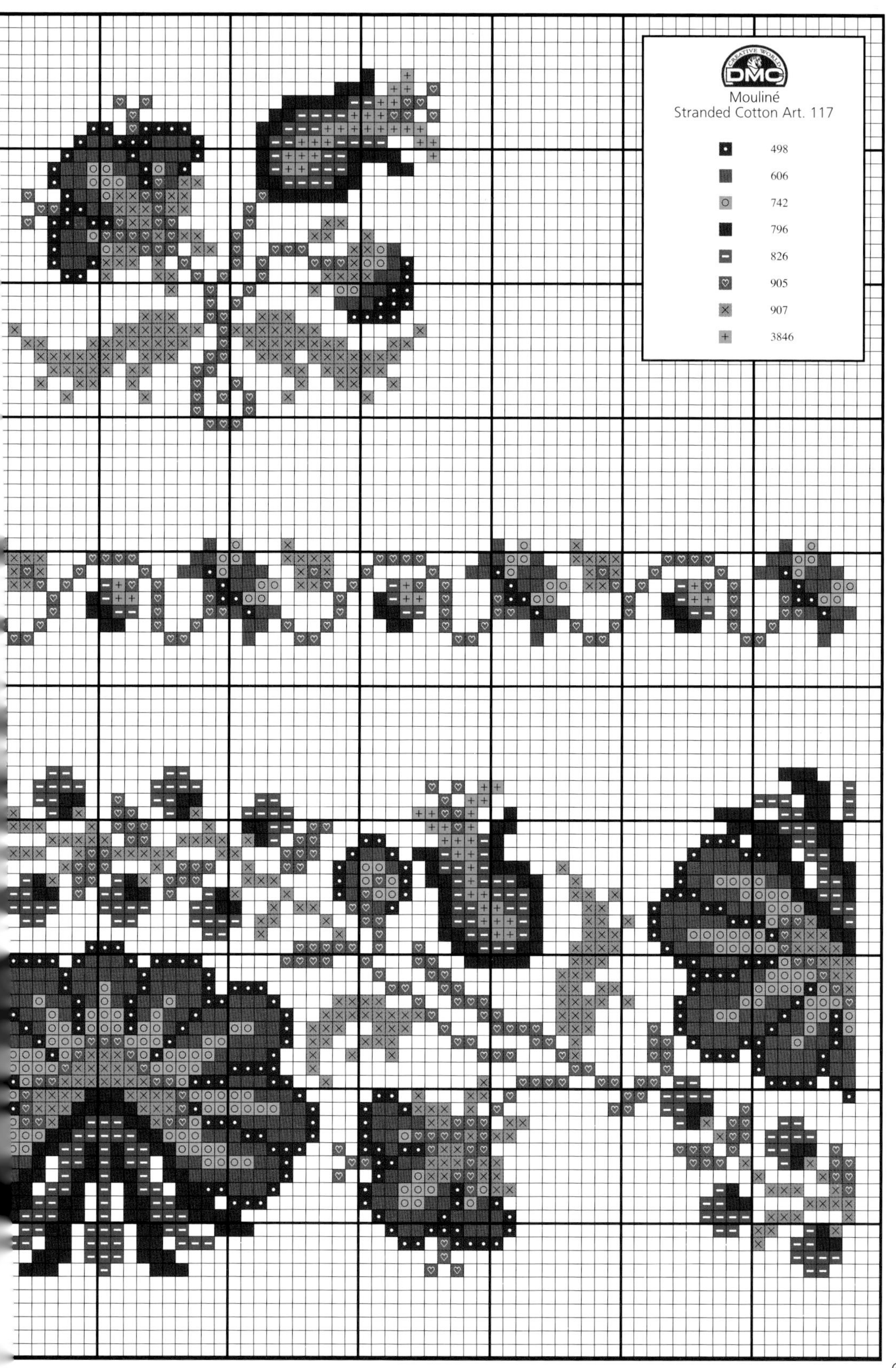
DMC
CREATIVE WORLD
Mouliné
Stranded Cotton Art. 117
498
606
742
796
826
905
907
3846

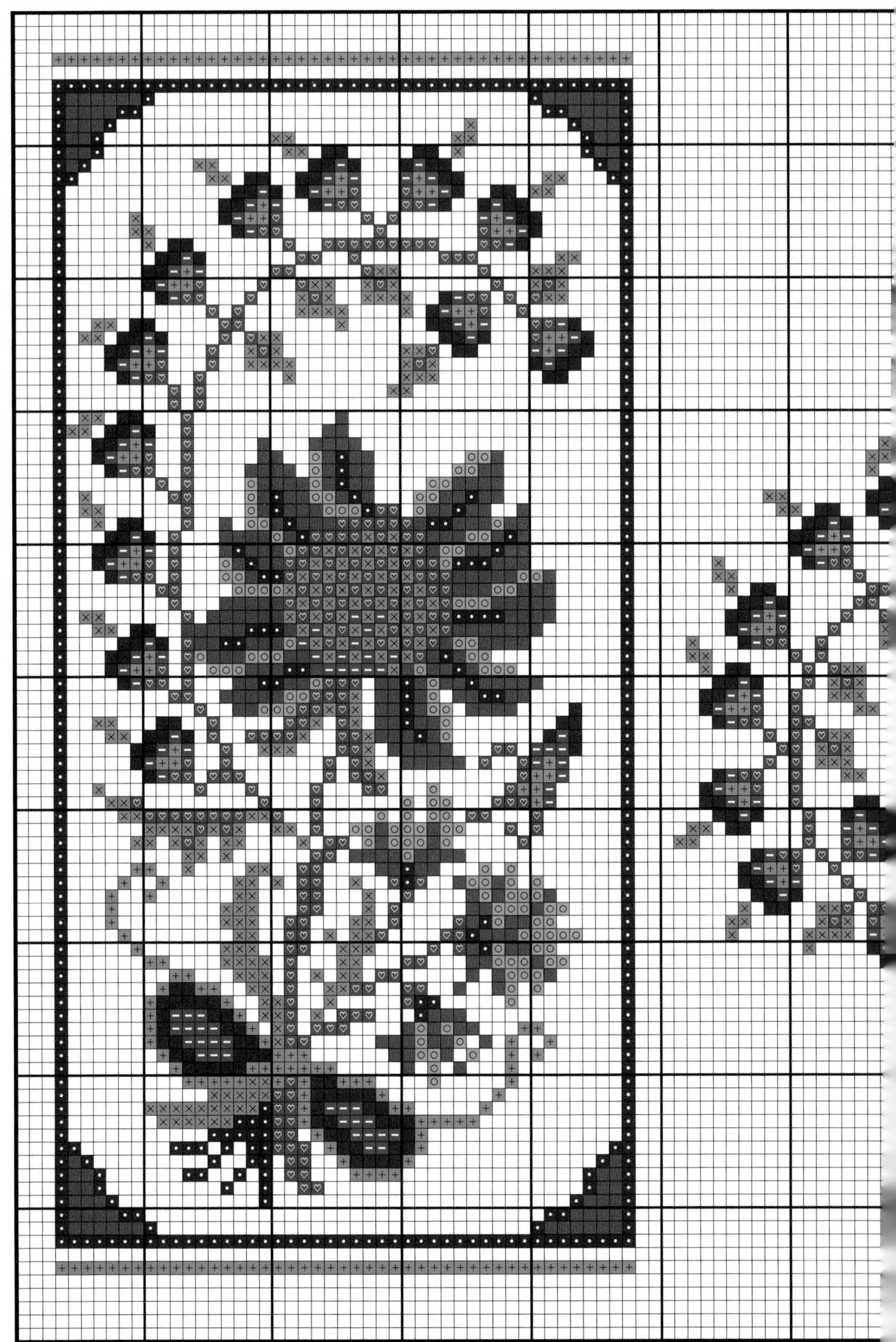

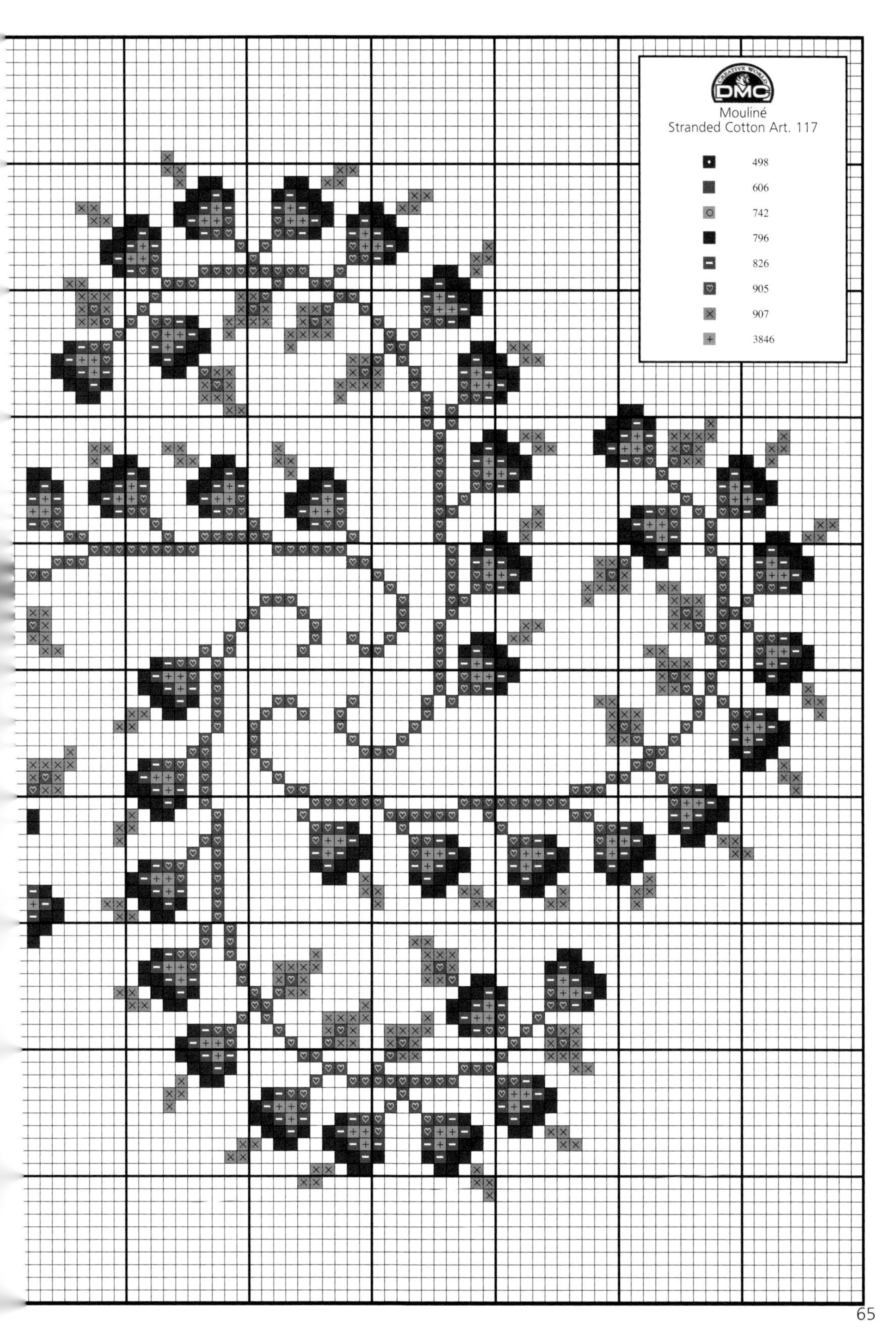
DMC
Mouliné
Stranded Cotton Art. 117
498
606
742
796
826
905
907
3846

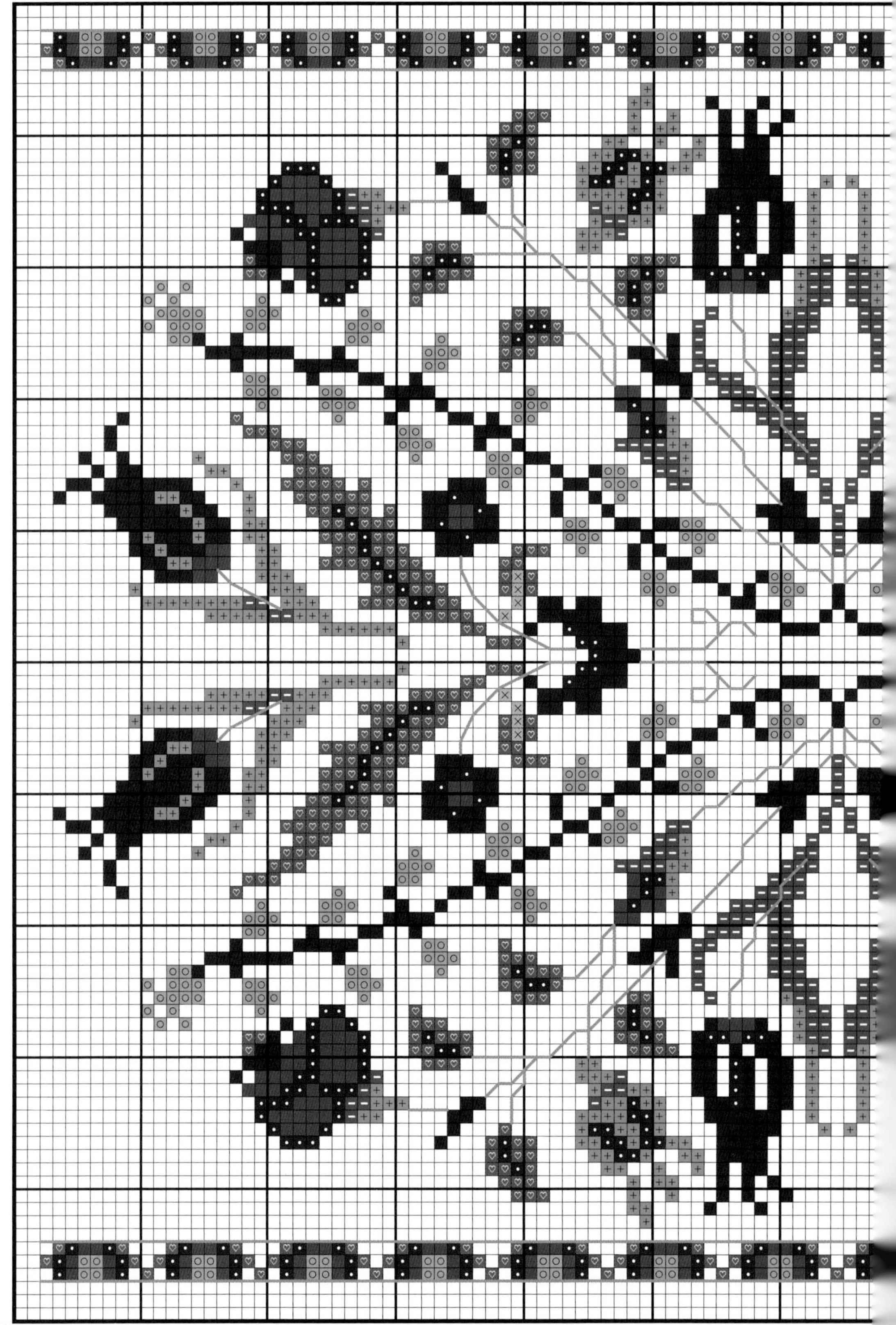

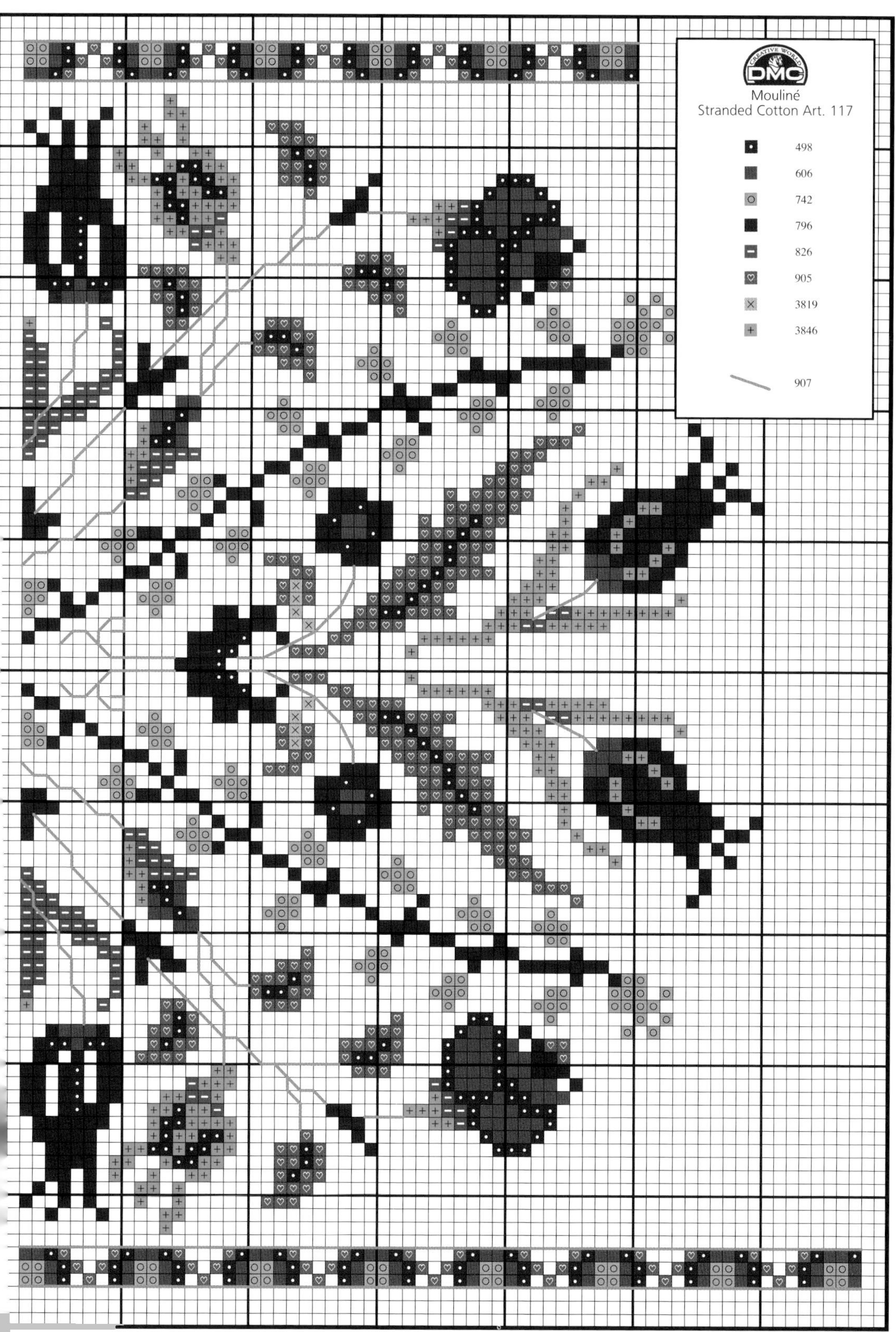
DMC
Mouliné
Stranded Cotton Art. 117
498
606
742
796
826
905
3819
3846
907

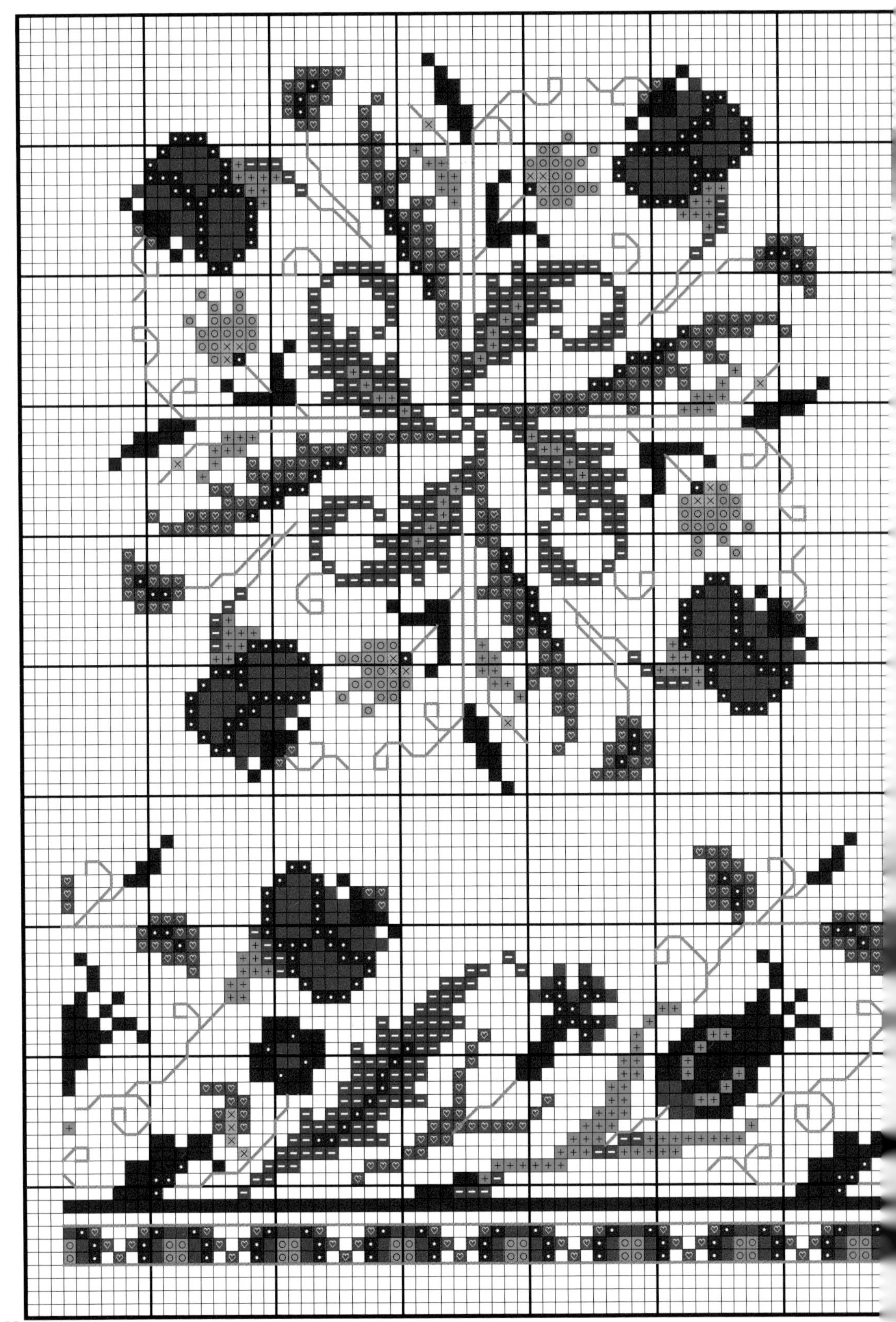

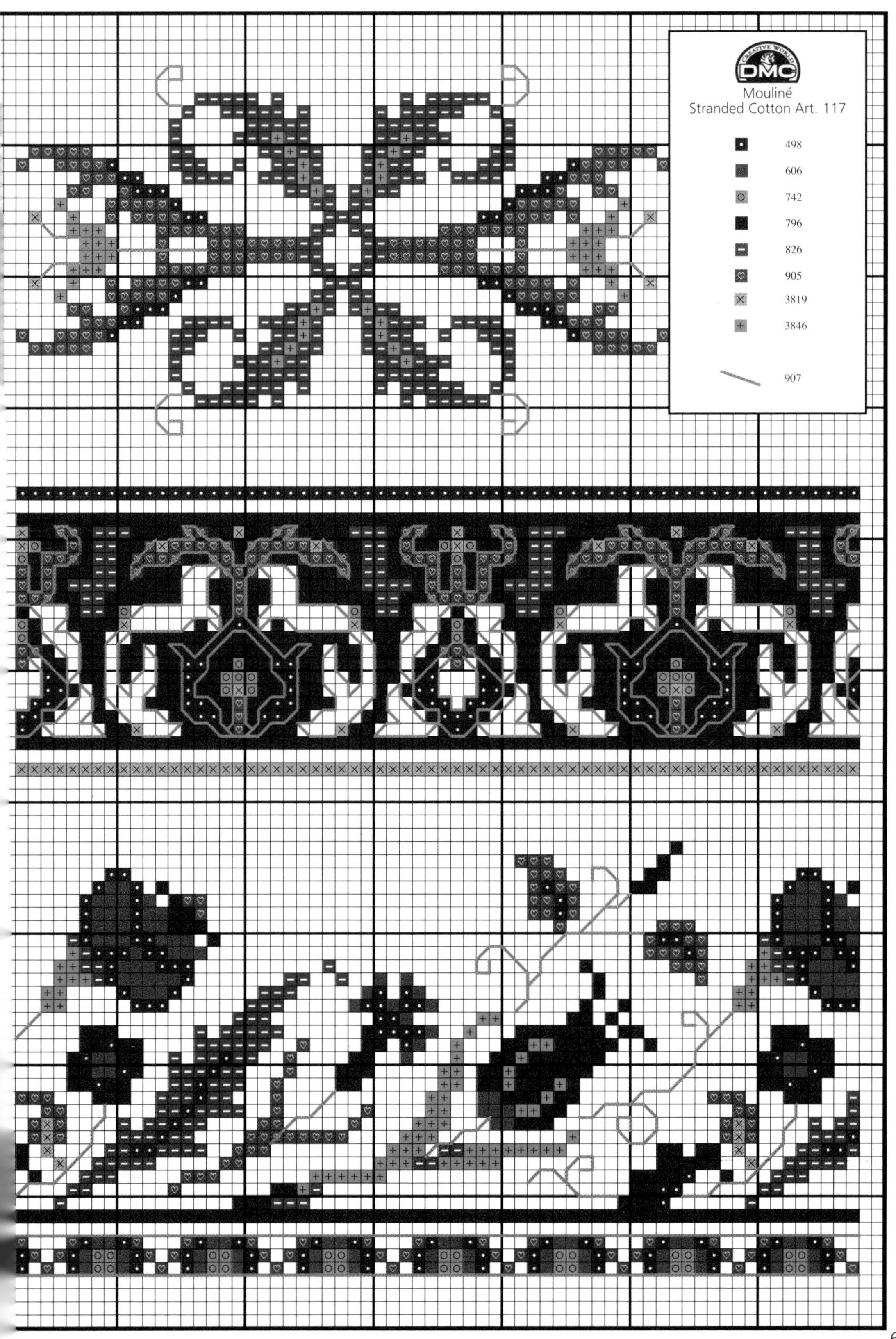
DMC
CREATIVE WORLD
Mouliné
Stranded Cotton Art. 117
498
606
742
796
826
905
3819
3846
907

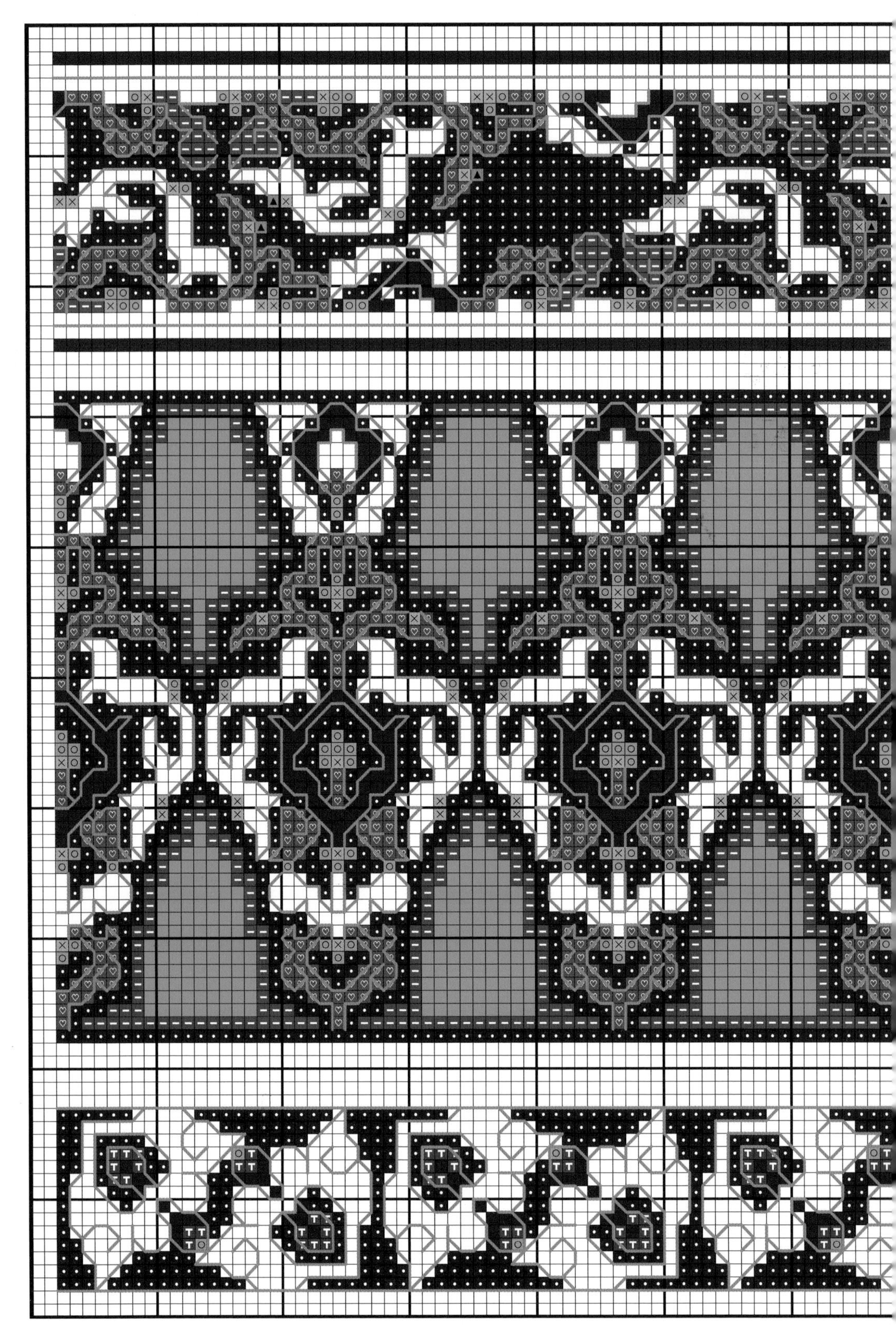

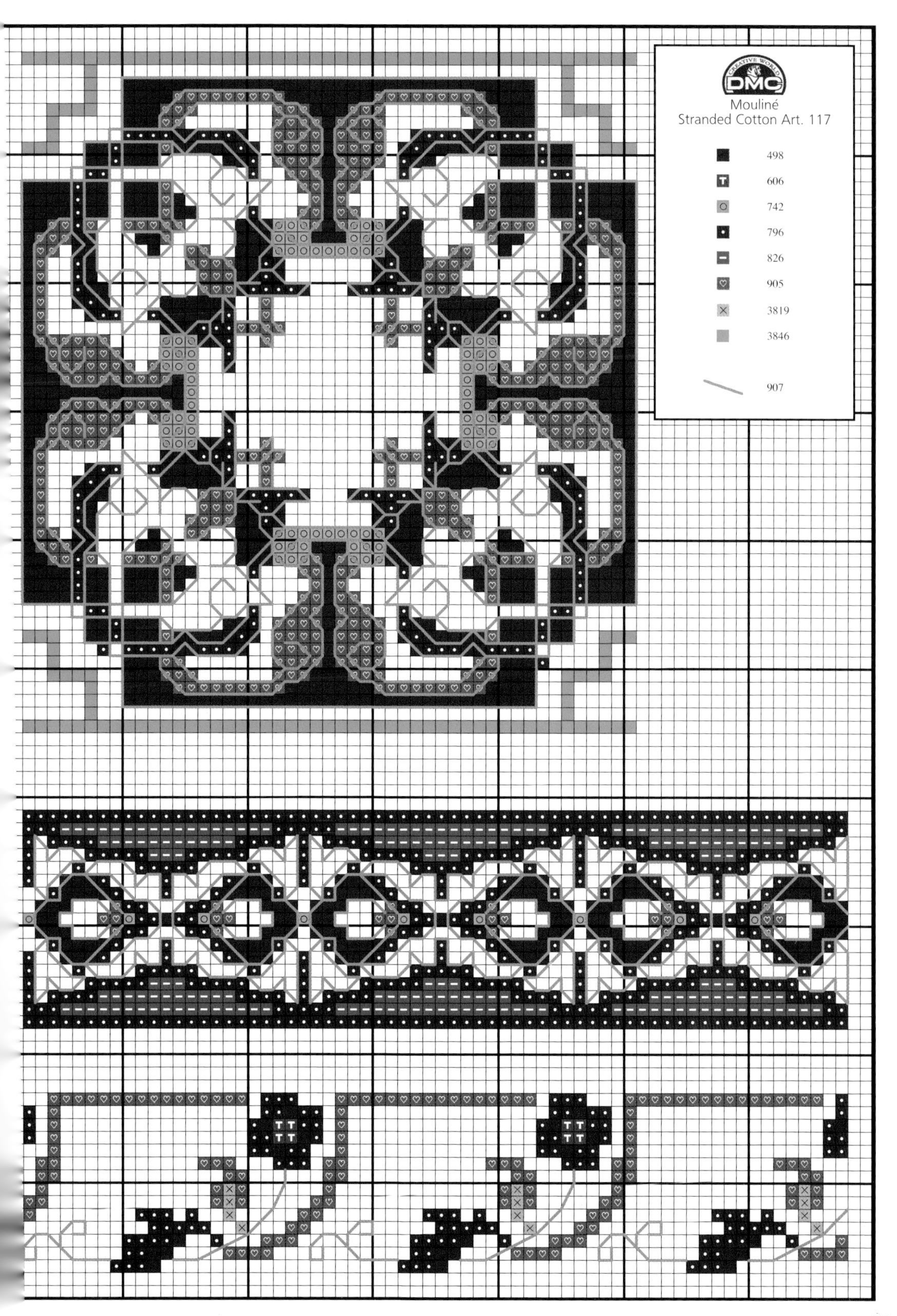
DMC
CREATIVE WORLD
Mouliné
Stranded Cotton Art. 117
498
606
742
796
826
905
3819
3846
907

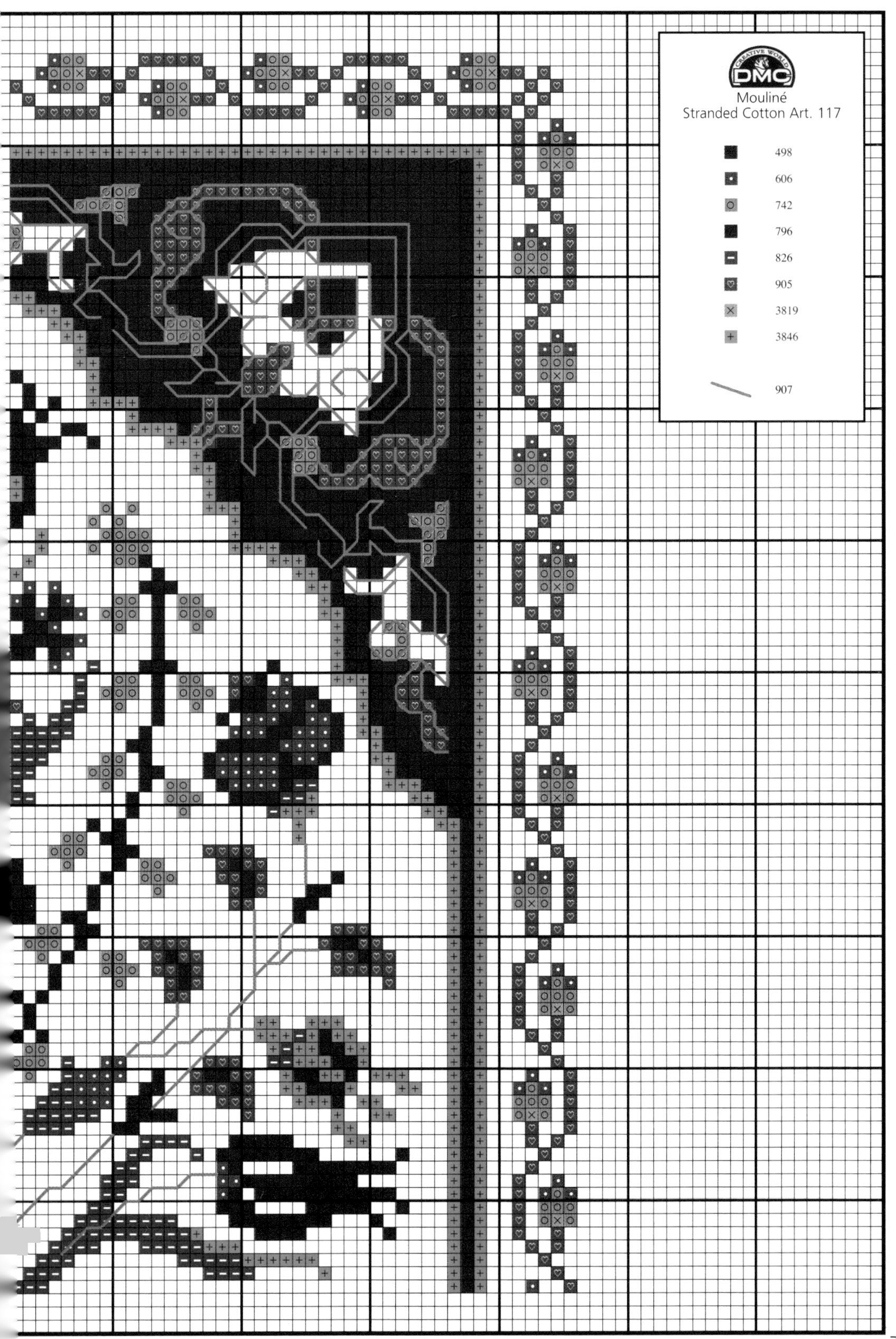
DMC
Mouliné
Stranded Cotton Art. 117
498
606
742
796
826
905
3819
3846
907

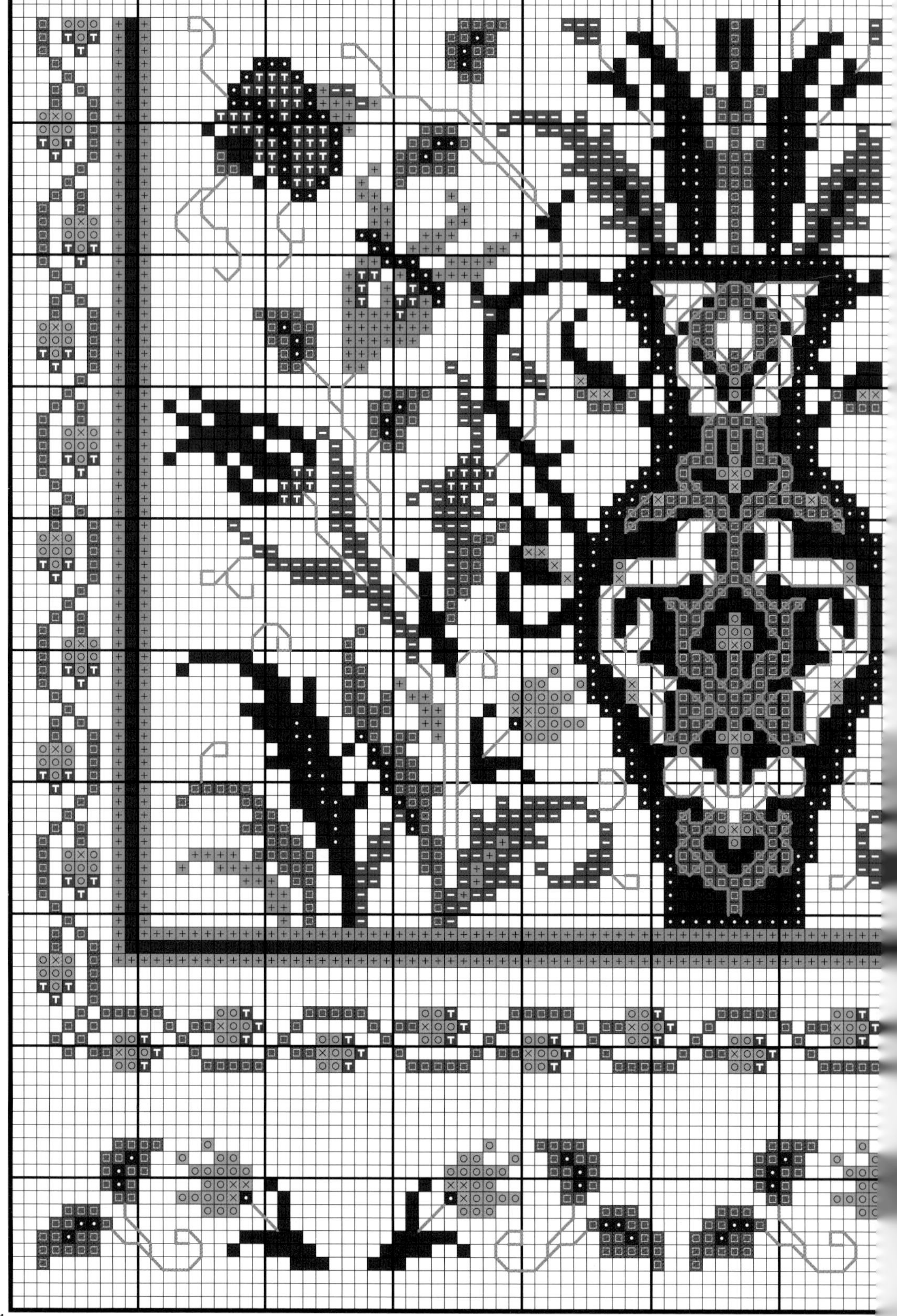

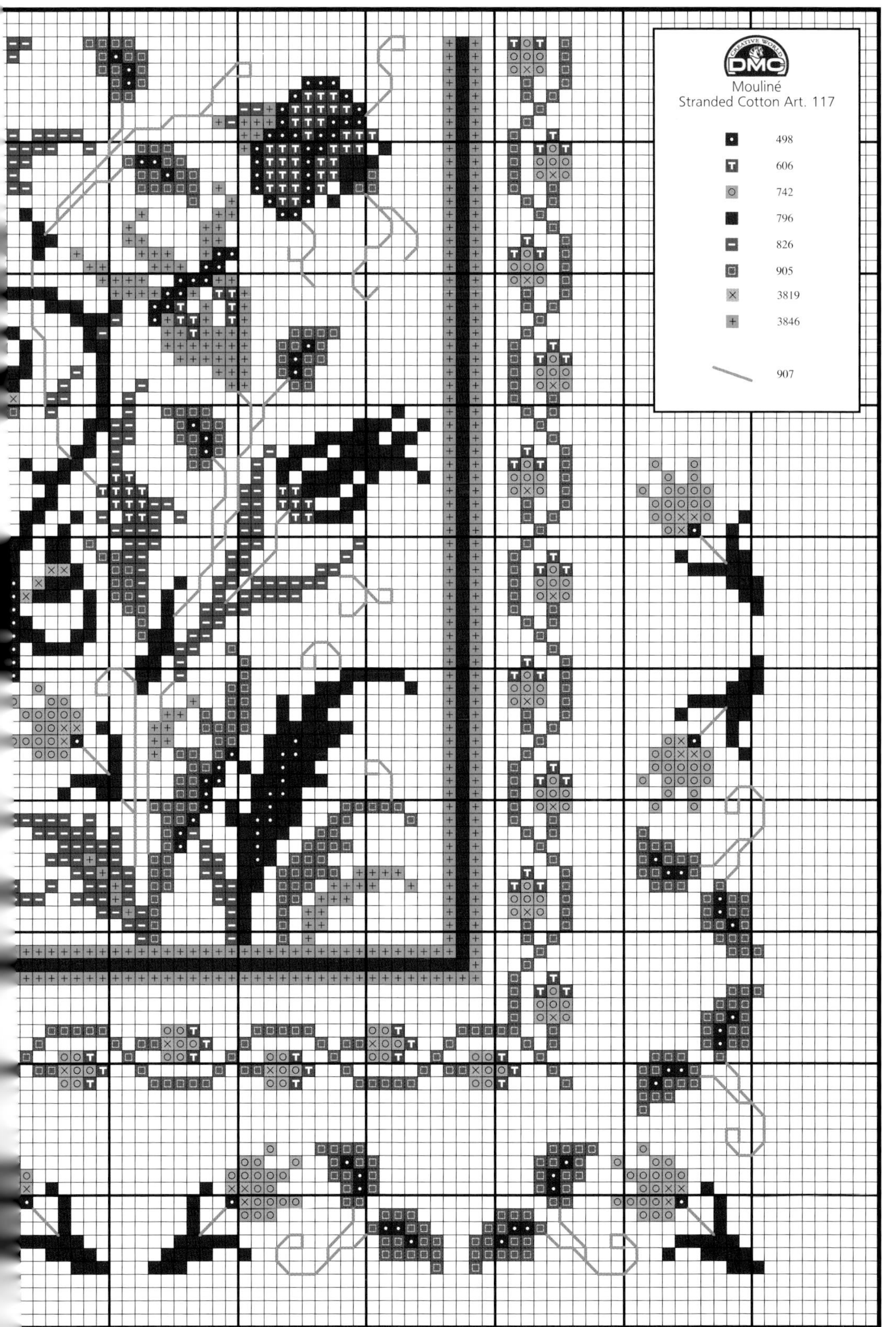
DMC
Mouliné
Stranded Cotton Art. 117
498
606
742
796
826
905
3819
3846
907

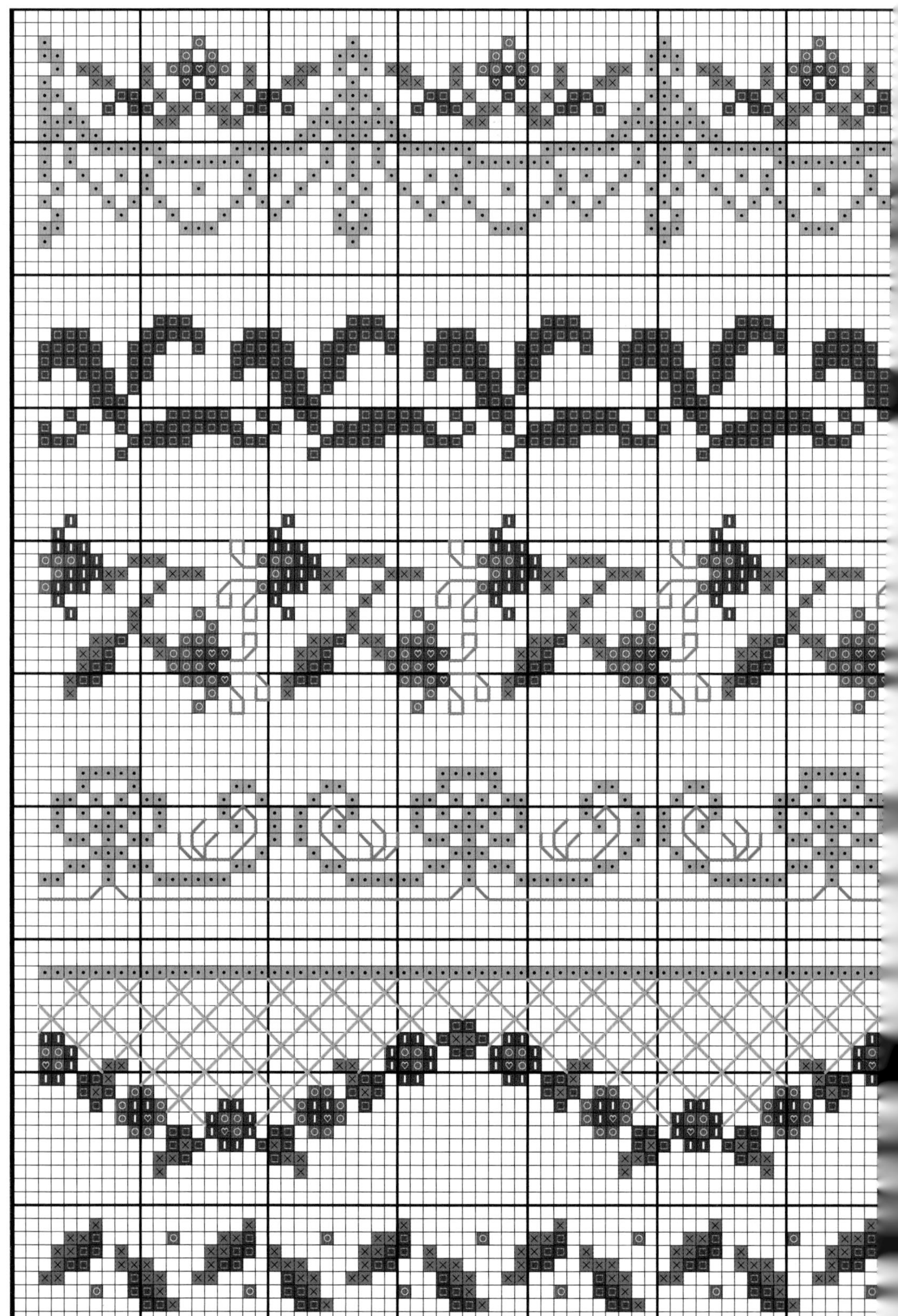

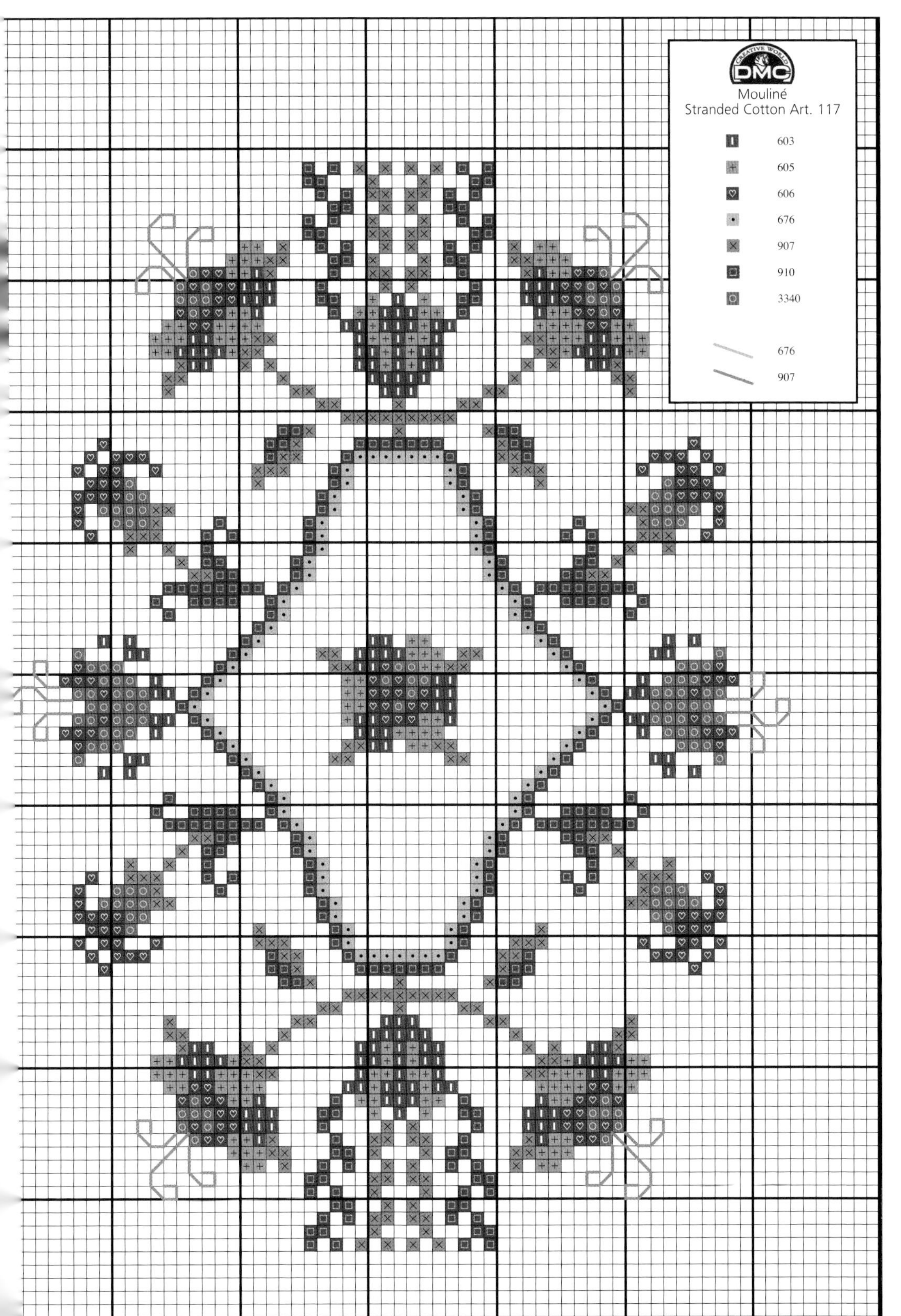
DMC
CREATIVE WORLD
Mouliné
Stranded Cotton Art. 117
603
605
606
676
907
910
3340
676
907

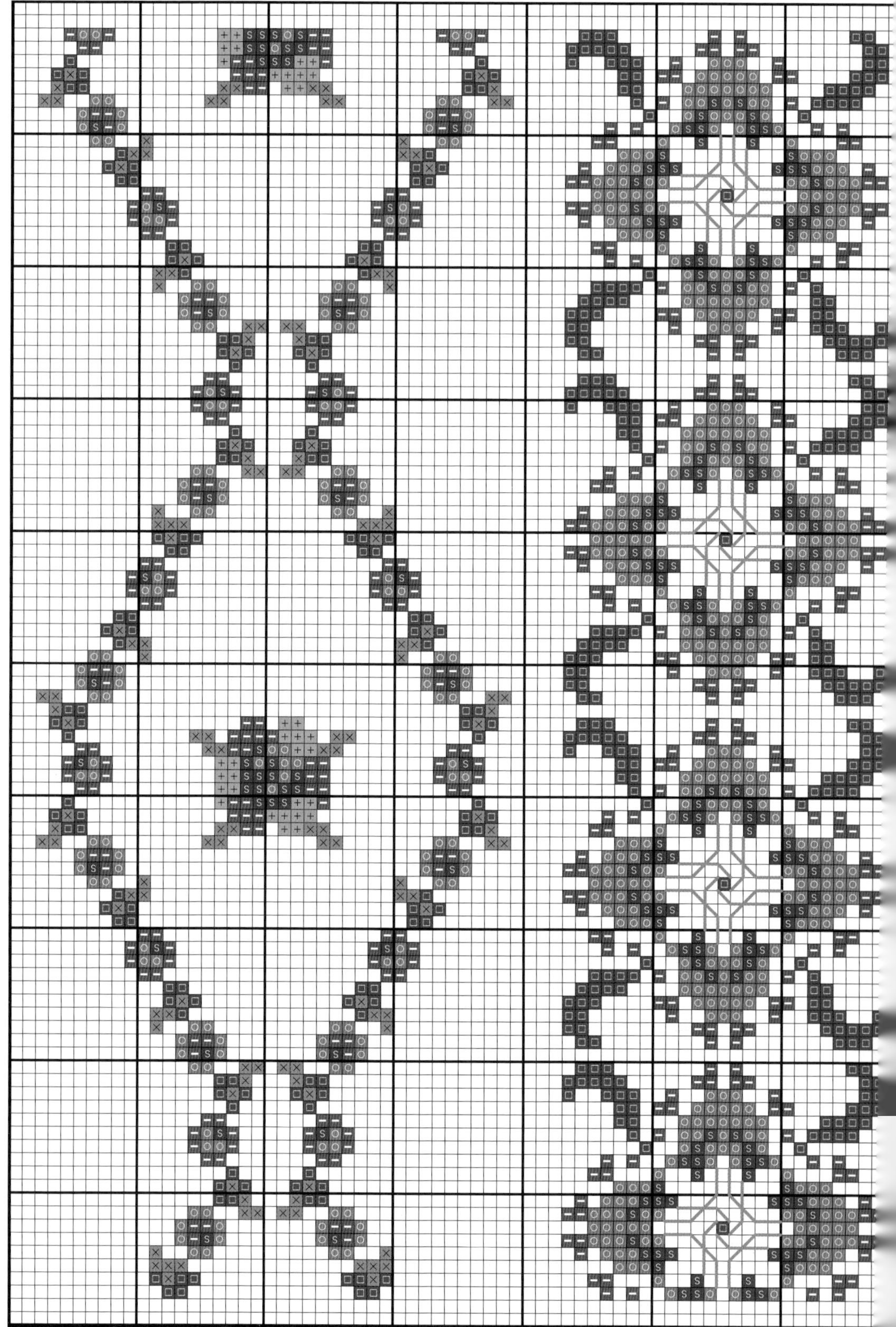

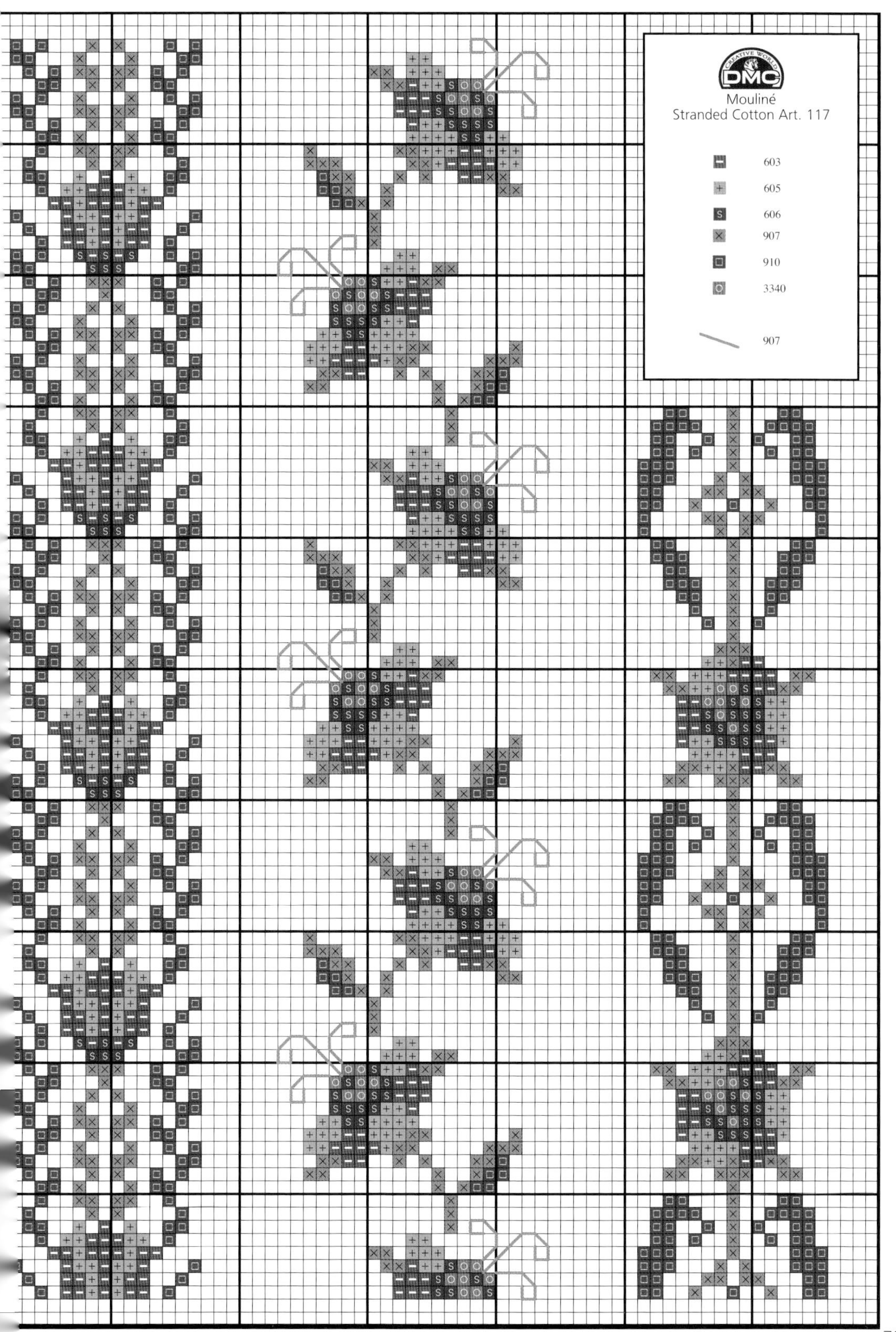
DMC
CREATIVE WORLD
Mouliné
Stranded Cotton Art. 117
603
605
606
907
910
3340
907

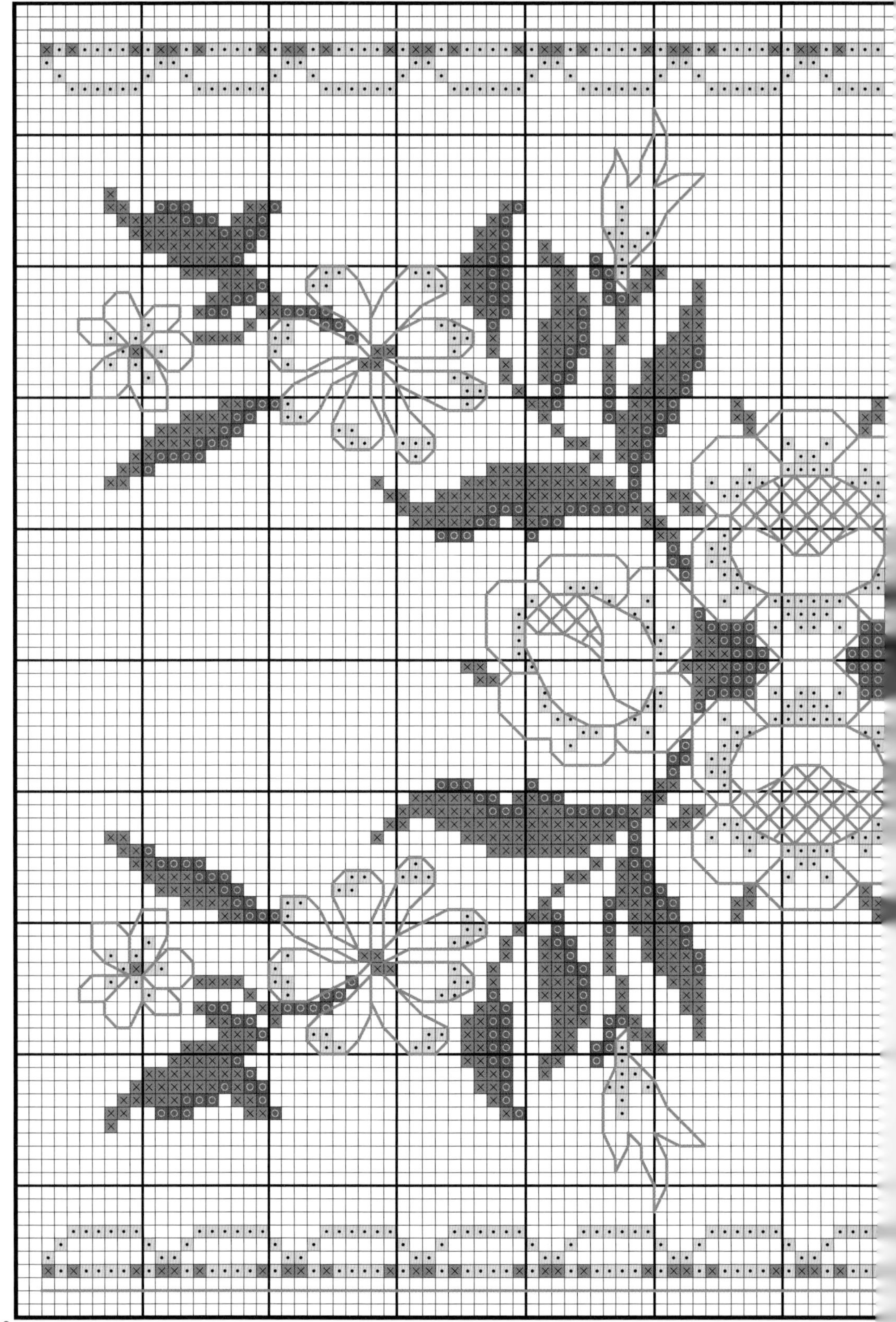

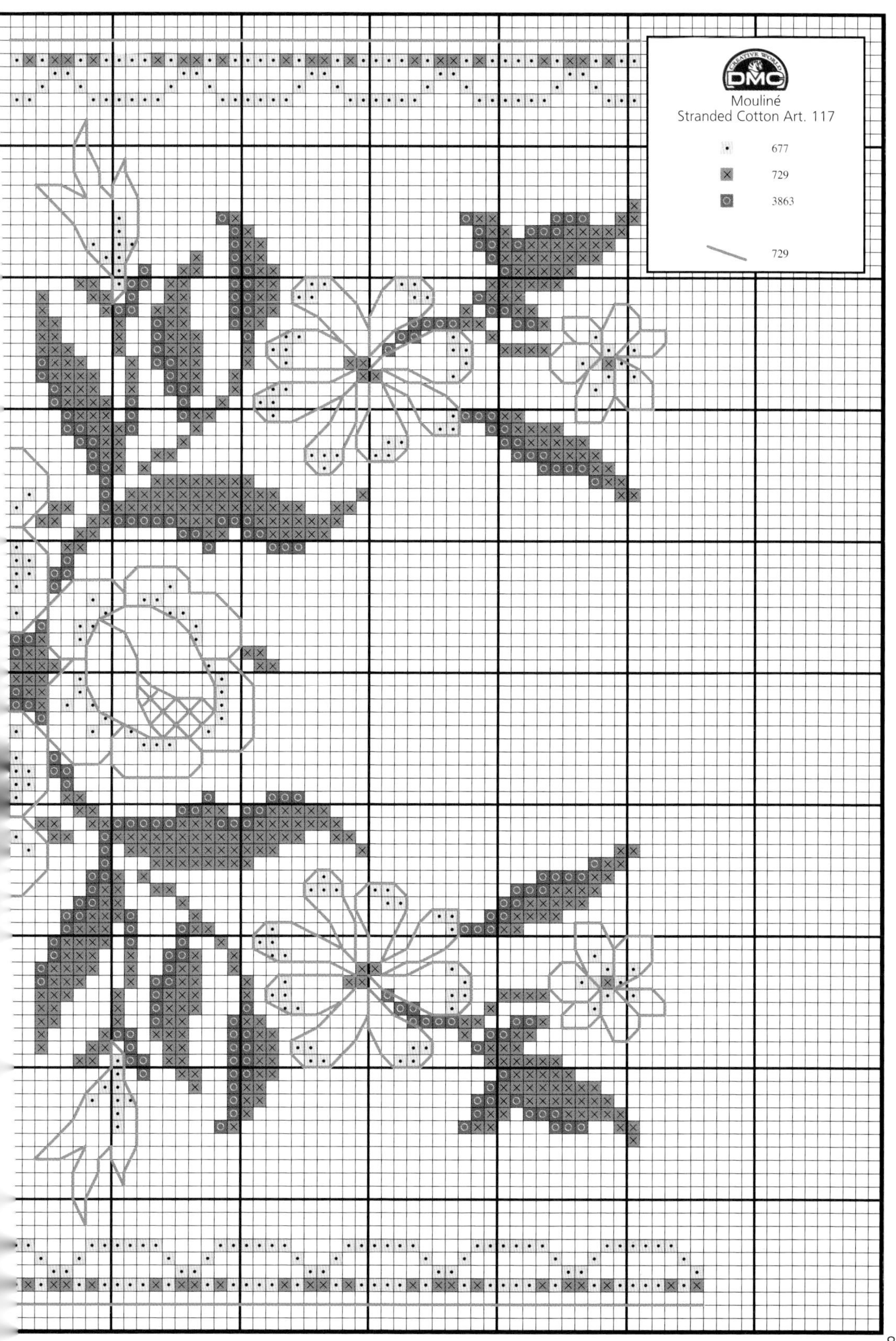
DMC
CREATIVE WORLD
Mouliné
Stranded Cotton Art. 117
677
729
3863
729

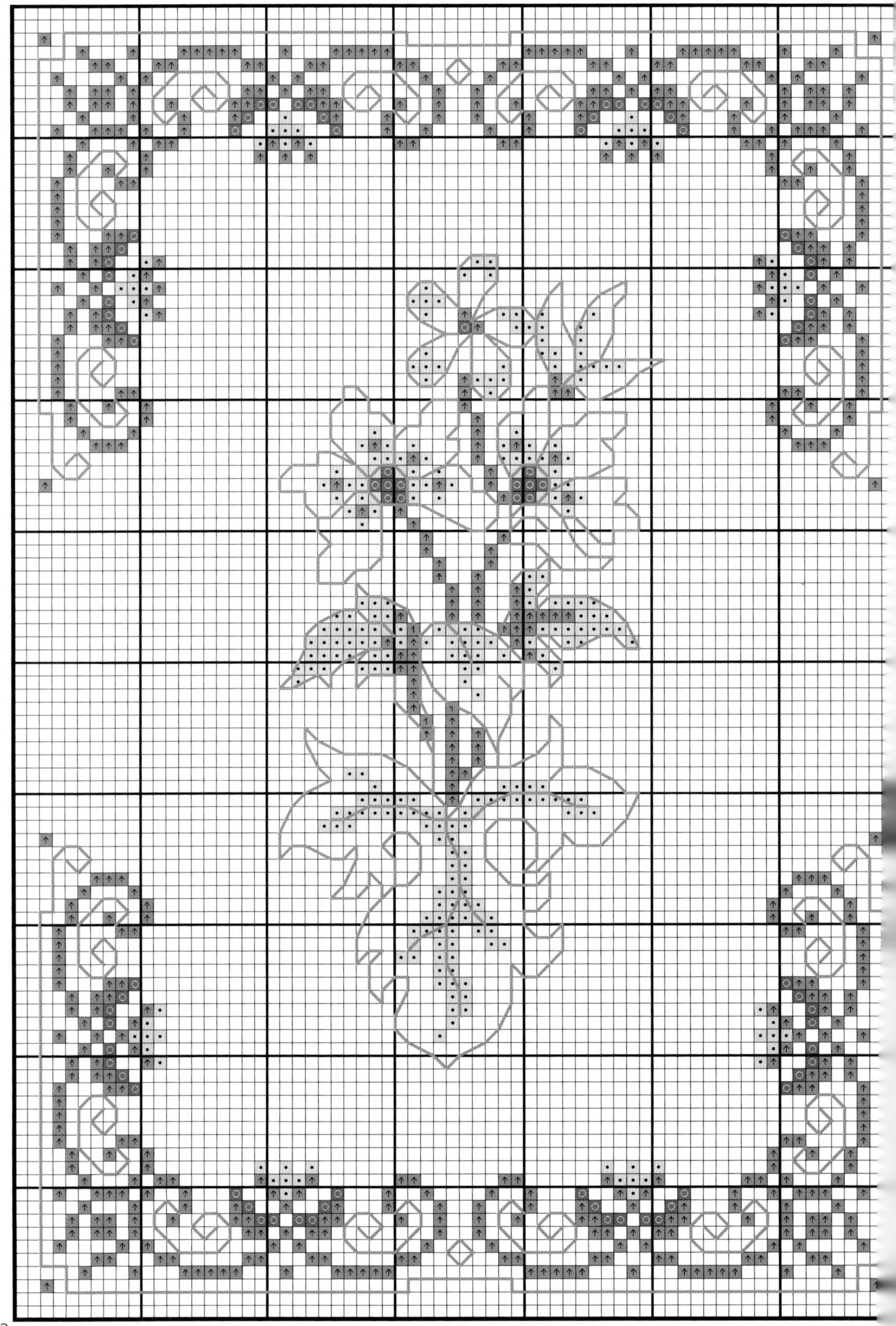

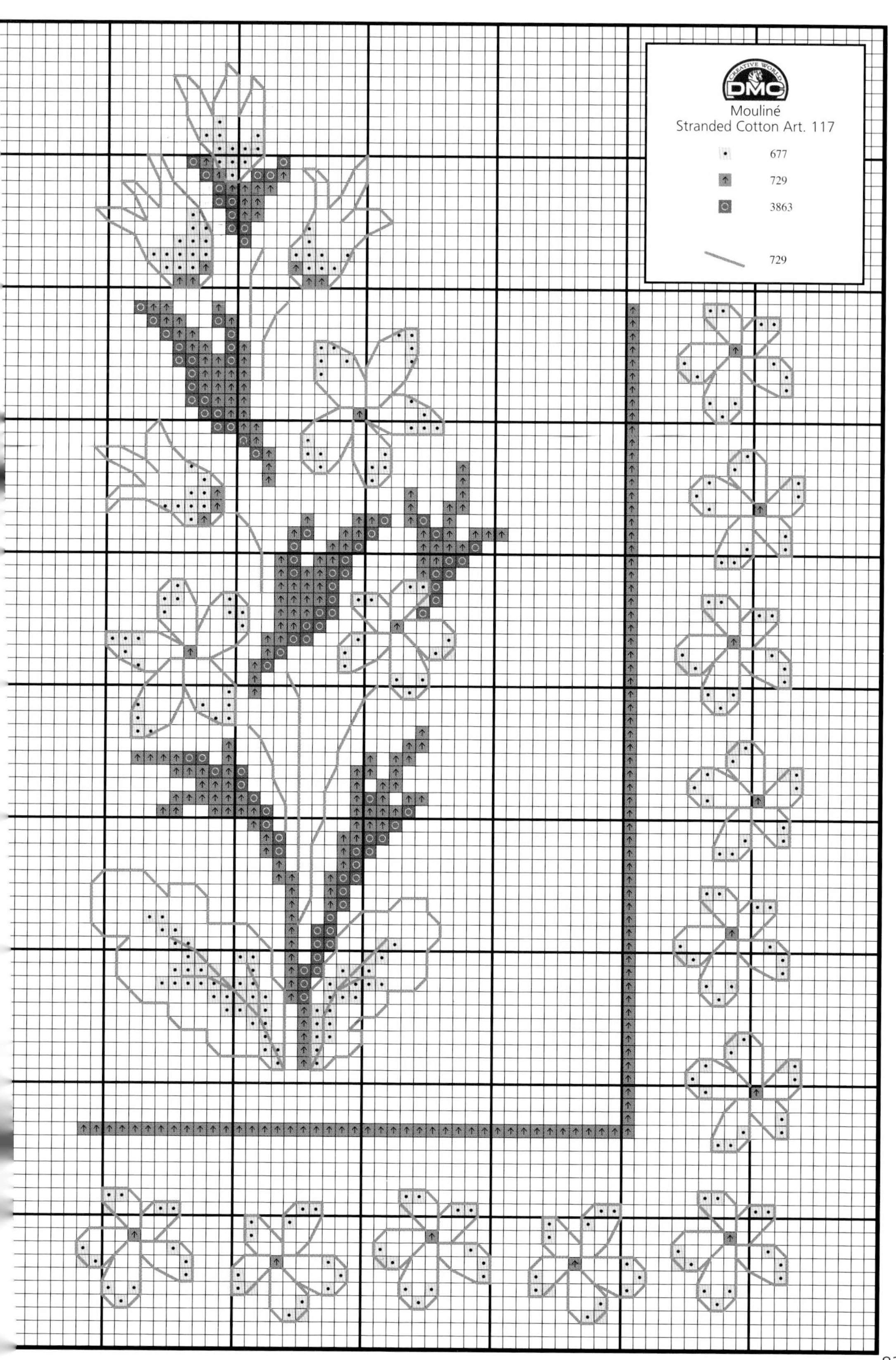
DMC
CREATIVE WORLD
Mouliné
Stranded Cotton Art. 117
677
729
3863
729

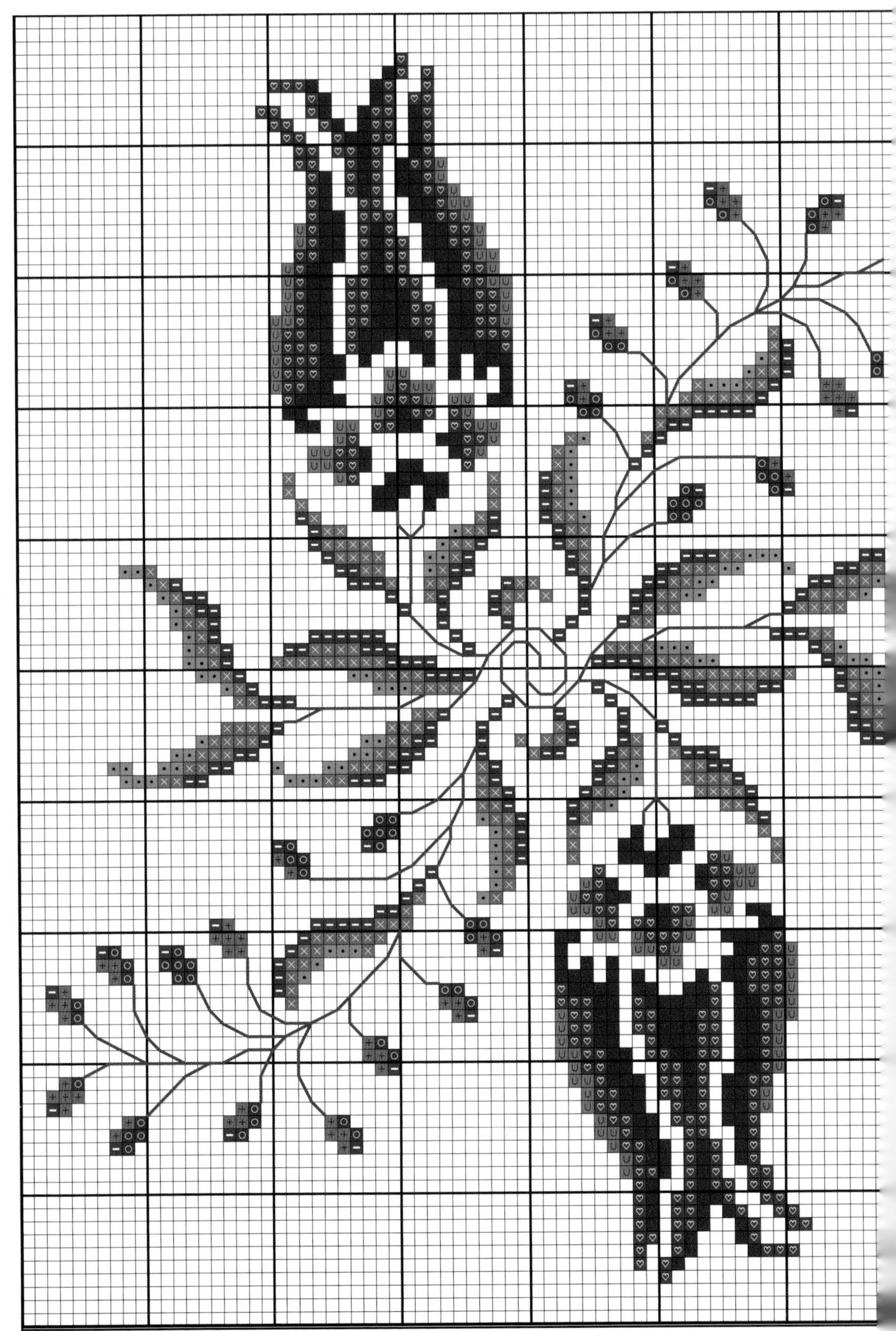

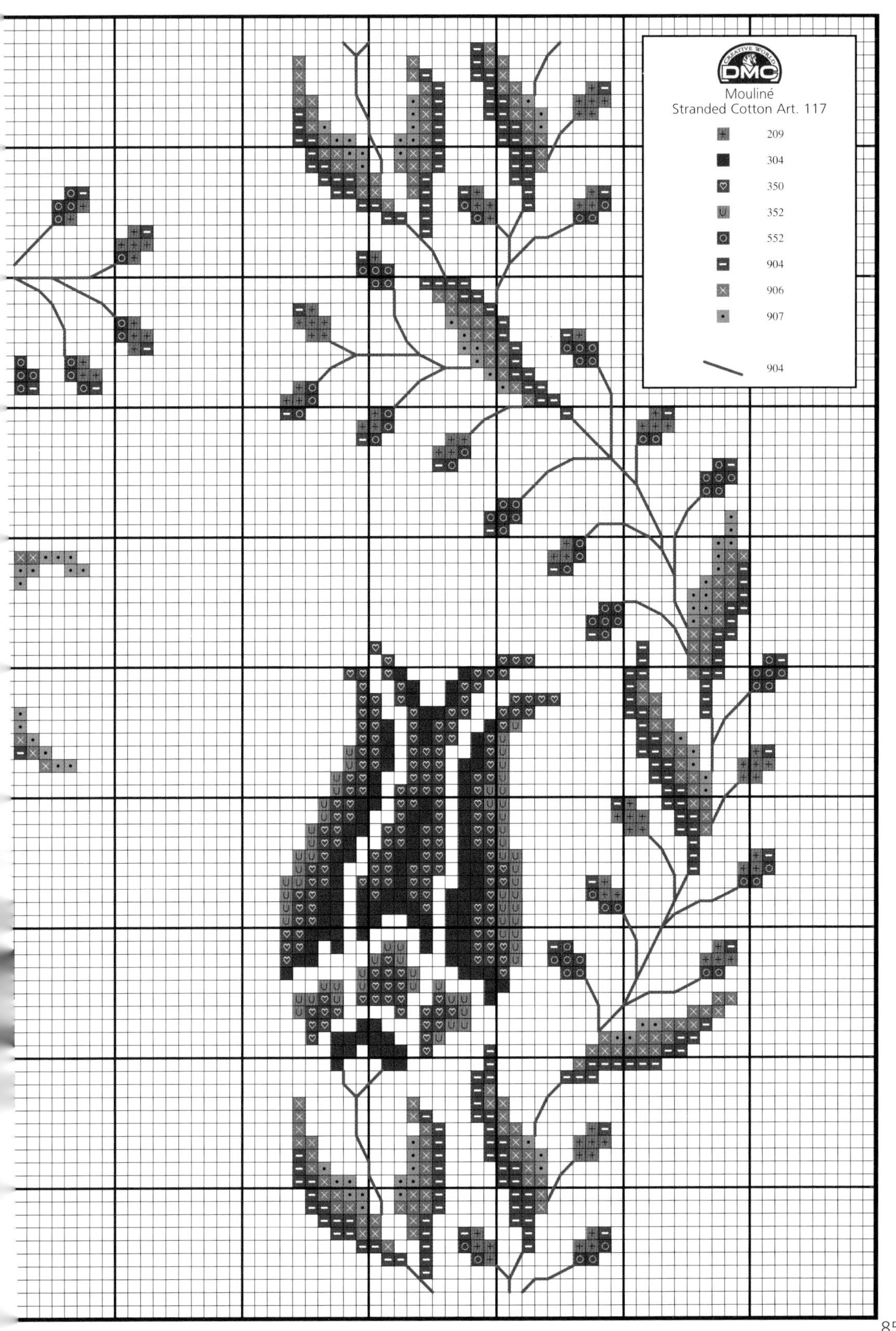
DMC
Mouliné
Stranded Cotton Art. 117
209
304
350
352
552
904
906
907
904

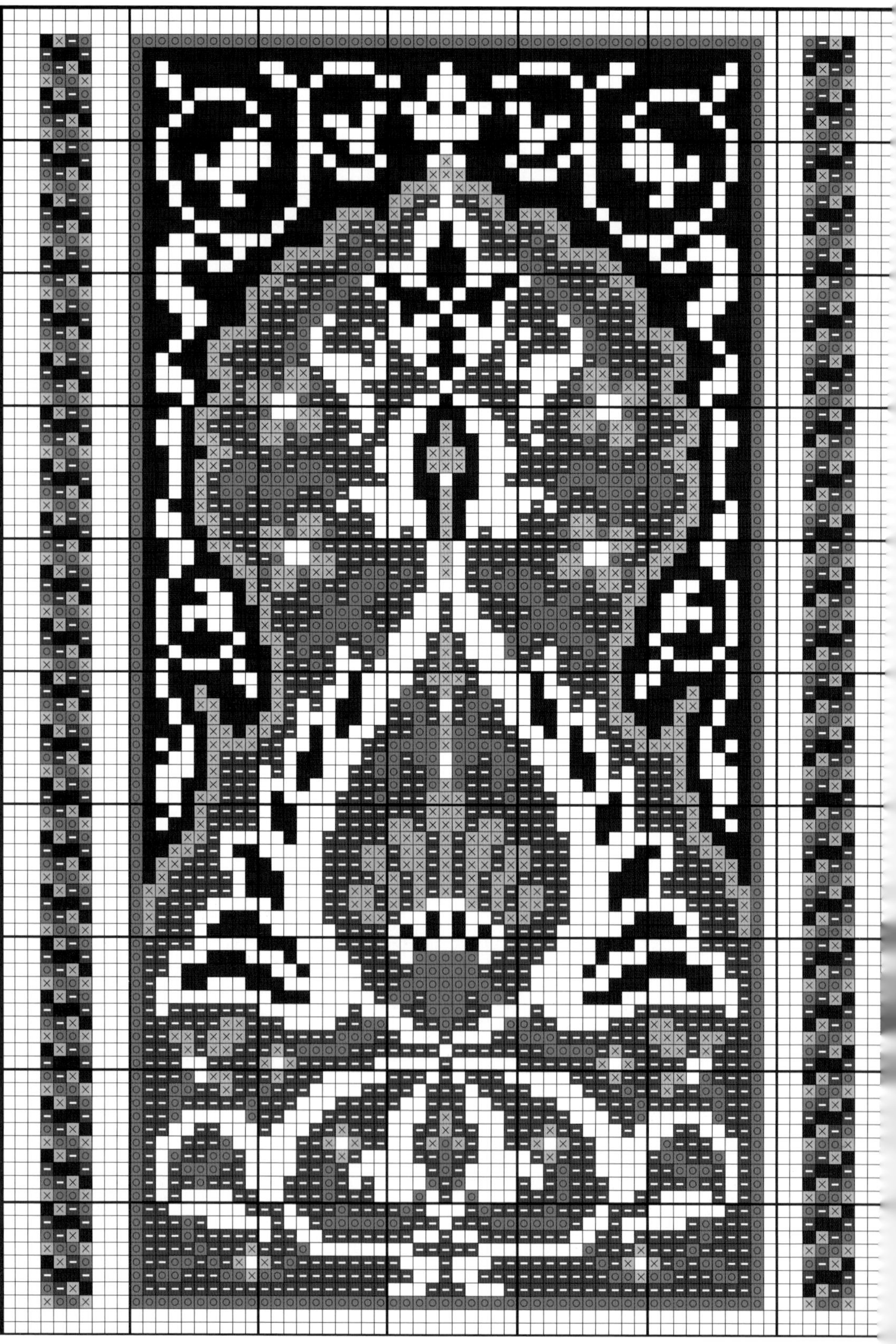

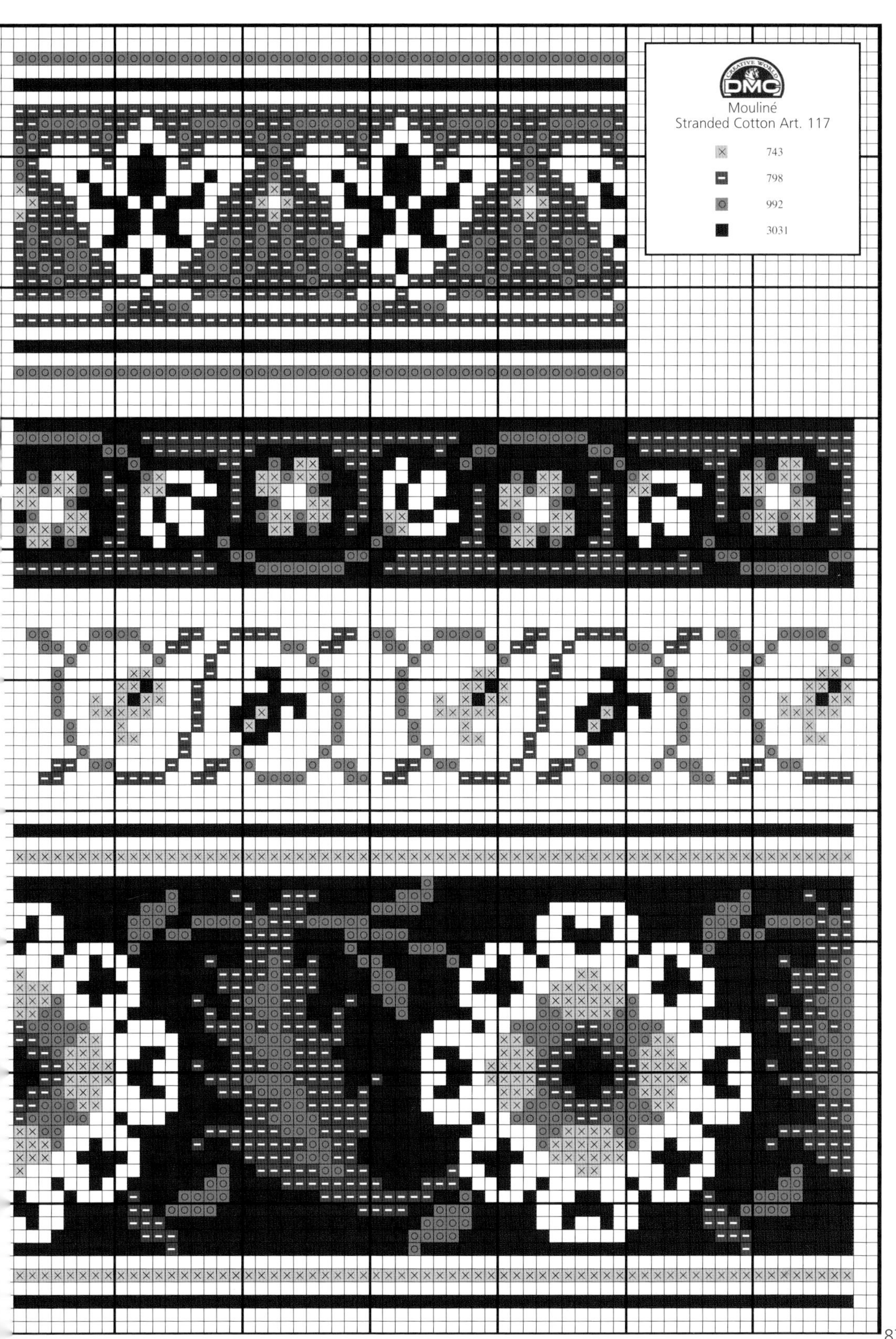
DMC
CREATIVE WORLD
Mouliné
Stranded Cotton Art. 117
743
798
992
3031

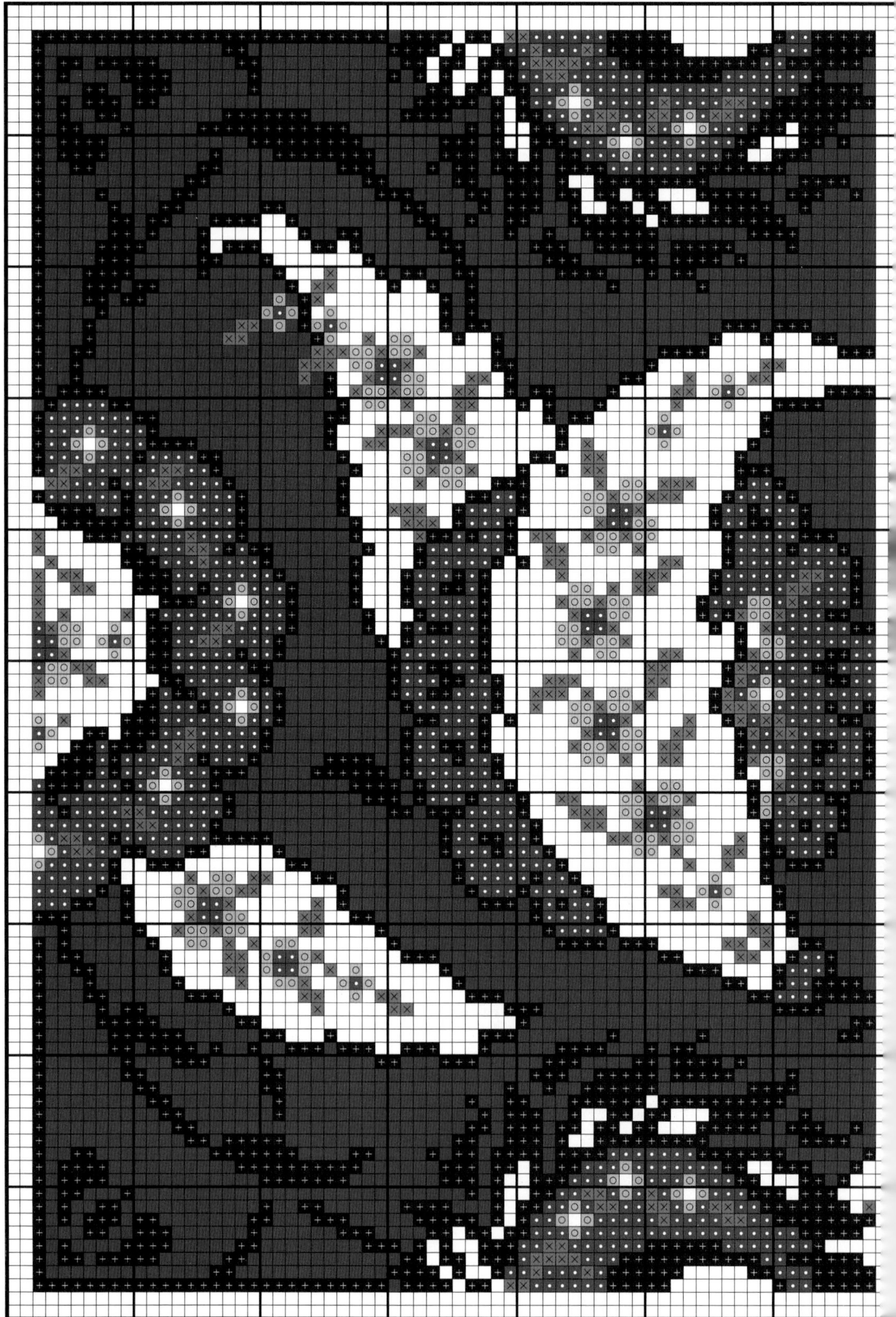

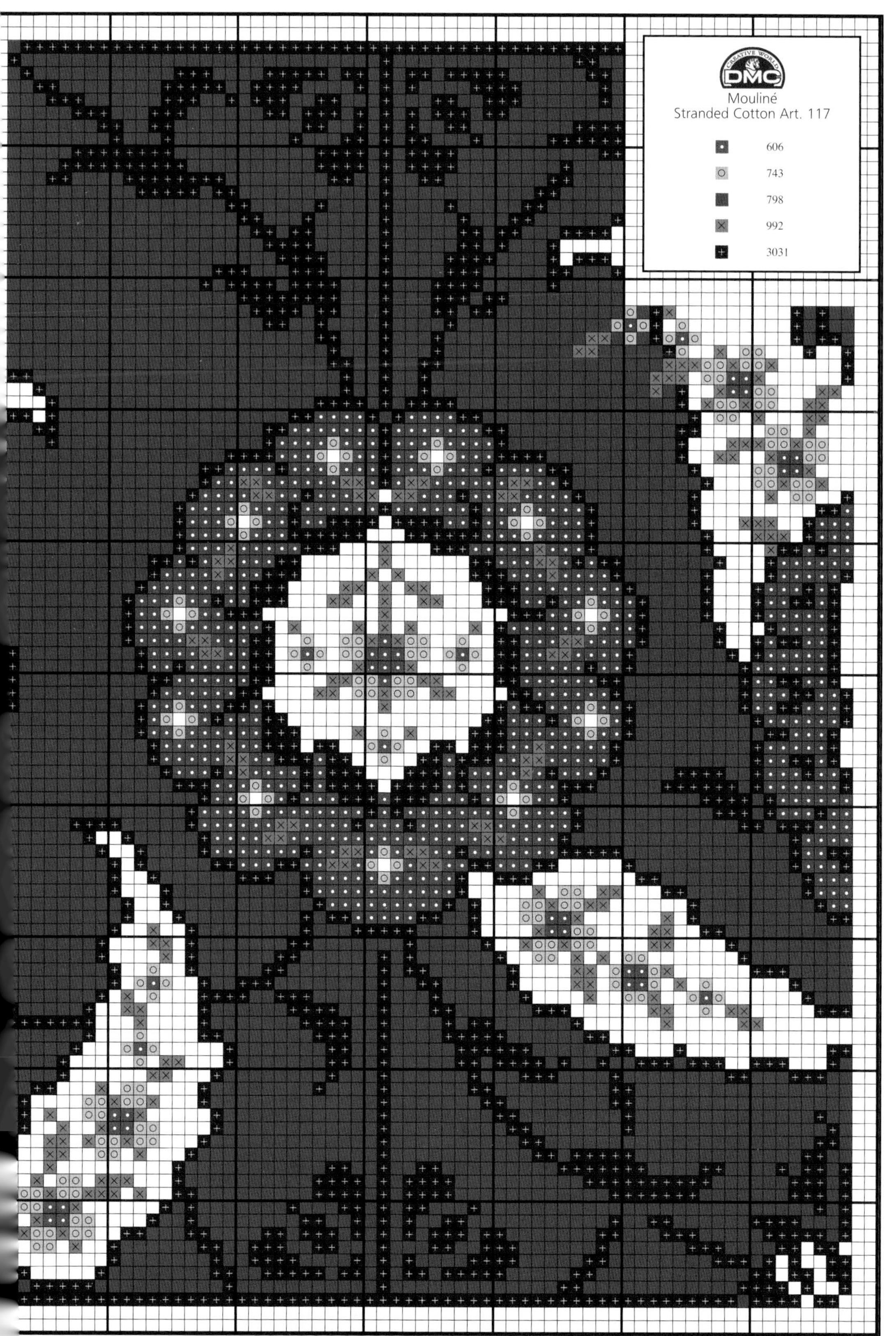
DMC
CREATIVE WORLD
Mouliné
Stranded Cotton Art. 117
606
743
798
992
3031

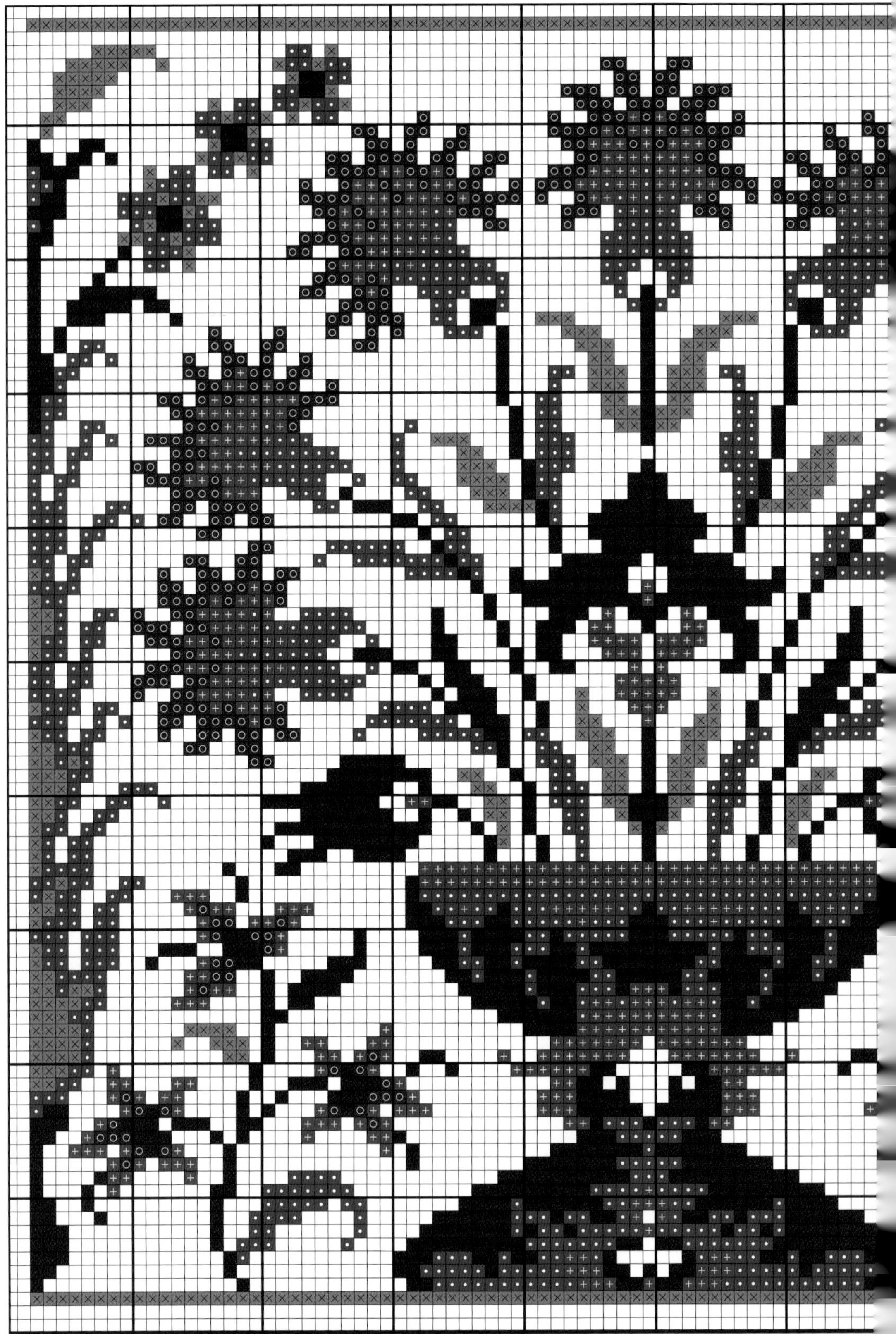

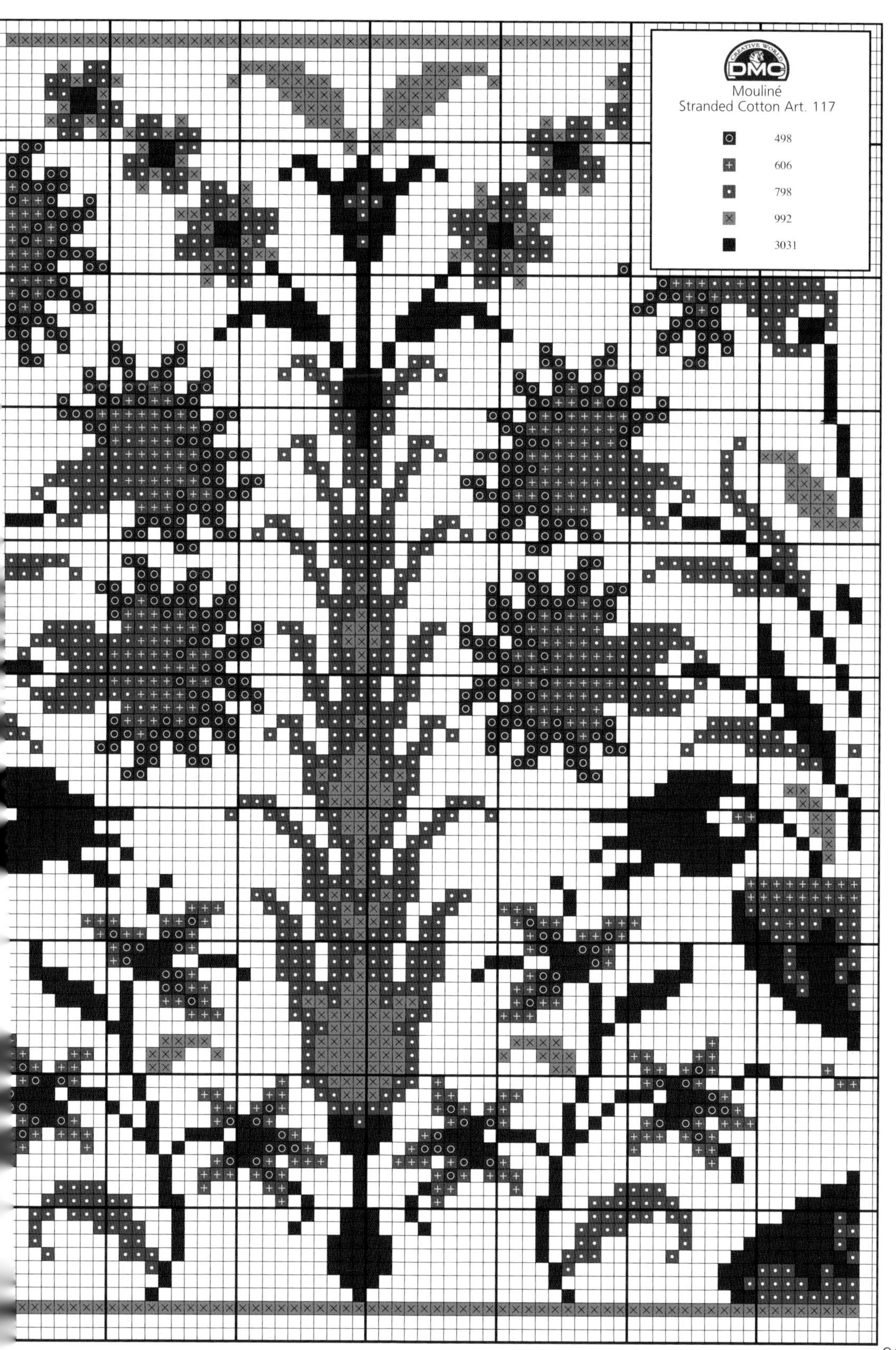
DMC
CREATIVE WORLD
Mouliné
Stranded Cotton Art. 117
498
606
798
992
3031

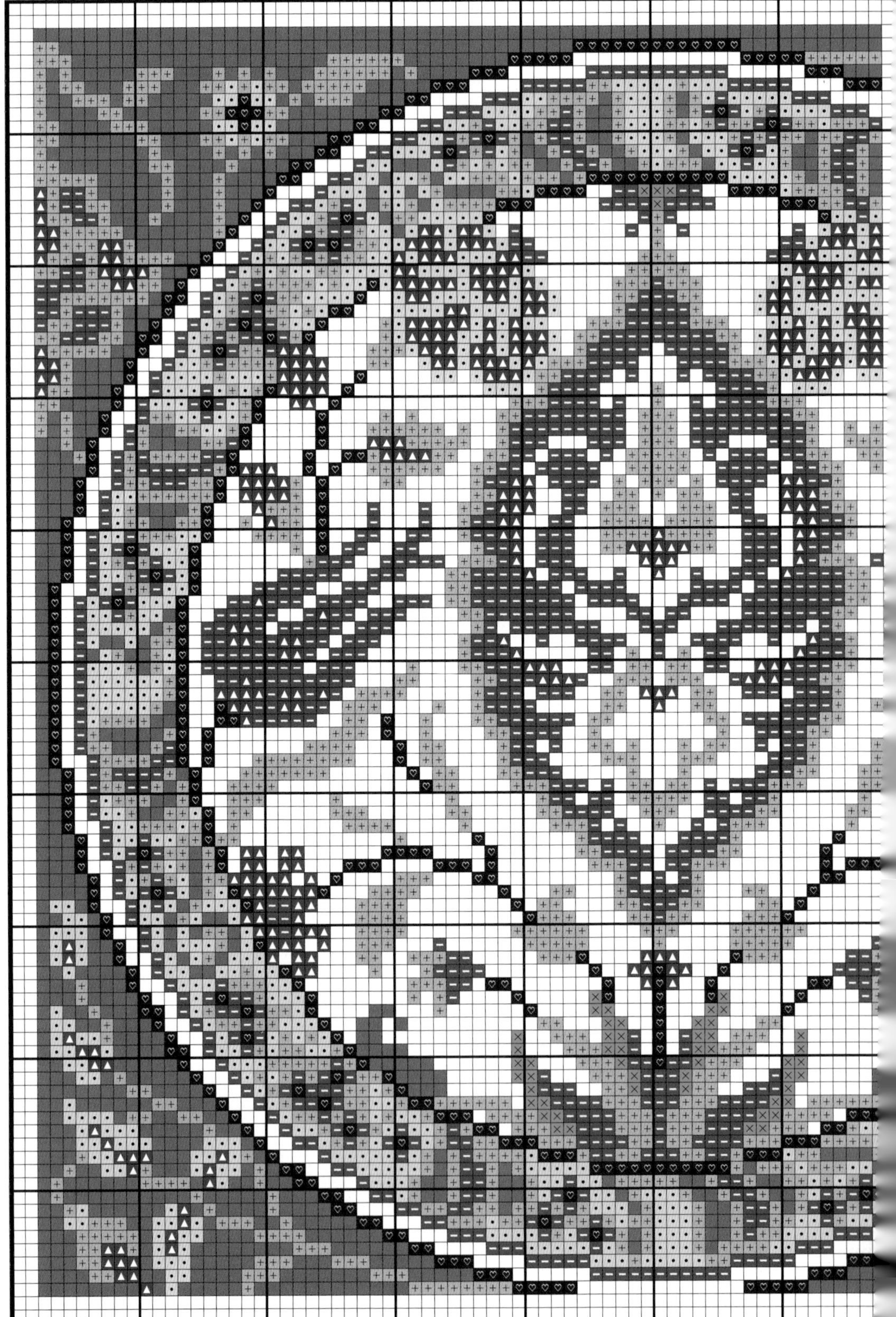

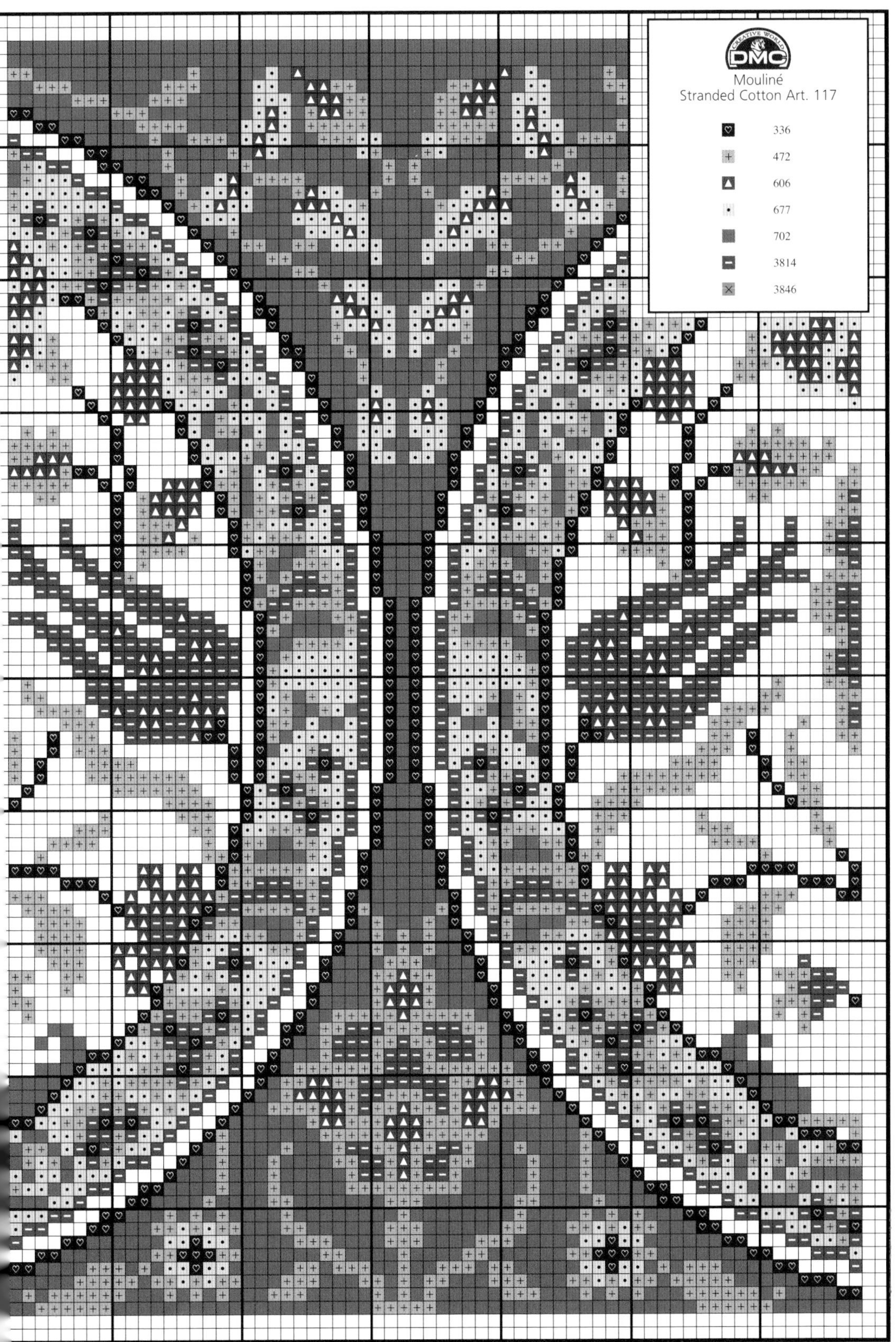
DMC
CREATIVE WORLD
Mouliné
Stranded Cotton Art. 117
336
472
606
677
702
3814
3846

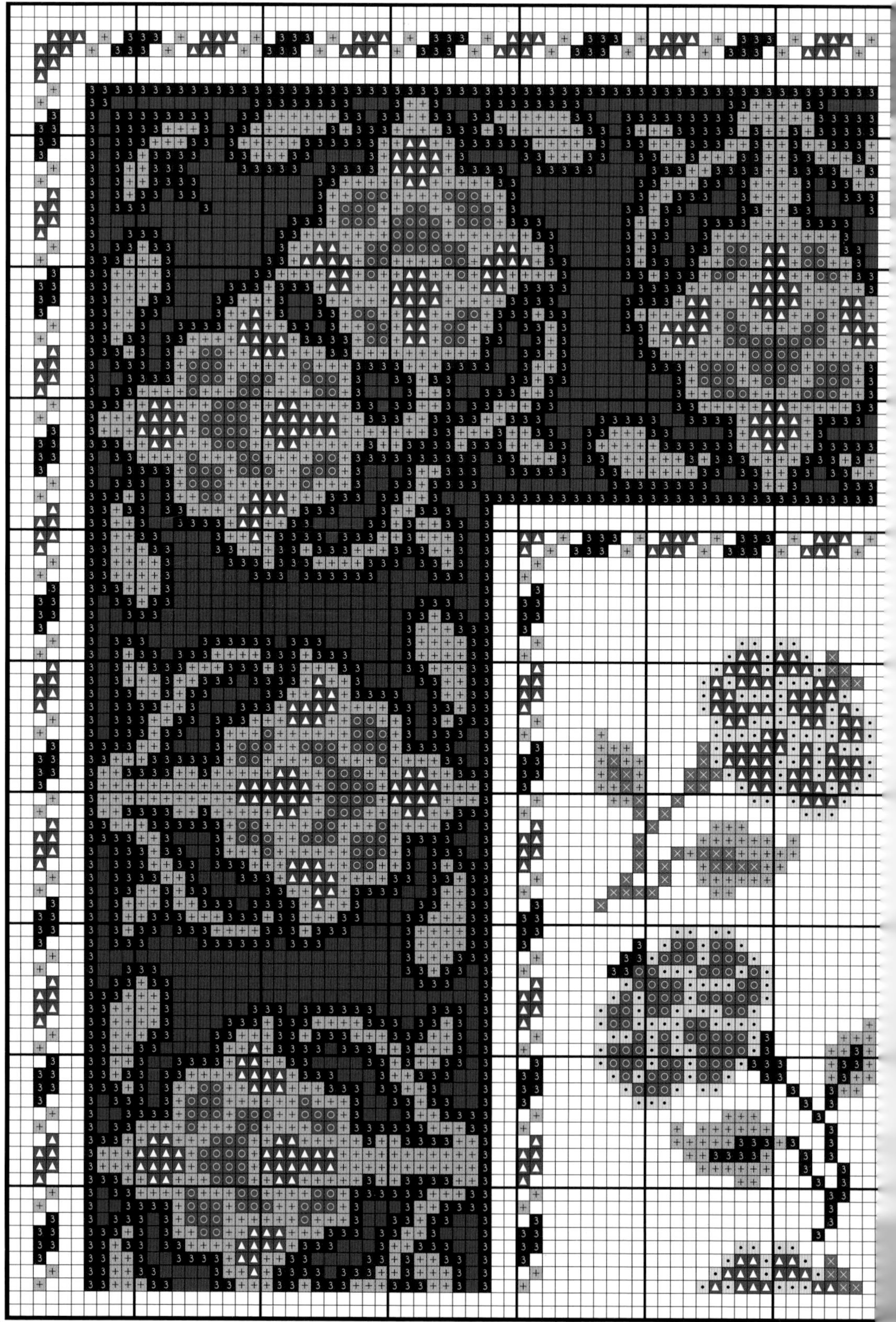

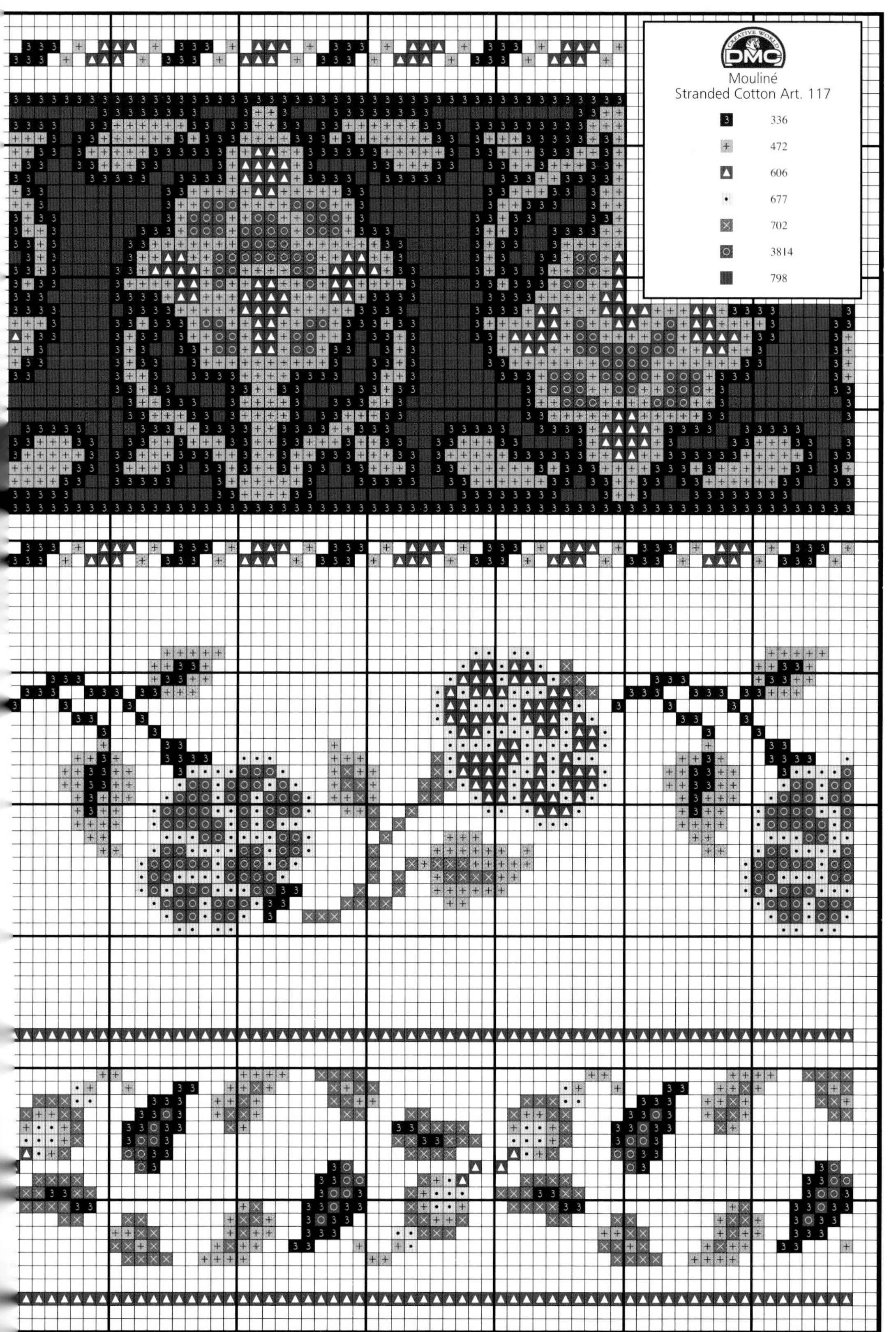
DMC
Mouliné
Stranded Cotton Art. 117
336
472
606
677
702
3814
798

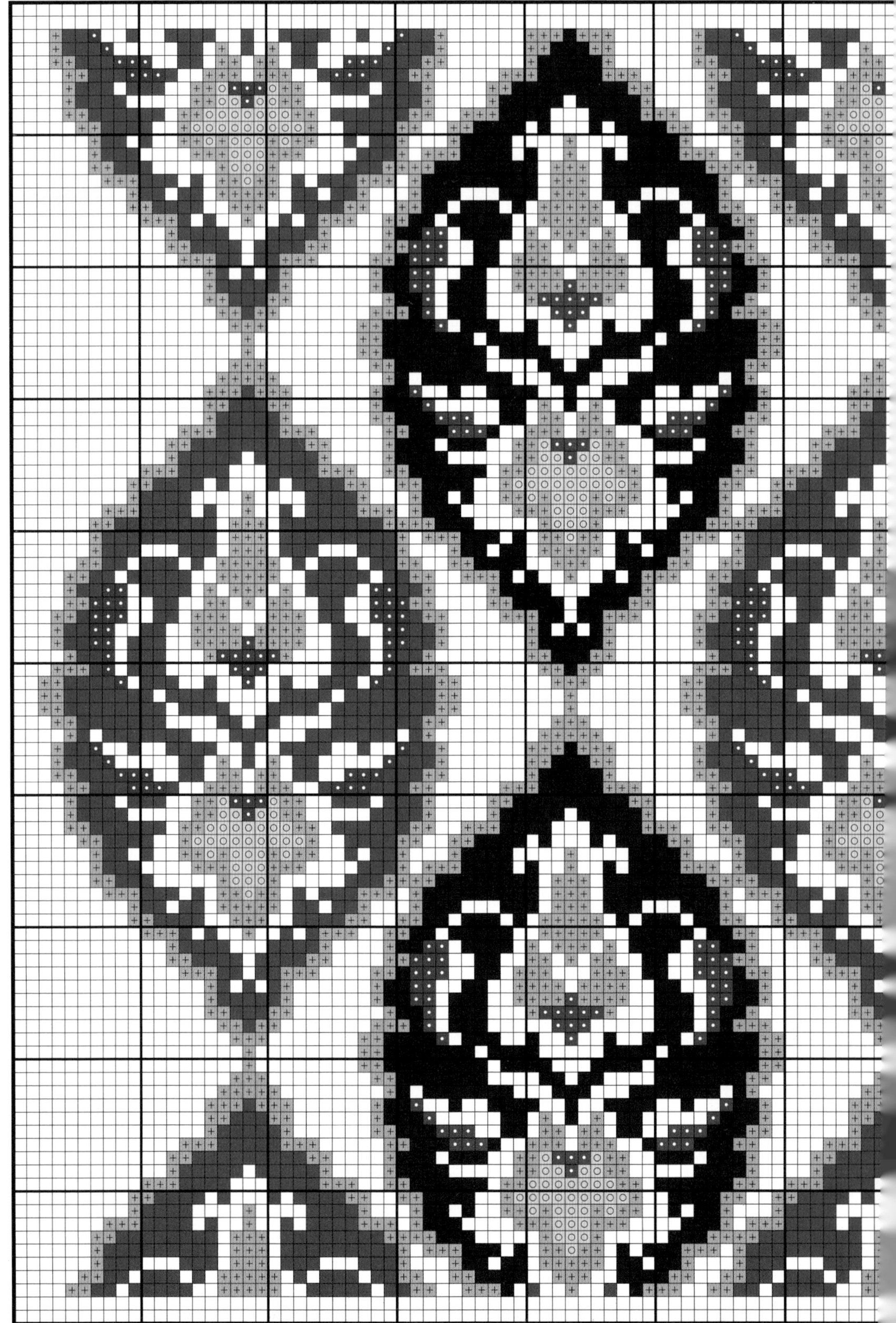

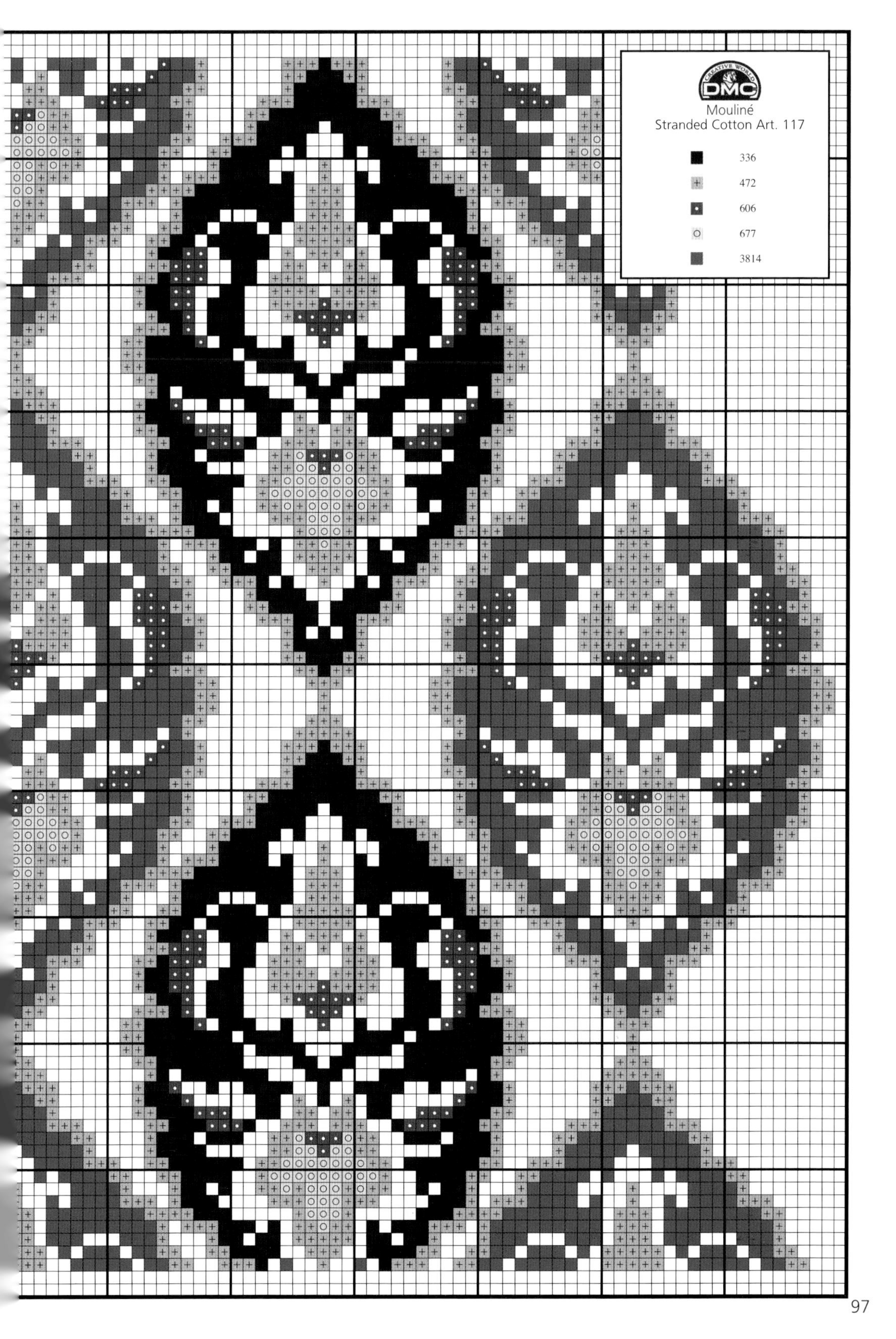
DMC
CREATIVE WORLD
Mouliné
Stranded Cotton Art. 117
336
472
606
677
3814

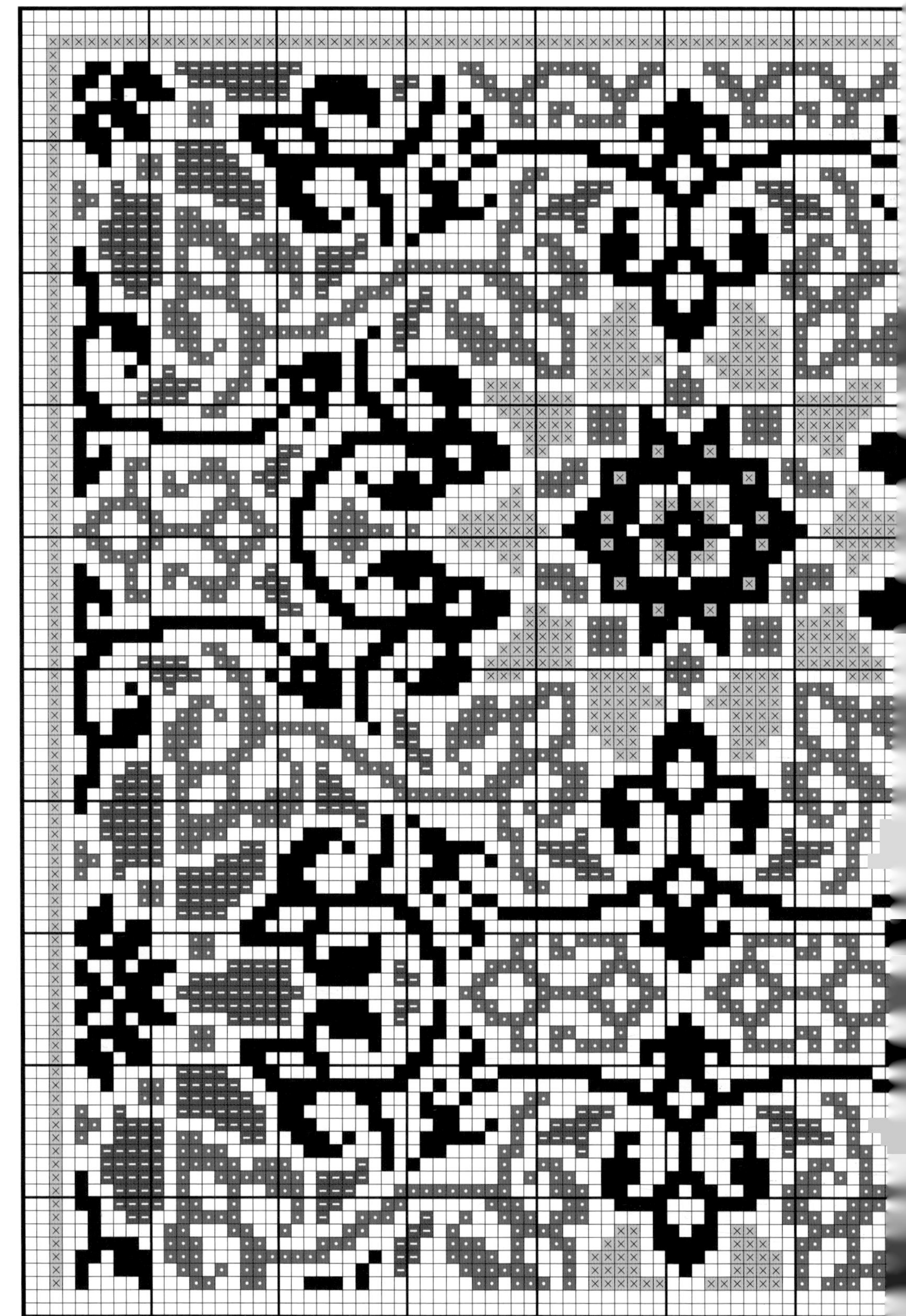

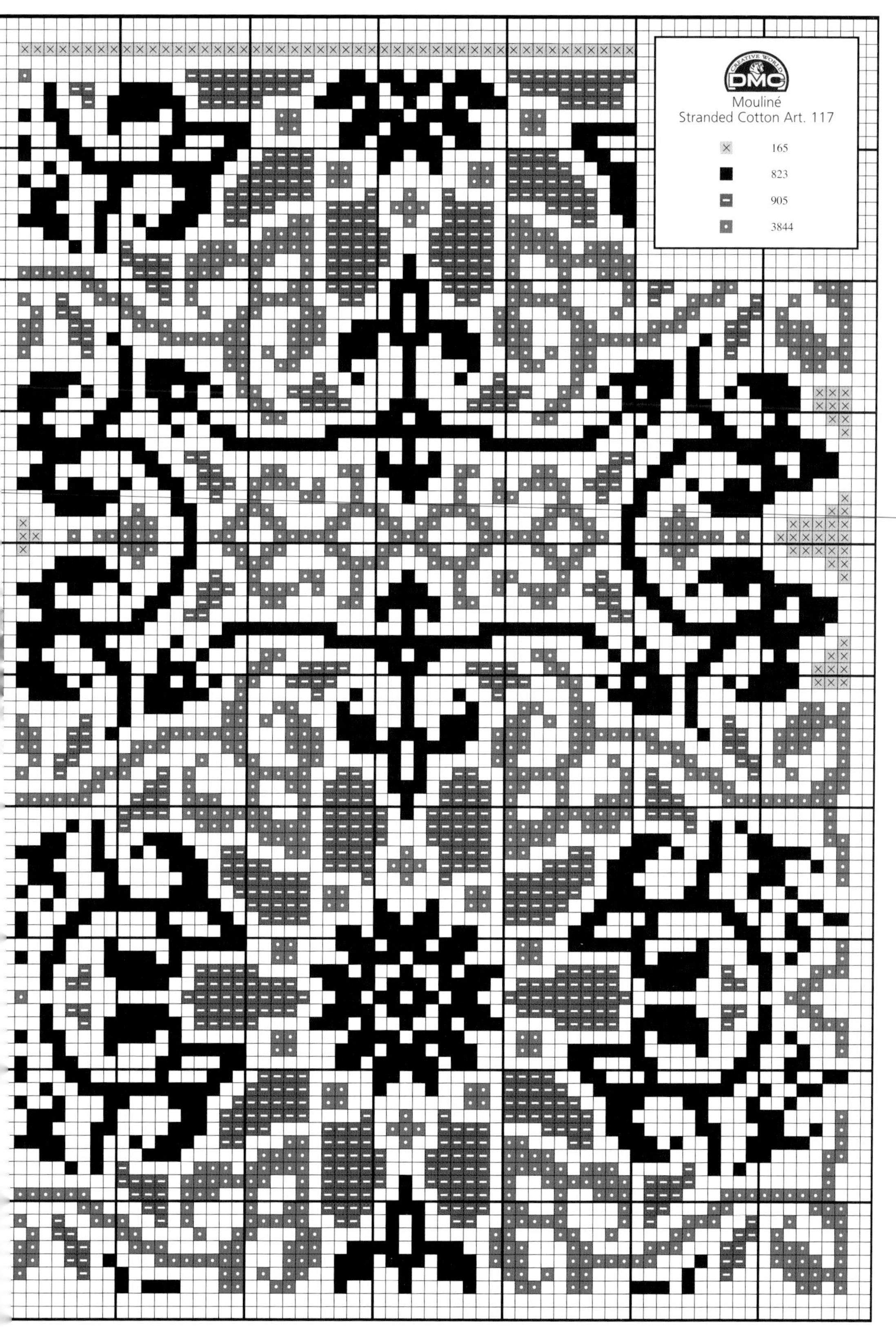
DMC
CREATIVE WORLD
Mouliné
Stranded Cotton Art. 117
165
823
905
3844

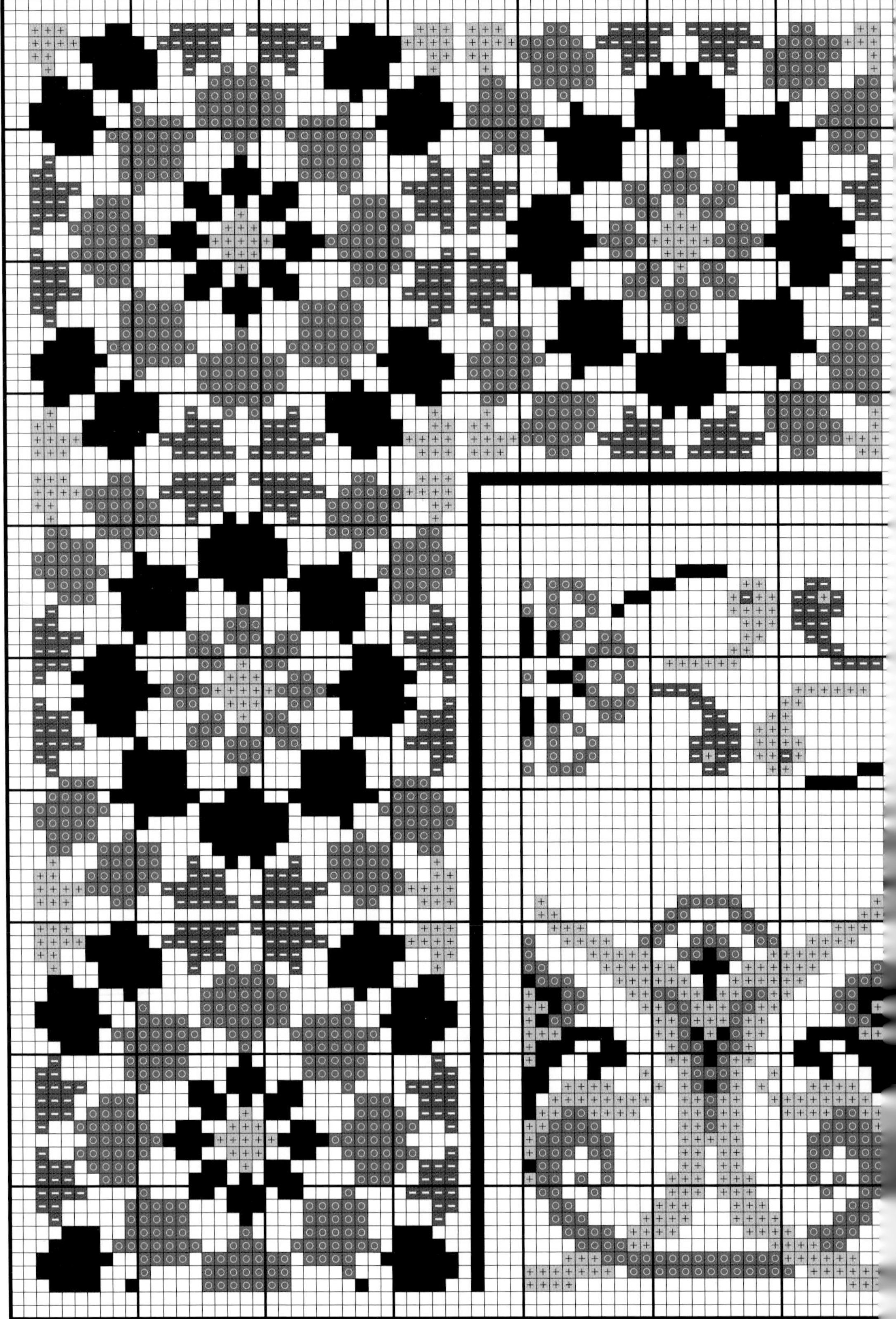

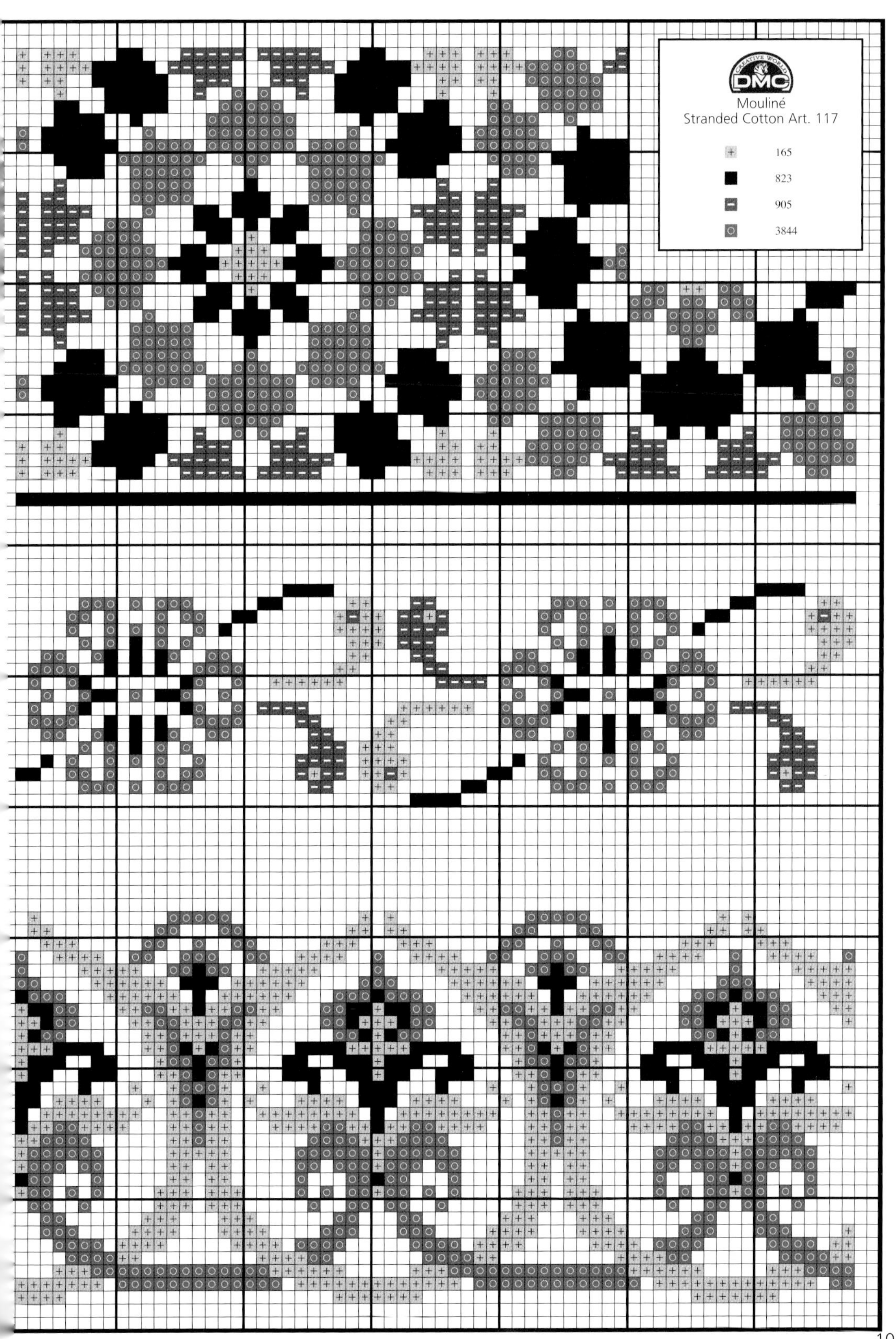
DMC
Mouliné
Stranded Cotton Art. 117
165
823
905
3844

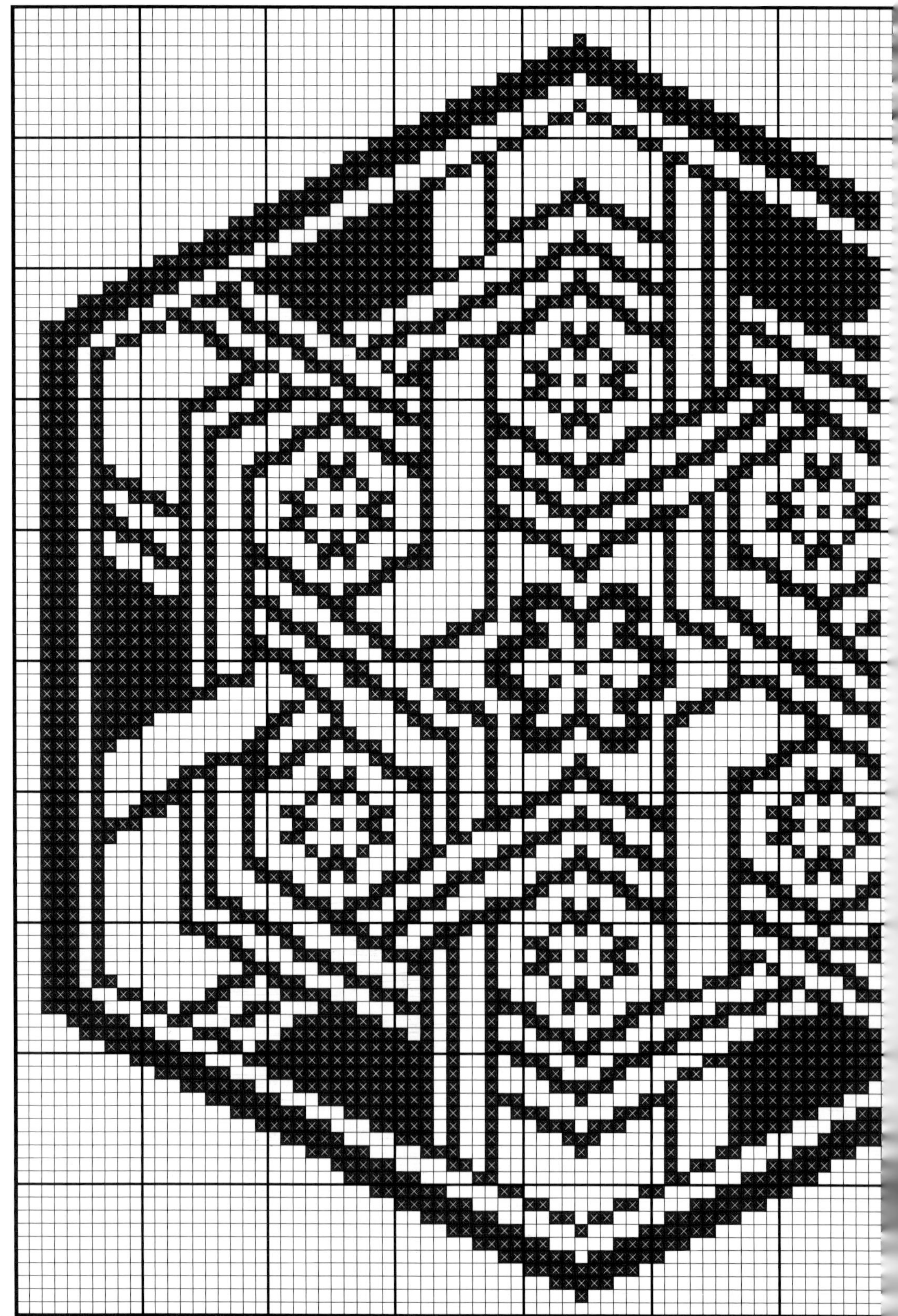

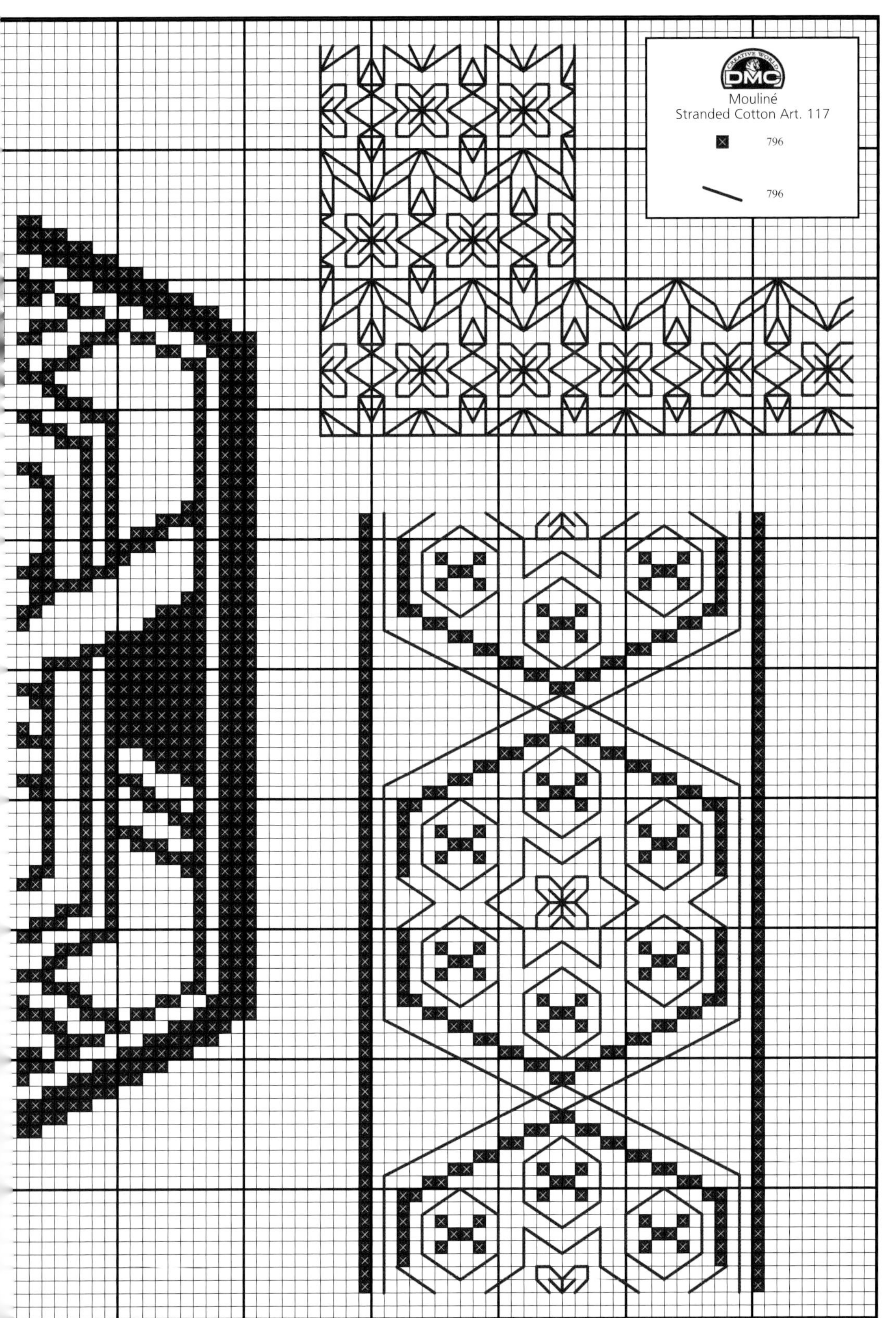
DMC
CREATIVE WORLD
Mouliné
Stranded Cotton Art. 117
796
796

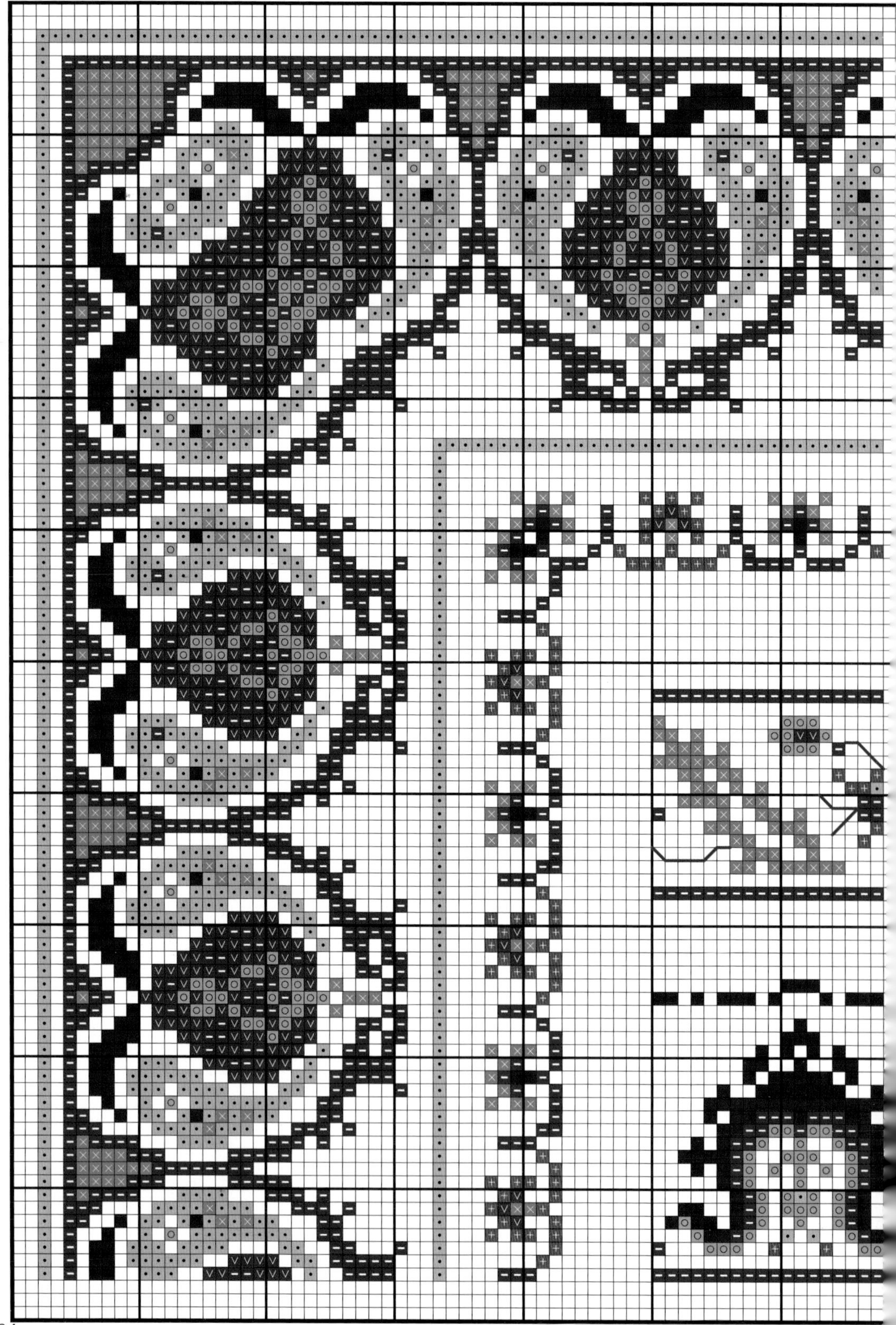

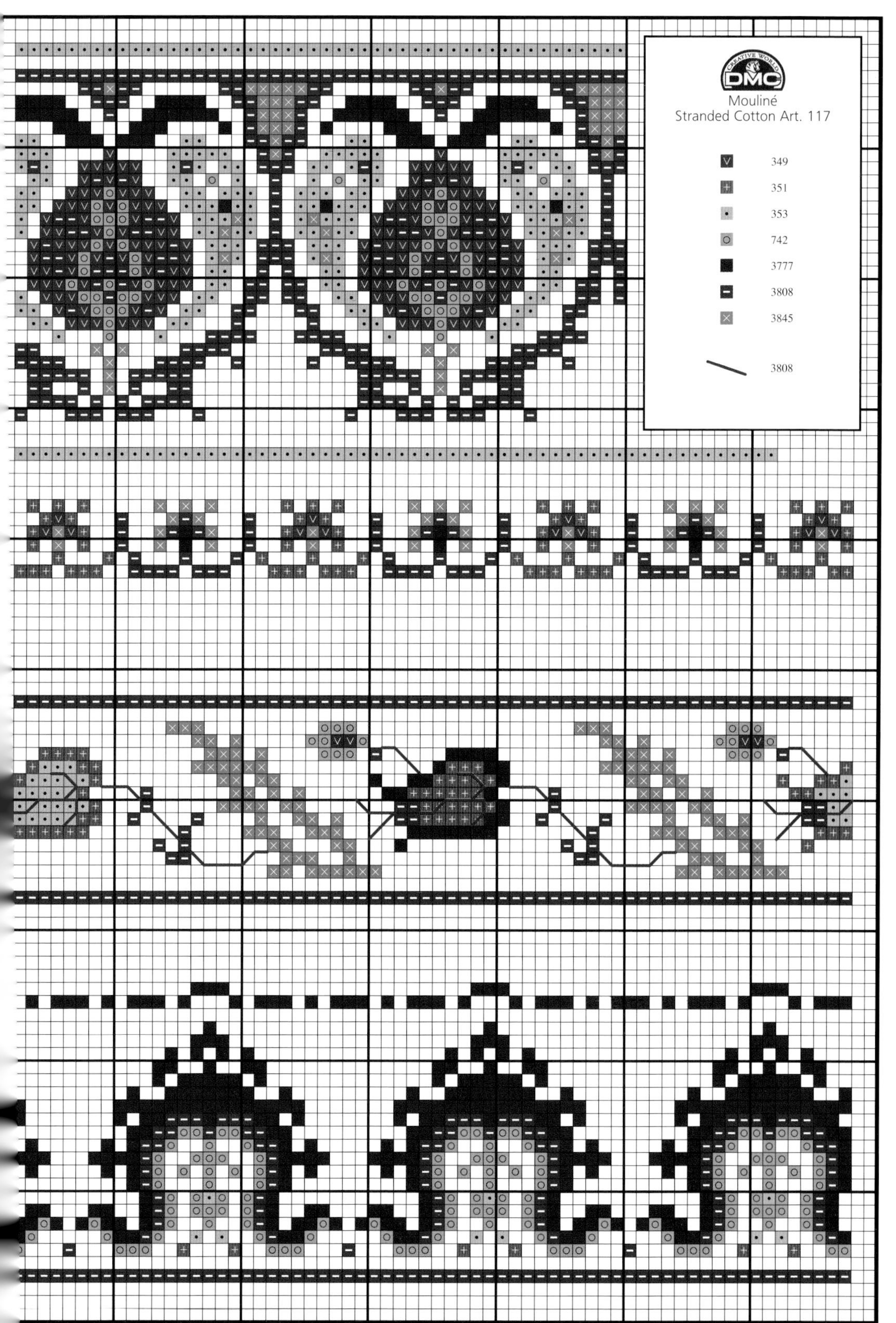
DMC
Mouliné
Stranded Cotton Art. 117
349
351
353
742
3777
3808
3845
3808

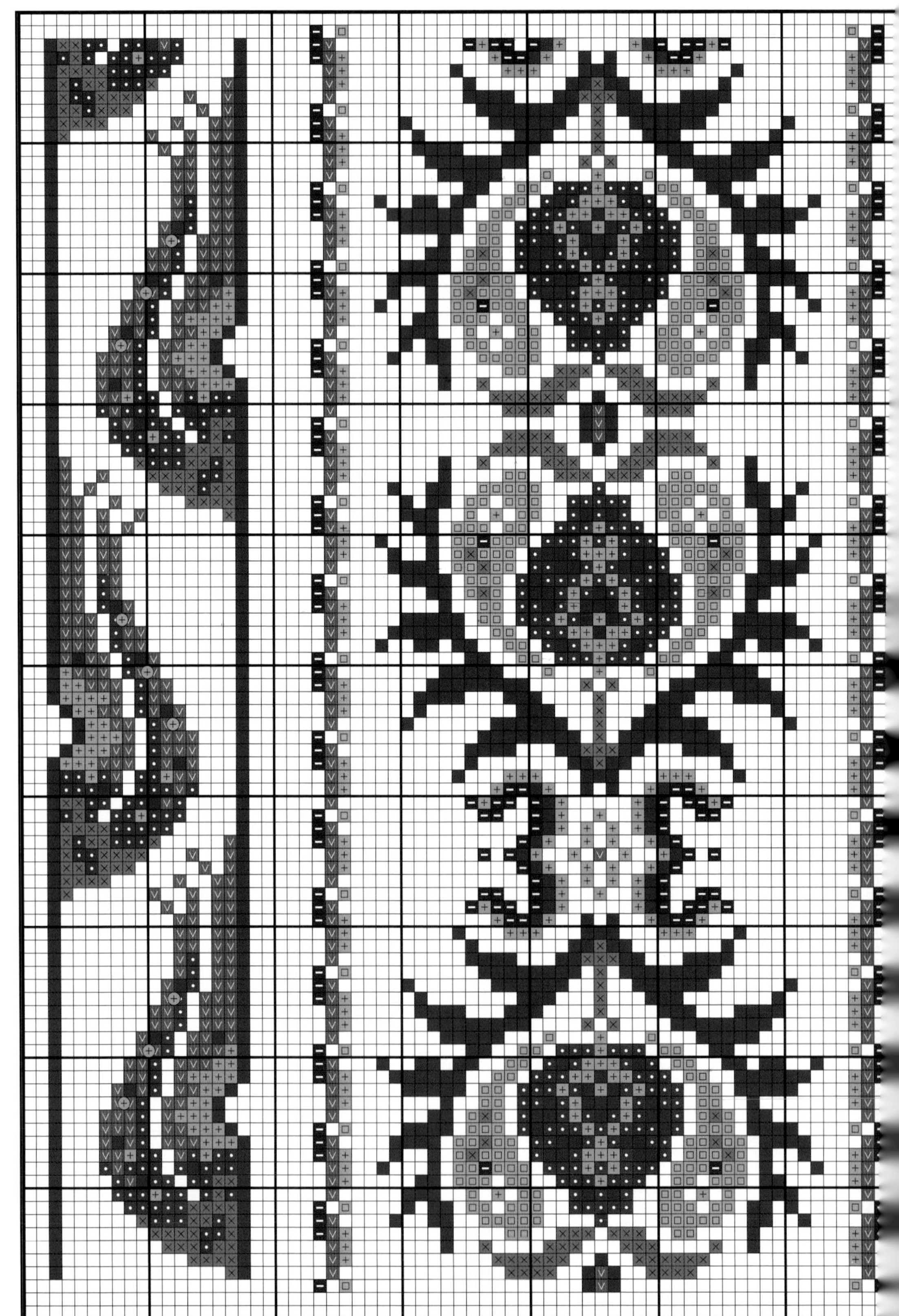

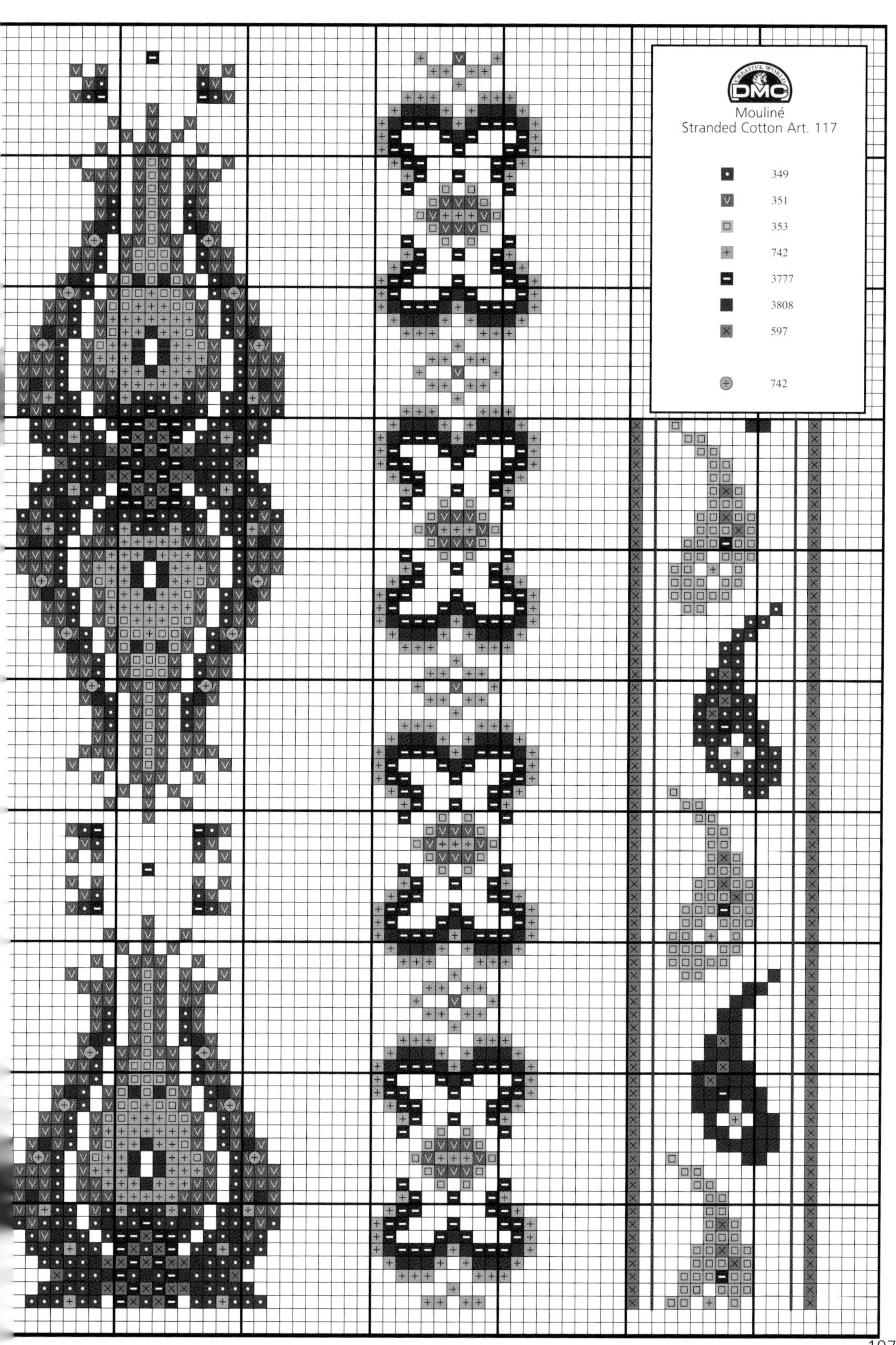
DMC
CREATIVE WORLD
Mouliné
Stranded Cotton Art. 117
349
351
353
742
3777
3808
597
742

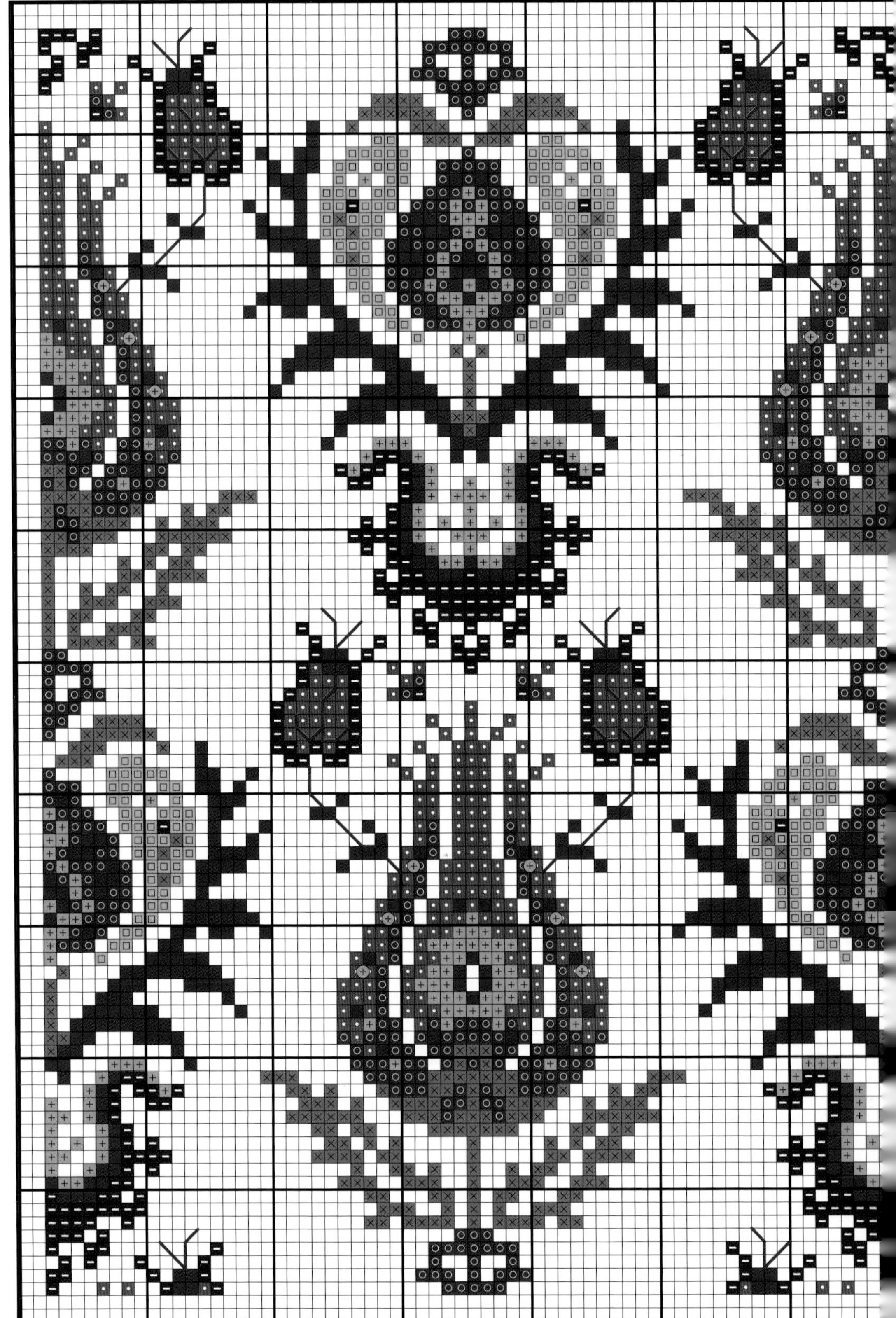

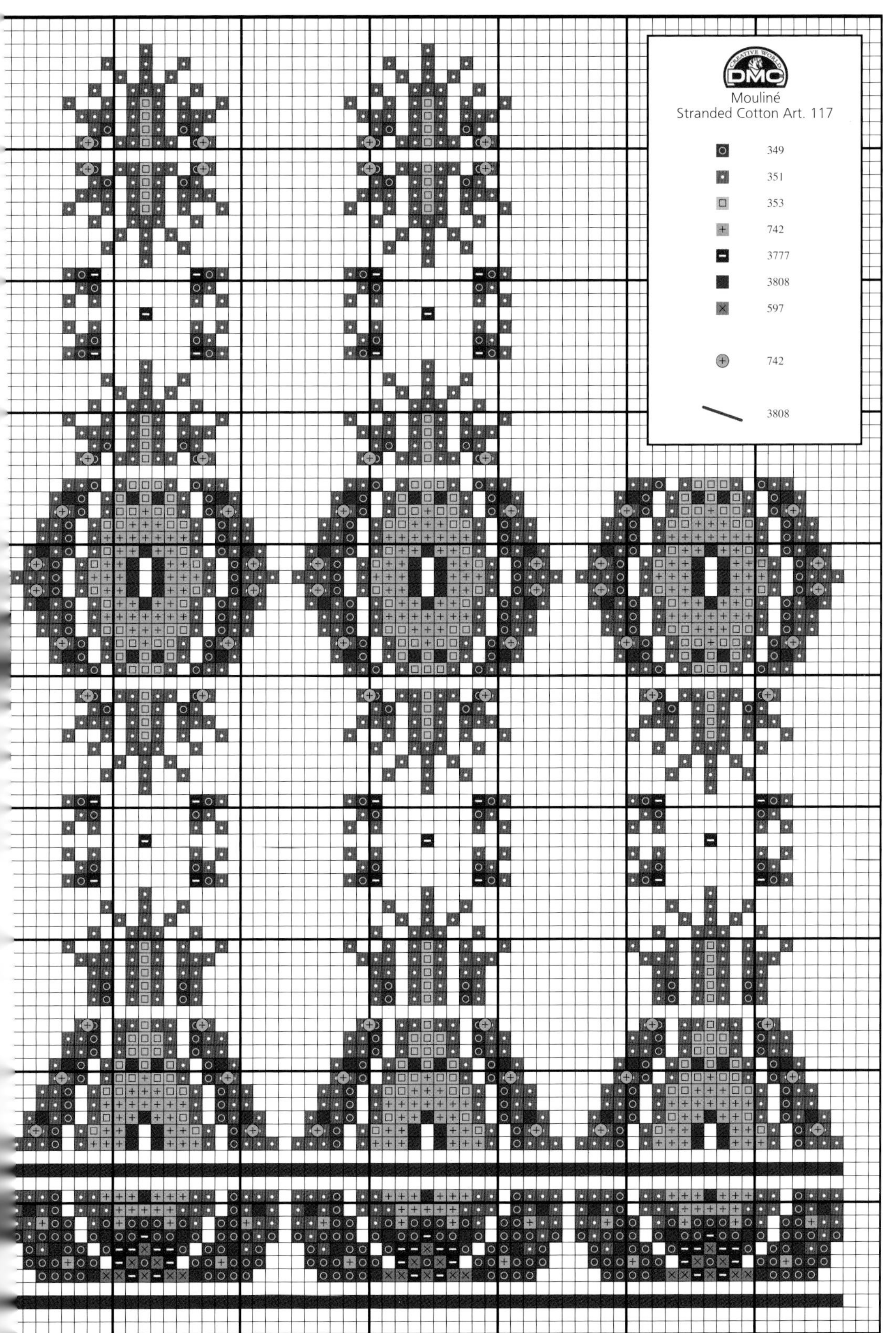

DMC
Mouliné
Stranded Cotton Art. 117
349
351
353
742
3777
3808
597
742
3808

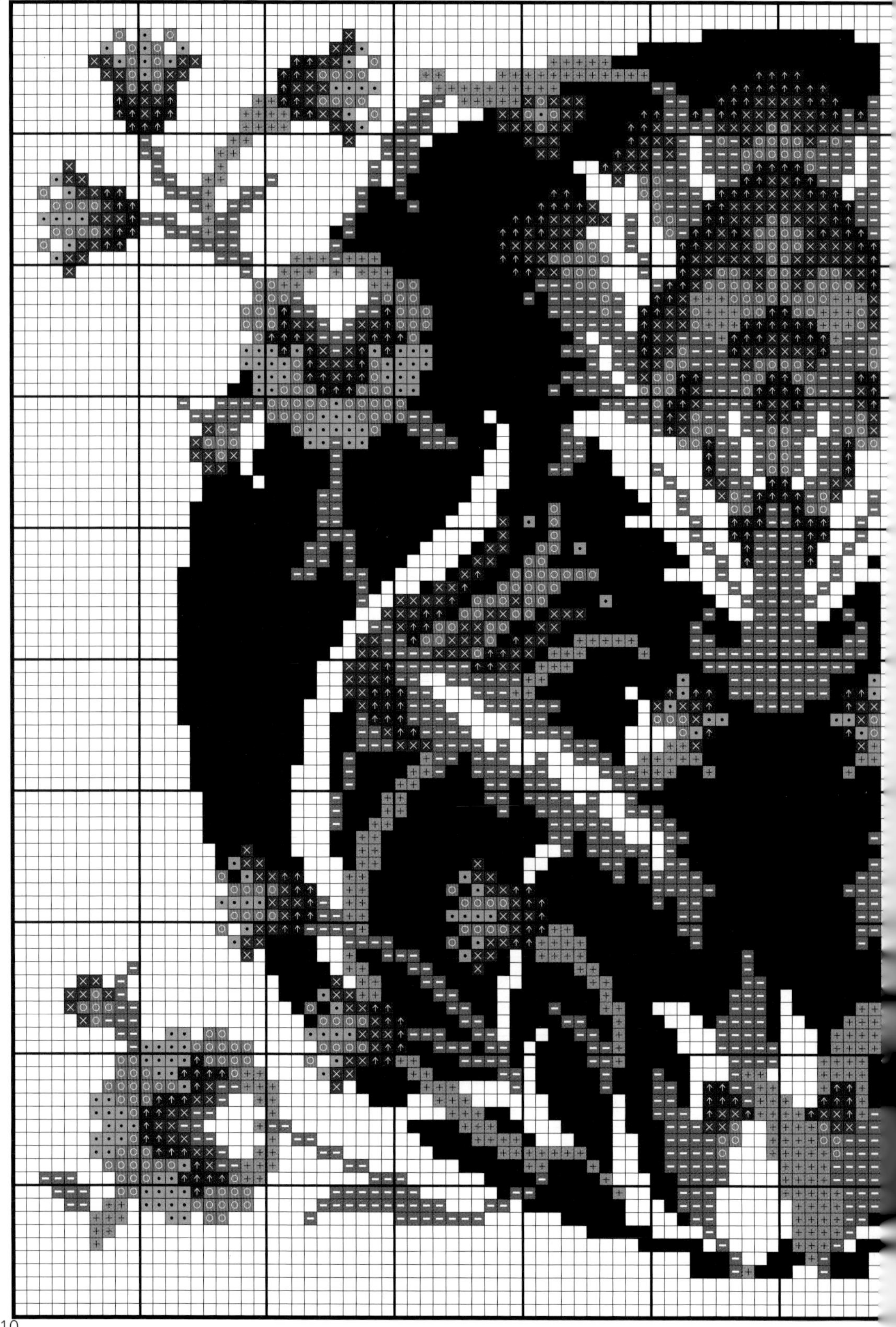

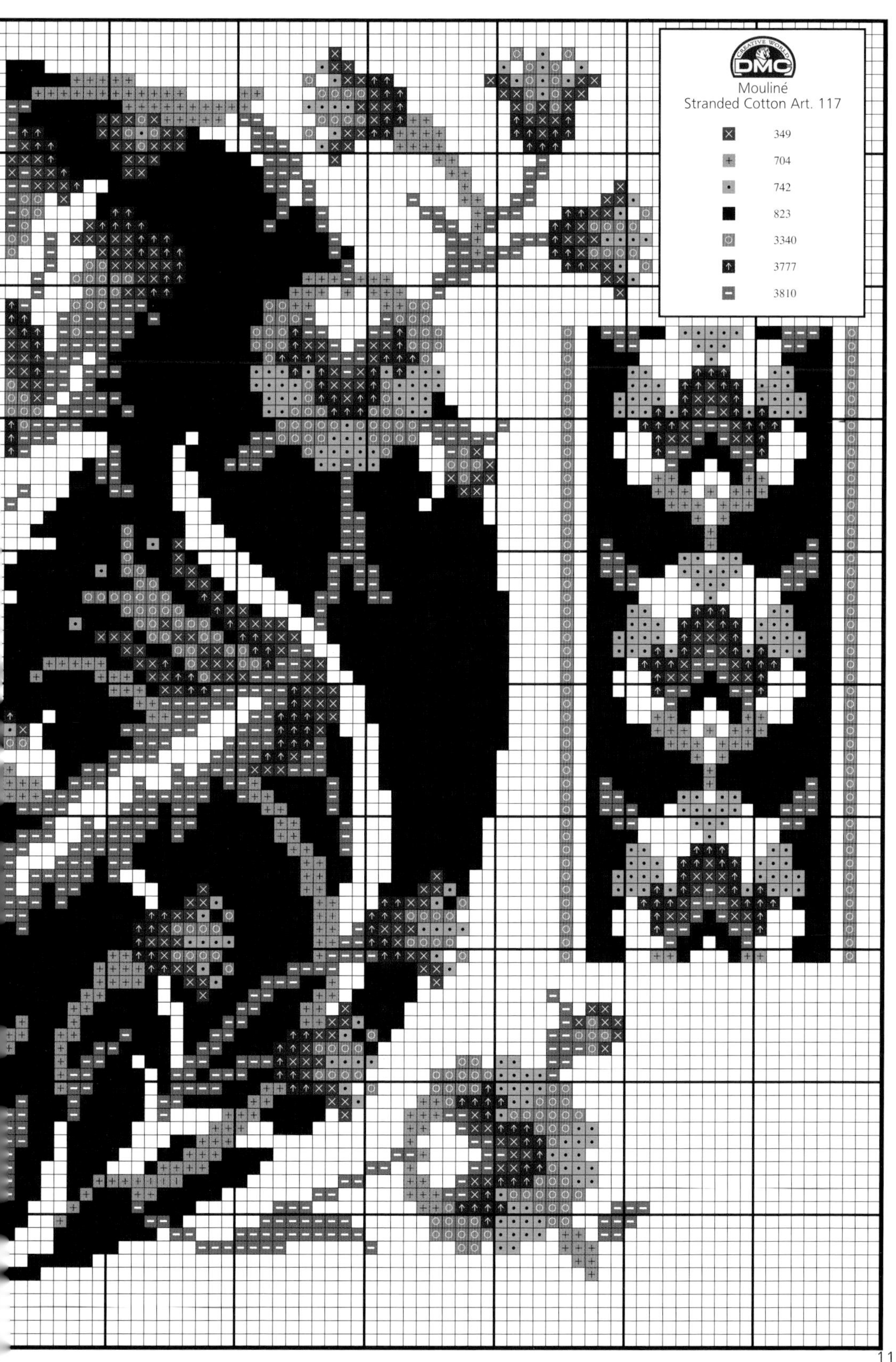
DMC
CREATIVE WORLD
Mouliné
Stranded Cotton Art. 117
349
704
742
823
3340
3777
3810

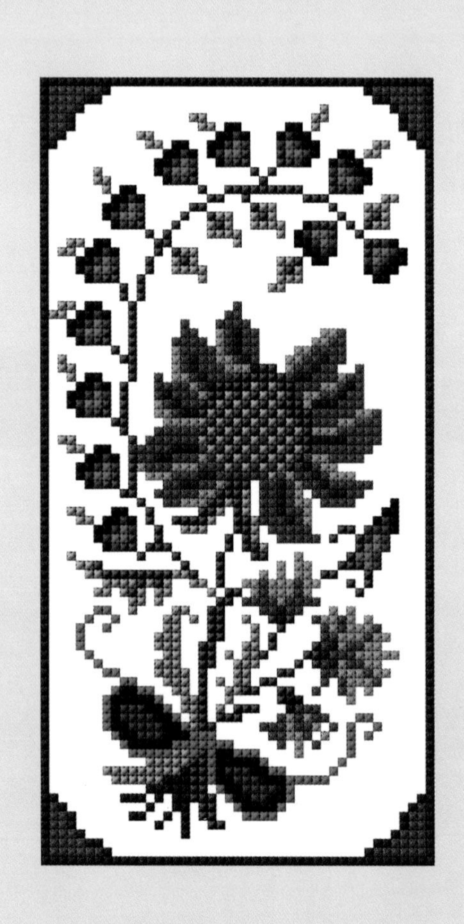